Practical Apologetics
How to carry out the Great Commission

By Alex Nicassio

"Always be prepared to make a defense to anyone who calls you to account for the hope that is in you.." 1 Peter 3:15

Practical Apologetics –
How to carry out the Great Commission

List Price: **$10.99**

Version 1.4.0 at 215 pages

ISBN-13: 13: 978-1495992971

ISBN-10: 10: 1495992977

BISAC: Religion / Biblical Reference / Handbooks

Authored by Alex R Nicassio MPA

Dedication – I dedicate this book to my dedicated and loving wife Kimberly Ann, who I met during RCIA. We were both helping to feed to homeless. She was a convert from the Baptist faith, and was convinced that the Catholic Church has the best answers for her questions. Our children and I thank her for her faithfulness to Christ and His Church as a gift from her grandmother Myra.

This book is the result of many years' research and presentations – any good presentation relies on an active audience! I would like to give an honorable mention to some of the people who have helped me in the development of this material:

Dr. Susan Nicassio, PhD in History
Lt. Col. David S. Englerth, US Army (ret.)
Charles Jones, Jr – Deacon
Allen Dresser, Bible Study Leader
Ginger Vislocky, Master Catechist
Nancy Brady, Enthusiastic Catholic

Nihil obstat pending

Other books by this author:
- *Writings of the Early Church*   ISBN-13: 978-1490474861
- *Adam – When the World Began*   ISBN-13: 978-1481807579
- *Martin Luther – Selected Writings* ISBN-13: 978-1502872500
- *20 things you should know about Jesus of Nazareth**
  ISBN-13: 978-1481807777
- *Foundations of the Bible*   ISBN-13: 978-1500101459
- *John 6:66*   ISBN-13: 978-1493571550

The Great Commission

"Then the eleven disciples went to Galilee, to the mountain where Jesus had told them to go. When they saw him, they worshiped him; but some doubted. Then Jesus came to them and said, "All authority in heaven and on earth has been given to me. Therefore go and make disciples of all nations, baptizing them in the name of the Father and of the Son and of the Holy Spirit, and teaching them to obey everything I have commanded you. And surely I am with you always, to the very end of the age." - Mt 28:16-20 (NIV)

"What is urgent is the evangelization of a world that not only does not know the basic aspects of Christian dogma, but in great part has lost even the memory of the cultural elements of Christianity." - Pope John Paul II

Be Ready

"Always be prepared to make a defense to anyone who calls you to account for the hope that is in you. But do this with gentleness and respect, keeping a clear conscience, so that those who speak maliciously against your good behavior in Christ may be ashamed of their slander." - 1 Peter 3:15-16

Salvation

"Outside the Church there is no salvation" (Extra ecclesiam nulla salus). - CCC 846

"The social duty of Christians is to respect and awaken in each man the love of the true and the good. It requires them to make known the worship of the one true religion which subsists in the Catholic and apostolic Church." - CCC 2105

"Wherever Jesus Christ is present, there is the Catholic Church" – St. Ignatius of Antioch, 110AD

"As I follow no leader but Christ, so I communicate with none save your Beatitude, that is, the seat of Peter (the Pope). For this, I know, is the Rock on which the Church is built. This is Noah's ark, and he who is not found on it will perish when the flood overwhelms all.." St. Jerome, to Pope Damascus 376 AD

If someone asks you what you believe, you should say:

The Nicene Creed

I believe in one God, the Father almighty, maker of heaven and earth, of all things visible and invisible.
I believe in one Lord Jesus Christ, the Only Begotten Son of God, born of the Father before all ages. God from God, Light from Light, true God from true God, begotten, not made, consubstantial with the Father; through him all things were made. For us men and for our salvation he came down from heaven, and by the Holy Spirit was incarnate of the Virgin Mary, and became man.
For our sake he was crucified under Pontius Pilate, he suffered death and was buried, and rose again on the third day in accordance with the Scriptures.
He ascended into heaven and is seated at the right hand of the Father.
He will come again in glory to judge the living and the dead and his kingdom will have no end.
I believe in the Holy Spirit, the Lord, the giver of life, who proceeds from the Father and the Son, who with the Father and the Son is adored and glorified, who has spoken through the prophets.
I believe in one, holy, catholic and apostolic Church.
I confess one Baptism for the forgiveness of sins and I look forward to the resurrection of the dead and the life of the world to come. Amen.

This is the common beliefs for all Christians, established at the Council of Nicea in 325 AD, and has been the basic belief for all Christians since then. This creed was adopted about 70 years before the canon of the Bible was established.

Table of Contents

Introduction 6
Chapter 1 – The Practice of Apologetics 12
Chapter 2 – The Church 27
Chapter 3 – Baptism 47
Chapter 4 – What did Jesus say to do to be 'Saved'? 62
Chapter 5 – The Last Supper 87
Chapter 6 – Judgment Day? 103
Chapter 7 – What Hard Proof Exists? 114
Chapter 8 – Where did our Bible come from? 135
Chapter 9 – The Eucharist 154
Chapter 10 – There is something about Mary…? 163
The Cheat Sheet and how to use it 178
Appendix 1: The Cheat Sheet: 181
Appendix 2: The list of the Popes 191
Appendix 3: A Chronology of Early Church Writings 194
Appendix 4: A table of the Early Church Canons 197
Appendix 5: Approved Eucharistic Miracles 200
Appendix 6: Approved Incorruptibles 203
Bibliography/Recommended Reading 205
Personal Notes: 212

Introduction

When someone suddenly shows up at your door (or anywhere else), and starts the conversation with "Are you Saved?" or "Are you assured a Heavenly reward?" most of us draw a blank. We suddenly find ourselves struggling to answer questions about things we have never heard of, and we doubt our faith and Church. How do you handle this situation?

In Short:
Apologetics is the art of understanding the Good News, and explaining it to others. Many Christians are lost, without an understanding of the Gospel, even though they claim to fully understand it. It is the duty of all Christians to properly understand the Gospel (good news) and once understood, to explain it to others so that they may participate in the new Covenant offered by Christ. Most Christians already participate in the Gospel, but many who think they *know* the Gospel are completely mistaken, and do not participate in the one Church established by Christ. They are cut off from the Body of Christ. Please reach out and help your lost brothers and sisters – How? Read on..

Long Version:
Why should I get involved? – I am sure that is what many of you are thinking. Why is one Church 'better' than another? Does God care if someone is Mormon, Jehovah's Witness or Catholic? Isn't it just a matter of opinion?

No.

If you <u>are not Christian</u>, or have not done as Christ instructed, you are not going to Heaven unless Jesus (the Judge) decides to show you leniency. You can be a wonderful person, and dedicated to your god(s) but there is one path to heaven, and that is through Christ. He has instructed us what to do to attain the kingdom, and that involves Baptism, Eucharist and His Church. Don't believe me? Keep reading..

If you <u>are a Christian</u>, you are supposed to believe what Jesus said – and act on His instruction. This is not a new situation – since the beginning, Christians have had to explain the Good

Introduction

News to a negative or skeptical audience, and generally we today are armed with not enough information and too many questions. Many of the great saints in history were famous for explaining the Faith, and opposing the ignorant (many of them ignorant of their own faith). The Church that Jesus established is the way to overcome the world and attain a heavenly reward. That Church is embodied by the Catholic Church.

I recommend that everyone, of any faith, strive to learn about *their* faith, so that they can be justified or condemned with some understanding of what they profess to believe in. It would be sad indeed to be condemned for your faith if you do not have an understanding of it... So how does someone learn how to stand up for what they believe in?

First – understand what you believe. You cannot explain something to someone else if you do not understand it yourself.

This book is packed with instructions from Jesus, but here are the top things to remember:

- Jesus died so that sins MAY BE forgiven, but ONLY if you follow His instructions:
    - Believe in Him – Jn 3:16
    - You must turn away from sin, and not sin again. [1]
    - You must be baptized as prescribed by Christ [2] for the forgiveness of your sins.
    - Then you will receive the Holy Spirit [3] by the laying on of hands [4]
    - Then continue to be Righteous [5]
    - If you do sin, you are required to get forgiveness for that sin [6]
- Must keep the Commandments [7]
- Must do good works [8]
- Jesus established ONE Church only,
    - Peter set as its head [9]

---

[1] Many references – example: Heb 10:26, Heb 6:5-6 – more in Appendix.
[2] Many references: Jn 3:5, Acts 2:38, Acts 19:3-6, etc.
[3] Acts 2:38 and many more
[4] Acts 19:6 and many more
[5] Mt 5:20 and many more
[6] Jn 20:20-24 and much more
[7] Jn 14:15, 1 Jn 2:3-4; 1 Jn 3:24; 1 Jn 5:3; Lk 18:18 and many more
[8] Rom 2:2-8, 2Cor 11:15, Rev 20:12-13, 1Pet 1:17, James 2

Introduction
- - o Led by Bishops[10]
    o The Church cannot fail[11]
    o The Church is the teaching Authority[12]
    o You must participate with the Church[13]
- You must eat the Body and drink the Blood of Christ
    o Not symbolically (Jn 6:66)
    o Without this, you have "No life in you"[14]
    o By this means, Jesus lives through us[15]
    o Through this we participate in the new Covenant[16]

Jesus established His Church almost 2,000 years ago, and since then, Christians have always worked towards a more complete understanding of the Faith. Although few *completely* understand it, a good understanding of the main elements is essential. Fully understanding the Church is a lifelong pursuit that few can master, but a good understanding of the basics is quite possible – reading this book is a good start!

Once you understand it yourself, then you have to understand how to relate the Good News to others – this process is called Catholic Apologetics.

---

[9] MT 16:18-19, and much more
[10] 1 Tim 3:1, Titus 1:7, 1 Pet 2:25, Acts 1:20
[11] Eph 5:25-26, Mt 16:18; 20:20
[12] Mt 18:17-18, 1 Tim 3:15
[13] 1 Cor 12:21, Rom 11:21-22, etc.
[14] Jn 6:32-58, Mt 26:26-27; Mk 14:22,24; Lk 22:19-20; 1 Cor 10:24-25
[15] Jn 6:56-57 - Whoever eats my flesh and drinks my blood remains in me, and I in them. Just as the living Father sent me and I live because of the Father, so the one who feeds on me will live because of me.
[16] Lk 2:22, 1 Cor 11:25, Heb 9:18, Heb 10:29

Introduction

What is Apologetics[17]?

Apologetics is a theological science which has for its purpose the explanation and defense of the Christian religion.

Apologetics means, broadly speaking, a form of apology – that is, an explanation. The term is derived from the Latin adjective, *Apologeticus*, which, in turn has its origin in the Greek adjective, *apologetikos*, the substantive being apologia, meaning "defense".

Catholic apologetics is the epitome of the Christian Apology, combining the arguments and considerations necessary to defuse misinformation and deliver truth. Using a comprehensive, scientific explanation of the Catholic Christian belief, the apologist delivers a calm, impersonal presentation of underlying principles is of the greatest importance, and the clarification of objections by opponents. By this means we light a candle instead of cursing the darkness.

An apologist does not address himself/herself to a hostile opponent for the purpose of refutation, but rather to the inquiring mind to provide and clarify information. Do not try to convict someone if they are angry, openly hostile or incapable of understanding. A proper defense of the truth in Christ is necessary, and may be accomplished quickly and easily by the delivery of a reasoned response. The aim is to give a clear and concise presentation of the facts which Christ's revealed religion – the Catholic Church - has presented since the beginning for every rational mind. We seek to lead the curious to recognize, first, the reasonableness and trustworthiness of the Christian revelation as realized in the Catholic Church, and secondly, their obligation to accept it.

---

[17] Derived from the Catholic Encyclopedia

Introduction
How do you properly use Apologetics?
In the initial chapters of this book, we will discuss how to go about learning, understanding and carrying out your duty to Christ and His Church through apologetics. You will be following these basic steps:
- Who are you talking to?
- What level of knowledge does the other person have?
- What religion do they believe in? (if any)
- Are they rational or not?
- Should you discuss these matters with this person?
- What can be said to redirect the discussion away from their talking points towards the Truth.
- What to do to direct the other(s) towards the Church.

Why do all of this?
If you are not studying at least an hour a day, and if you do not have a very good grasp of Scripture, then you are missing out on a 'good' understanding of the Gospel. As a Catholic, you may be aware of how the whole thing works, because the Church has developed an excellent system of devotions and practices that guide the faithful to be good Christians, but even with this system in place, many people fail to put this faith into practice in their daily lives. Learning the details of why we do what we do can change your heart, and give greater depth to your participation in the Church. Learning Apologetics can develop your understanding and make you a better disciple[18] of Christ.

Do people need your help?
Yes. Urgently.

"What is urgent is the evangelization of a world that not only does not know the basic aspects of Christian dogma, but in great part has lost even the memory of the cultural elements of Christianity." - Pope John Paul II

Theology is not merely a theoretical preference in churches, as many would believe today. In the USA, we are drilled daily to be tolerant – to believe that there is no single Truth. We are told

---
[18] 'Disciple' comes from the word 'Discipline' so that you might become disciplined and obedient to the Gospel.

Introduction

in many ways that "Everyone is entitled to their own personal truth, and none of us has any rights to believe or to profess that there is one greater Truth." Everything is relative, we are told.

Of course, if you want to believe that 1+1=11, our society is quick to correct you. The tolerance we are told to practice only applies towards religion, oddly enough. Our society considers religion to be stupid and worthless – so we 'tolerate' it because none of it holds Truth. But our society is wrong about that.

Most Americans profess to be Christian – currently about 76%[19]. If you profess to be a Christian, then you are obligated to do what Christ taught – as stated over and over in the New Testament. Of the 36,000 Christian churches in the world today, only the Catholic Church (and those in union with the Church) have the 'fullness of the Truth'.[20] To quote the Catechism:

*"The social duty of Christians is to respect and awaken in each man the love of the true and the good. It requires them to make known the worship of **the one true religion** which subsists in the Catholic and apostolic Church."*[21]

In this book, we will cover many topics lightly, and some in greater depth. This is a starting point for you – not an ending point. Luckily there are MANY books available to assist you in your life long journey of understanding. People I have worked with in the past have become much more conscious of the depth and beauty of our Catholic Christian Faith and at almost every gathering someone says "Why don't they tell us this stuff? It makes so much more sense with all the details!" Put the time into this, and you will reap astonishing rewards.

---

[19] Barry A. Kosmin and Ariela Keysar (2009). "American Religious Identification Survey (ARIS) 2008" (PDF). Hartford, Connecticut, USA: Trinity College.
[20] CCC paragraph 819
[21] CCC paragraph 2105

Chapter 1 – The Practice of Apologetics

There are thousands of religions in the USA today, with more coming every day. Everyone seems to believe they have a right to establish their own religion, and they train their congregations to convert others to their tiny faiths, while chipping away at the Church. To find out what a person or church believes, you are going to have to ask the right questions.

In Short:
Who has the right to establish a Church? Only Jesus – He created the term[22], and established His only Church. With a bewildering array of religions in the world, a random person asking you a question about your faith could be coming from anywhere. If you choose to try to share the Good News with someone else, the first consideration had to be finding out where that person is, theologically speaking. Are they Christian, or not. If they profess to be Christian, are they really? Knowing where to start is half of the battle. Help them to understand their own beliefs, and kindly offer them information to help correct their errors.

Long Version:
"Brother, are you Saved?"
How often have you heard this expression? Just how far from reality is this question, with its assumptions and mistaken bible interpretations piled upon another, the questioner probably does not understand his own question – it is just what they say to begin the process of evangelization.

What is the question really mean? "Are you a fundamentalist Christian" is the actual question. If you answer yes, then he/she will see if you will join his/her church. If you say no, then the conversation will follow a series of memorized questions, with the intention of making you convert to Fundamentalism, and join his/her church.

So either way, the intent is to get you to forsake your Church to join the fundamentalist's church. This constant migration of

---

[22] This is fully explained in Chapter 2 – The Church

Chapter 1 – The Practice of Apologetics

Protestant Christians from one church to another is why there are so many little churches spread all across the country, each with its tiny embattled congregations. If you are to understand what the questioner's goal is, you have to understand what faith they belong to. Once you understand this, you can understand the best answers to their questions, and how to pose questions of your own.

There are many religions in the world today – many who profess themselves to be Christian as well. A breakdown of the major religions[23] is as follows:

World Religions
- Christianity – 2,200 Million
- Islam – 1,600 Million
- Hinduism – 1,100 Million
- Chinese Religions – 932 Million
- Buddhism – 488 Million
- Judaism – 14.5 Million

Worldwide Christian Religions
- Catholic- Christianity 1,100 Million
- Orthodox/Eastern Christian 240 Million
- Conservative Protestant 200 Million
- Liberal Protestant 150 Million
- African Christian Sects 110 Million
- Pentecostal 105 Million
- Anglican 73 Million
- Jehovah's Witnesses 15 Million
- Latter Day Saints 12 Million
- Unity, Christian Science, etc. 2 Million

As you can see, Catholicism is the Big Church, and that is with good reason. Even with the reduction in numbers in recent years, the Church has always been seen as the repository of the

---

[23] From the CIA fact book 2012

Chapter 1 – The Practice of Apologetics

Christian Faith. Islam has been steadily growing over the years, also, but Christians are still much more numerous.

In comparison, let's look at the breakdown of faiths in the USA today, and the odds that they will attempt to confront you -

Major Religions of the USA, as of 2008 Census

Religion	% of USA	Notes	Creed?	Bishop
Catholic	25.10%		Yes	Yes
Baptist	15.80%	Saved - Bible only fundamentalist	No	No
Christian Unspecified	7.20%	Could be anything	No	No
Methodist	5.00%	Bible and some church - varies	Yes	Some*
Lutheran	3.80%	Bible and some tradition - varies	Yes	Yes*
Non-denominational	3.50%	Saved - Bible only fundamentalist	No	No
Pentecostal – Unspecified	2.40%	Saved - Bible only fundamentalist	No	No
Protestant – Unspecified	2.30%	Could be anything	Some	No
Presbyterian	2.10%	Bible and some tradition - varies	Yes	Yes
Agnostic+Atheist	1.60%	No Christian God	No	No
Mormon/Latter Day Saints	1.40%	Non Christian cult - mystery religion	No	Yes*
Jewish	1.20%	Non Christian Faith	No	No
Others	1.20%	Could be anything	Some	No
Episcopal/Anglican	1.10%	Bible and some tradition - varies	Yes	Yes
Evangelical/Born Again	0.90%	Saved - Bible only fundamentalist	No	No
Churches of Christ	0.80%	Saved - Bible only fundamentalist	No	No
Jehovah's Witness	0.80%	Non Christian cult - apocalyptic	No	No
Muslim	0.60%	Non Christian faith	No	No
Buddhist	0.50%	Non Christian Faith	No	No
Assemblies of God	0.40%	Saved - Bible only fundamentalist	No	No
Seventh-Day Adventist	0.40%	Bible Only Schismatic group - apocalyptic	No	No
United Church of Christ	0.30%	Ecumenical Bible/faith based	Yes	No
Church of God	0.30%	Saved - Bible only fundamentalist	No	No

* The office exists, but not part of Apostolic Succession. They are selected without direct lineage to Apostles.

The religions in **bold** face are trained regularly to evangelize, while the others do not focus as much on evangelization. Mormons spend at least 5 hours a week in study or going out to evangelize, while the Jehovah's Witnesses study 5 hours a week and go door to door another 5 hours a week.

I also included in this table if they accept the Nicene Creed (c.325 AD) or if they have Bishops of any kind. These points are important when talking to someone of these faiths, as they are essential elements of the Christian Faith.

This information is for guidelines only – a starting point to ask questions. Many people who belong to these faiths do not understand their church's structure. Let's focus on Christian denominations – other faiths are too far from Christianity to convict easily. If faced by non-Christians, just be kind and answer questions that are not confrontational. Disengage when

Chapter 1 – The Practice of Apologetics

possible – do not deny Christ, but do not enter into a confrontation either.

Who established their church?

Religion	% of USA	Notes	Who Established	When Established
Catholic	25.10%		Jesus	c. 31 AD
Baptist	15.80%	Saved - Bible only fundamentalist	John Smyth	1609 AD
Christian Unspecified	7.20%	Could be anything	Anybody	
Methodist	5.00%	Bible and some church - varies	John Wesley	c. 1784 AD
Lutheran	3.80%	Bible and some tradition - varies	Martin Luther	c. 1521 AD
Non-denominational	3.50%	Saved - Bible only fundamentalist	Anyone	
Pentecostal – Unspecified	2.40%	Saved - Bible only fundamentalist	Alma White	c. 1936 AD
Protestant – Unspecified	2.30%	Could be anything	Anyone	
Presbyterian	2.10%	Bible and some tradition - varies	John Calvin	c. 1560 AD
Agnostic+Atheist	1.60%	No Christian God	None	
Mormon/Latter Day Saints	1.40%	Non Christian cult - mystery religion	Joseph Smith	c. 1820 AD
Jewish	1.20%	Non Christian Faith	Moses	c. 1230 BC
Others	1.20%	Could be anything	Anyone	
Episcopal/Anglican	1.10%	Bible and some tradition - varies	Henry VIII	1534 AD
Evangelical/Born Again	0.90%	Saved - Bible only fundamentalist	Howell Harris	c. 1735 AD
Churches of Christ	0.80%	Saved - Bible only fundamentalist	Alexander Campbell	c. 1830 AD
Jehovah's Witness	0.80%	Non Christian cult - apocalyptic	Charles Taze Russell	c. 1870 AD
Muslim	0.60%	Non Christian faith	Muhammad	c. 610 AD
Buddhist	0.50%	Non Christian Faith	Siddhartha Gautama	c 500 BC
Assemblies of God	0.40%	Saved - Bible only fundamentalist	John Calvin	c. 1914 AD
Seventh-Day Adventist	0.40%	Bible Only Schismatic group - apocalyptic	Ellen G. White	1863 AD
United Church of Christ	0.30%	Ecumenical Bible/faith based	Many People	1957 AD
Church of God	0.30%	Saved - Bible only fundamentalist	R. G. Spurling	c. 1886 AD

The Catholic Church was established by Jesus Himself, and its first leader, after Jesus ascended, was Peter. Sometimes the answer to this is "If Peter was the first Pope, who was the second?" Here is the answer – St. Linus, in 67 AD. To see who followed, in order, I have provided you with a table of the Popes in Appendix 2.

If you examine it, we have a clear line of authority all the way back to our founder, Jesus Christ. Although the Orthodox Churches can also trace their lineage back to the days of Jesus, the fact remains that Peter was selected to be the leader of the Church, and he moved to and died in Rome. His successors remained in Rome, (with a short relocation to France) and the direct line back to the first Pope remains in the Catholic Church.

Chapter 1 – The Practice of Apologetics

Given this information, we should now understand where our Church stands in the big scheme of things, and once you know where the other churches stack up, you have a starting point to discuss things – if you have not completely defused the other party by this point!

Assure others that this is a clear, well documented and legitimate succession of leaders – quite unique in History! What other organization has had a consistent organization for virtually 2,000 years?

Who can set up a church?

The question to ask anyone is – who has the authority to establish their own church? The Bible is quite emphatic that the Church is to be unified, and only under one leader. In the New Testament, that leader is Peter. How can it be that these days everyone feels empowered to compete with the Church Jesus established? Where is the biblical basis for setting up a schismatic church on your own? Where is the Bishop and his authority from Christ Himself? Where in the Bible does the term 'Pastor' come from? The Early Churches had 'Pastors', but they were Priests, Bishops and Deacons. We will talk about his more in chapter 2, but keep in mind that no one has the authority to "invent a church"!

What are your goals?

Paul famously wrote that he is "all things to all people" in Corinthians. The full section is:

[19] *"Though I am free and belong to no one, I have made myself a slave to everyone, to win as many as possible.* [20] *To the Jews I became like a Jew, to win the Jews. To those under the law I became like one under the law (though I myself am not under the law), so as to win those under the law.* [21] *To those not having the law I became like one not having the law (though I am not free from God's law but am under Christ's law), so as to win those not having the law.* [22] *To the weak I became weak, to win the weak. I have become all things to all people **so that by all***

Chapter 1 – The Practice of Apologetics

possible means I might save some. [23] *I do all this for the sake of the gospel that I may share in its blessings."* [24]

Paul is explaining that he knows his audience, understands what they believe (as we explained in Chapters 1 and 2) and he has a goal – to share the Good News that some might be saved from their error. You should have the same goal, and perhaps, learn from Paul a good way to share it to others.

What is our Goal?

The goal and intent of Apologetics is to deliver the Good News – The Gospel is that the "Kingdom of God is at hand":

Jesus was going throughout all Galilee, teaching in their synagogues and proclaiming the gospel of the kingdom, and healing every kind of disease and every kind of sickness among the people. [25]

The Gospel is not a single statement, but the entire message of Christ, as contained in the 4 Gospels. The entire message is the Good News – it is not a single phrase, much though some churches want to make it a single statement (like Jn 3:16 or Rom 1:16). It is not easily summarized, but Paul attempts to in 1 Corinthians 15:3-7:

"For I delivered to you as of first importance what I also received, that Christ died for our sins according to the Scriptures, and that He was buried, and that He was raised on the third day according to the Scriptures, and that He appeared to Cephas (Peter), then to the twelve. After that He appeared to more than five hundred brethren at one time, most of whom remain until now, but some have fallen asleep; then He appeared to James, then to all the apostles; and last of all, as to one untimely born, He appeared to me also."

Does this sound familiar? It should – some of it is in the Nicene Creed – the Nicene Creed is, essentially, a summary of the Good News. That is why we recite it each week. That is why it is considered the basic summary of our faith. This creed is ancient, and intended to ensure all Christians understand at least the basics. Today, some do not accept even this most basic creed.

---

[24] 1 Cor 9:19-23 NIV
[25] Mt 4:23

Chapter 1 – The Practice of Apologetics

Likewise, an integral part of the Good News is that there is one Christ, one Gospel and one Church, as Paul says in 1 Cor 1:10-13:

"Now I exhort you, brethren, by the name of our Lord Jesus Christ, that you all agree and that there be <u>no divisions</u> among you, but that you be made complete in the same mind and in the same judgment. For I have been informed concerning you, my brethren, by Chloe's people, that there are quarrels among you. Now I mean this, that each one of you is saying, "I am of Paul," and "I of Apollos," and "I of Cephas (Peter)," and "I of Christ." **Has Christ been divided?** *Paul was not crucified for you, was he? Or were you baptized in the name of Paul?"*

Here Paul clearly supports the undeniable emphasis from the earliest days that there is only one Church established by Christ, and we are not to separate into different sects established by different leaders (Paul, Apollos or Cephas/Peter, as listed above).

Today many Christians do exactly what Paul warned against – they identify themselves with religions founded by men – Martin Luther, Henry VIII, John Smyth, Joseph Smith, John Wesley, Alma White, John Calvin.. the list goes on. None of these people have the authority to establish a church – and belonging to one of these churches separates people from the one Church that Jesus established.

There is one Church, and our job, as members of that one true Church, is to gently pull people back to unity.

That is your goal.

Therefore, avoid distractions to topics that are not in line with the Gospel. If they want to bash Mary, calmly and politely ask if that is what they believe is necessary for salvation? Keep them on relevant points, not just a tirade of hateful of jargon against the Church. The basic goal of your conversations should be that Christ's Church is embodied in the Roman Catholic Church, and that the elements of that church – [1] Tradition (including the Bible), [2] the Magisterium and teaching authority from Christ Himself and finally [3] the Sacraments are 3 essential elements in the life of a Christian if he or she is to attain the Heavenly Reward they are seeking.

The following chapters contain details so that you can more deeply understand these essential components of Christ's Church,

Chapter 1 – The Practice of Apologetics

but it is essential to learn a couple of specific points so that if you get confused, you can always circle back around to them. These basic points were mentioned in Chapter 1 – sections are assigned to each of the basic beliefs in the Cheat sheet. Study these references, and read the entire chapter that each is in, because many of the people you might talk to will try to provide another explanation for each that may sound plausible, but are in fact completely wrong.

Should you talk to this person?

Before attempting to hold a conversation with someone, ask yourself the question "Is this a good idea?" Please consider at least the following aspects of your companion and environment before beginning to talk about this subject:

1. Is this a safe place to talk, if something went wrong?
2. Is this person rational or not?
3. Is this something that, in the event that offence is taken, will have long term negative impacts on you or your family?

We are all anxious (I hope) do help others, and if you are reading a book on Apologetics, you are probably interested in helping others to discover the Truth. As we know from the history of the Church, even the most careful of us are stoned to death from time to time.

Although there are certain advantages to becoming a Martyr, we should make all reasonable efforts to avoid this in practice. Stepping in the way of danger when it can be avoided is unwise. Often the subject can be handled in another way with the same effect, so keep your eyes open.

An example might be someone coming to the door and wanting to come inside to talk to you about 'Jesus'. You might be eager to do this, but consider your personal safety in the event that an altercation breaks out. You would be surprised how quickly an apparently calm person can become hostile and violent.

Another example might be a family member, who you earnestly want to convert or become faithful, but if you directly challenge them, they may make your life miserable and oppose the Church on the basis that you were 'rude' even if your were kind and polite.

Chapter 1 – The Practice of Apologetics

That is not to say that you wave the white flag and run, but sometimes 'discretion is the better form of valor'.

Some ideas might be:
1. Have an information sheet prepared to answer questions, not answer them yourself.
2. Have other printed materials available, and 'leave' them in places where they might be found.
3. Play Apologetics Videos or Audios where others can hear.
4. Read the Bible in places where others can see.

There are many ways to start a conversation without being obtrusive, and wherever possible avoid conflict, or back off when things get too aggressive.

Properly Understanding Scripture

Conversations often get derailed because of a difference of opinion about the meaning of a specific scripture. You must remember that many people spend hours each week reading over and over the same small chunks of scripture, and they *believe* that they understand those scriptures. Through a process of taking statements out of context and using a 400 year old translation (King James) the meaning can be warped to the point that it is meaningless. Always insist on the following:

- Scriptures referenced must be in Modern English – no 400 year old translations allowed! The King James Version is preferred by many because it is hard to understand. They want that uncertainty to mask their lack of understanding.
- We must agree that the Bible is inerrant regarding the Faith – this is to limit their reference to other sources. We believe the meaning of the Scripture is inerrant in matters of Faith and Morals, *but individuals' understanding* of scripture is certainly not inerrant.
- Jesus told us things we need to know – He was not lying or attempting to mislead us. If He said it, it is important, and must be done. You cannot skip the 'hard teachings' because they are tough to follow. Quite the opposite.

If you can get agreement on these 3 points, this should be and easy conversation. Remember – this is OUR book! The Catholic

Chapter 1 – The Practice of Apologetics

Church *wrote* the New Testament, then pulled together the entire Bible and has studied it for almost 2,000 years.

When you present something (like John 6:53 regarding the Eucharist) the other party will typically flinch and say that it means something entirely different (like 'Have Faith') or just admit that they do not know. A common term used to excuse 'I do not know' is that something is a 'Hard Saying' of Christ, or 'that is a mystery that will only be revealed at the end of time'. If you let them off the hook, you cannot win them for Christ.

Gently offer that there is an answer, for 2,000 years, that explains each of these. That question is fully answered in Christ's Church.

Read in Context

The scriptures were not written yesterday – we have to understand the context. The original message was delivered to people in a time long gone. It was not specifically written to you! The message certainly can be understood to mean something to us, but to properly understand it, we have to understand the 4 ways to read scripture and understand it – those are[26]:

1. **Literal Sense:** "[T]he meaning conveyed by the words of Scripture" (Catechism, no. 116), the actual event, person, thing described in the biblical text. The literal sense gives rise to the following three "spiritual senses."

2. **Allegorical Sense:** How those things, events, or persons in the literal sense point to Christ and the Paschal Mystery.

3. **Moral Sense:** How the literal sense points to the Christian life in the Church.

4. **Anagogical Sense:** How the literal sense points to the Christian's heavenly destiny and the last things.

We must therefore not only read and understand the entire chapter from which we are reading, but also understand the person writing the book/letter, who he is writing to and what the

---

[26] CCC 115-119

Chapter 1 – The Practice of Apologetics

intended message is. Possibly most important, we have to understand that all of the Scriptures are intended to fit together like a puzzle, with no missing pieces. The Fundamentalist or Schismatic often wants to accept only one part of the puzzle, and leave everything else out. They (with very good intentions) read through the scriptures skipping over anything that they do not understand. I cannot say how many times people tell me how simple the Bible *really* is. I am always tempted to say "Sure, if you ignore the content, it is very simple indeed!"

I never have said that to a person, but I say it in my head a lot. I do not say it to people because there are so many truly good people out there that are lost and looking, and they deserve every chance to come home to Christ's Church. I do not what to hinder that by a cross word. But I cannot agree to something that is not true, and we should all stand for Truth.

When faced with someone who claims to fully understand the Bible, I like to give this example:

"Do you know what a Rainbow is? Yes, it is a sign of the Noetic covenant (the covenant with Noah) but we get the name from the Hebrew, which is Rain Bow, or a weapon of war used by God to create destructive rain on the Earth. It is this weapon that God used to create the flood, and to show that He would not use it again in that way, He puts it in the sky so we can see it as a sign of his covenant agreement not to destroy the world again by rain. Did you know that? It is in the Bible, and it helps to understand the purpose of the Rainbow, but without that piece of information, you thought it was a simple empty symbol, but now you understand that it is a weapon of God. It is through study of the details of scripture that we can come to properly understand the message of God. The Bible does not explain itself, and it is not simple to understand, but it is the wisdom of the ages in one volume. It requires study and learning to comprehend."

The fact is that very few people really understand much about scripture – radical Protestant Fundamentalists in particular know many lines of scripture, but they have no understanding of what the message is, simply because the actual message of the Cross is at odds with their beliefs – the beliefs of *Sola Scriptura* and *Sola Fideles* are clearly not only not 'biblical', they are not even Christian beliefs.

Chapter 1 – The Practice of Apologetics

What can we talk about?

The top 3 items that can best tackled to introduce your conversation partner to the Church and why they need her will be discussed in this section.

- Top 3 Items
    - Church
        - Who Established YOUR church?
        - When and How the Catholic Church was established
        - Why Catholic Church?
    - Salvation
        - Saved? What does that mean…?
        - Problems with assured Salvation
        - What do you have to do?
    - Sacraments
        - Baptism
        - Eucharist
        - Forgiveness of Sin

If the person you are talking to is Christian and knows their faith (as above) you can ask the questions below:

- **Who established your church?**
    - If they say Jesus – look it up and tell them who did.
    - If they say someone else, ask them why they would have authority to defy Christ's Church and make their own?
- **Does your church accept the Bible – word for word?**
    - Yes – then where is your Bishop?
        - If they have none, point to NT (1 Tim 3:1, Titus 1:7, 1 Pet 2:25, Acts 1:20)
        - No Bishop, no valid Church.
    - No – then what do you believe?
- **Does your church accept the Nicene Creed?**
    - Yes –
        - Then where is your Apostolic Succession?
        - Are you 'catholic'? Universal & United.
        - Do you accept one baptism to *forgive sins*?
        - The Bible is not mentioned in the Creed.

Chapter 1 – The Practice of Apologetics

- Salvation by Faith Alone is not in Bible or Creed. Quite the opposite.
- No –
  - Creed was adopted and accepted by ALL Christians in 325 AD. Only recently did anyone deny the Creed. It preceded the Bible by about 70 years.

Many Christians are not clear about what they believe – some are just following a script they were taught, and once you get off the script, they are pretty lost. Therefore, the first requirement to having a rational conversation is to get the other party off of their talking points. In this situation, the principal questions to continue to ask someone about their church are:

Do you believe Jesus is God – a part of the Trinity?
- If they choke on any of that, they are borderline Christians at best.
- Jesus is God (Jn 1:1-2)
- There is a Trinity (Mt 28:19)

What do they do to go to Heaven?
- Faith Alone – look at James 2:20 and 24
- Accepting Jesus as Personal Savior
  - Where does the Bible say that?
  - What about Baptism (Jn 3:5, CCC 1263)?
  - Eucharist (Jn 6:50-66)?
  - Good works (James 2)?
  - Keeping the Commandments (Lk 18:18-22, MT 19:16)

When you sin, how are they forgiven?
- I ask God for forgiveness (Counter with 1Tim 2:5 - "One mediator between God and man" – you are not that mediator! You cannot directly ask God for anything.)
- Jesus paid for all my sins (Counter with Mt 18:18, Jn 20:22-23). Your sins are washed away in Baptism, but you can make more!

Always keep to the main points, and do not get distracted with side issues. A popular method for some groups is to lay into Mary or the Saints as an attempt to divert away from topics they do not want to talk about. Offer to provide them information on

Chapter 1 – The Practice of Apologetics

these issues, if they want, but the first and most important issue has to be Salvation, the Church and the Sacraments. Without these three items, Mary or any other topic is not worth talking about. Let them hate whomever they like (that generally puts the matter in its place – no one wants to be someone who 'hates' Mary.)

Rehearse

Practice makes perfect – read the material, study the scriptures and watch EWTN specials. Read items from Catholic Answers. Recruit your Catholic friends to help you to understand the teachings of the Church. Recruit your protestant and non-Christian friends to explain their beliefs without interruption. Take notes – show your interest and concerns. Practice listening to the things you do not want to hear, so that you may learn to counter and understand the error in their understanding. If you do not know the answer to a question, make the effort to understand. Do not feel slighted when they show no interest in the Truth – your job it to introduce them to the Truth, not to force anyone to believe anything. The Holy Spirit will convict them of the Truth if it is possible, but for many it is not. Possibly above all, practice your humility and grace under pressure. Remember that on Judgment day, you can say with a clear conscience that you did your part to spread the Gospel.

Know your Faith!

Everyone hits the rocks sometimes – you are going to be hit with arguments and ideas you do not have an answer to. Change your heart to consider something you are not prepared for a *challenge* not a setback. Always try to be collaborative, not aggressive. Try to work this out together, not against each other. Assume the other person is genuinely trying to serve God, and genuinely try to help them.

Final Advice for Preparation

I have been actively engaged in Apologetics since 1988, when I found a copy of Karl Keating's book[27], and read it over and over until it fell apart. I had never seen anything like it, and I

---

[27] Keating, Karl. Catholicism and Fundamentalism: The Attack on "Romanism" by "Bible Christians" (Ignatius Press, 1988)

Chapter 1 – The Practice of Apologetics

used it to convert many of my friends to the Church. I go to visit schismatic and non-Christian venues from time to time and talk to people there to see what can be done to help them, and I learn a lot.

There are a lot of dedicated and genuinely good people out there, who are seeking the Truth, but no one tells them where to look. You can help these people if you know what you are talking about, and share it with compassion.

You do not need to convert anyone to the Church – just plant the Truth in them with a pleasant and positive attitude, and that Truth will eventually grow in them. You may never know the full impact of your work, but I believe that on the last day you will be happy with the souls you have brought to Christ out of the shadows of ignorance. I have been blessed to know many converts over the years, and I hope to help many more. I pray that you too reach people in need.

Remember that you must share Christ's message with love and compassion – never with aggression or anger. No one is perfect – if you make a mistake, just apologize and walk away.

Chapter 2 – The Church

There are many weird misperceptions about the Christ and Scripture that lead to wrong thinking. Once a Christian believes that Jesus of Nazareth was the divine Son of God, then certain other beliefs should follow – but many seem to forget Who God Is and the Plan. You really think Jesus left without thinking about His Church? Did he rely on a Bible (that would not exist for almost 400 years) or did He set up Peter as the head of His Church? Jesus did not hand out a Bible to His followers and ask them to read it and make up their own minds..

In Short:
Christ came with a plan, and left with a plan – that plan was to establish the Church to be led and run by Humans, but reporting to an earthly authority who was set by Christ Himself. That Church is incorruptible by design, and will remain until the return of Christ. Think not? You think God can deliver to you a 'perfect book' but He cannot run a Church? Making an assumption that Christ's Church (as established by Him) can be corrupted beyond repair is saying that Christ was not competent to establish His own Church properly. Wow. Do you think Jesus was incompetent? I don't – why would you?

Long Version:
Let me start with my own clumsy attempt at a parable – based on one Jesus taught. It goes like this:

The master of a great farm lived in a far off land, and although the people who work the land generally accept his ownership of the land, they often refuse to pay him homage as they should. When the master sends overseers to instruct them, they refuse to listen to them and beat them until they leave. One day the master sent his son, thinking that they would accept him and his leadership, but the people conspire against the son, and kill him as well, thinking that that will be the end of it. It was not – the son returned from the dead and appointed a leader for those who would be obedient. This new leader for the obedient farmers was empowered to make decisions in the absence of the son until he returned. This new leader would dedicate himself to the service of the son, and would do his best to be a good leader in

Chapter 2 – The Church

the place of the master and his son. For this reason, the decisions of the leader would be acceptable to the master, because (even though the leader is not the master or his son) the leader was doing his best to follow the directions related to him by the son. As the leaders died and were replaced by other leaders, they all followed in the footsteps of the original leader who dedicated his life to properly serving the master and his son. In this way, the leader could not mislead the people, because he was entrusted with the responsibility and authority to make decisions on behalf of the master and his son. In this way, the best efforts of the leader, though fallible himself, becomes infallible. One day the son will return to reward the obedient and punish the disobedient.

Christ came with a plan, and left with a plan – do not think any event in His incarnation was an accident. His arrival at that place and time was set in the very beginnings of time – if you know about Daniel, the prophecy of 70 weeks told the Jews exactly when the Messiah would arrive and where. The passion was carefully planned to the last detail to fulfill predictions of the Messiah. Events could not have happened in a different way – the plan of redemption had to happen the way it did. No detail was left to chance.

This plan included an eternal and earthly Church to do the will of Jesus. The early Church operated as Jesus instructed – they gathered, shared things in common and replaced fallen leaders to ensure the continuation of His Church. Peter was set up as the leader of this Eternal Church, and it was made to withstand even the gates of Hell itself because it was given the power and authority of Christ himself. It is for this reason that the Church is the great institution that can withstand all enemies, and who resisted and overcame the most powerful enemies the world has even known, from the Romans to the Nazis and the Communists. Despite incredible odds against it, the Church Christ established continues unabated and indomitable.

What is the Church?

You probably think you know the answer to that question, but did you know that Jesus created that term, based on a single term used in the Torah?

Chapter 2 – The Church

So, did the Jews at the time of Christ have a 'Church'? No, they did not – not as we would identify a Church. The communities would have a Synagogue or 'meeting place' and there was the Temple in Jerusalem. Note that all of the Jews, even though they may have been in a different political/religious group, they generally shared the same Temple and meeting places. Essenes typically did not go to the Second Temple, and lived separately in community, but the Priests, Scribes, Pharisees and Sadducees all shared venues. None of the Jews had a 'Church'. Hence the old question – Did Jesus ever attend Church? No, He did not, as the first Church was 'created' at Pentecost.

In Mt 16:13-20, the Christ established an entirely new organization, which was written in Greek as 'Ekklesia[28]'. This is a translation of the OT Hebrew word 'Qahal[29]' (קהל) or 'they who are called out'. Scholars conclude that the qahal must be a judicial body composed of representatives of the 'edah[30] (literally 'the swarm' or the people of Israel). This word (qahal) appears first in Exodus, and is used to describe a group within the Jews who were wandering in the wilderness following the Exodus from Egypt. The function of this 'leadership group' was to direct the People of God as they wandered through the wastelands, looking for the Promised Land. Moses would gather them together to give instructions and to learn the disposition of the People. It was to these people that many of the miraculous events of the Exodus were shown, and they shared it with their people. All 500,000 of the people did not gather to see and hear everything that was going on – someone had to look after the mundane events and leave the high spiritual matters to their representatives in the Qahal. Sound like a parallel to something else? Yes indeed – the purpose of Christ's Church was exactly that – a group of people whose purpose was (and is) to lead the People of God out of this world towards the Promised Land. Not everyone can or should become a great religious leader – there are people selected for that work (the qahal) and the rest of us listen to them (we are the 'edah).

---

[28] Ekklesia: εκκλησια – H – 'Those called out'
[29] Qahal: קהל – Strong's Number H6951 – 'Those called out'
[30] Edah: עדה – Strong's Number H5712 – 'the swarm' or 'the people'

Chapter 2 – The Church

Why does this matter? The selection of the word for 'Church' is vitally important to understanding Christ's intent for this group. The fact that He used the little used word from Exodus and not 'Temple' or 'People of God' is astonishingly important – He was revisiting Exodus again, as much of the establishment of the Church did. The Eucharist was a Passover Meal with new implications; the Baptismal Sacrament recalled the crossing of the Red Sea; The presentation of the Law is affirmed but expanded, and many more examples. Why use the work Qahal instead of 'edah?

In short – Qahal means 'Leaders of the People of God', while 'edah means 'The People of God'.

If Jesus had used the word 'edah in Mt 16 the meaning of the message would have been <u>very different</u>. He would have been saying that Peter was the rock on which the People of God would be built. The Church would be all of the people of God. BUT that is not what Jesus said.

Jesus called His Church the Qahal – the leaders of the People of God. Peter was the foundation rock of this group. Think about it – Jesus asked Peter if he loved Him more than the other apostles, and He asked that Peter strengthen the other apostles as well – not all believers, but the Apostles. This group would assume the role of the Qahal of Exodus – they reported to a leader (Moses/Peter). Their leader spoke to God to get instructions (Moses/Peter), the leaders would get their instructions from their earthly leader (Moses/Peter) and relate those instructions to their flock, the 'edah (People of God). The difference is enormous. Christ instructed that not only was Peter the leader of His followers, but that the Apostles were the Qahal, who were empowered to lead the People ('edah). The people are not empowered to lead themselves! Their job is to follow the Church (Qahal) and their teachings faithfully[31].

In the beginning, the new Church of the 'People of the Way' also attended the Temple, but their leaders were the Church. The sheep followed their shepherds, and the shepherds were the Qahal or Ekklesia. We today define a church to be the people who form the body of the believers, but when Jesus used the term He was

---

[31] 2 Thess 2:14-15 – "It was for this He called you through our gospel, that you may gain the glory of our Lord Jesus Christ. So then, brethren, stand firm and hold to the traditions which you were taught, whether by word of mouth or by letter from us."

Chapter 2 – The Church

referring to the Apostles headed by Peter – the Bishops that would represent the People of God. The leaders of this Church would be known as the Ecclesiastic authorities – the leaders of the Church – Priests, Nuns, Monks, Deacons and Bishops.

When the Christ created the concept of Church based on the wandering people who escaped Egypt, He was making some clear statements.

- This was a New Exodus
- Peter was established as the new Moses
- He was leading them through the wilderness towards the Promised Land

People of the Way

Jesus said: *"I am the way, and the truth, and the life. No one comes to the Father except through me..[32]"*

Paul referred to the Christians as People of the Way as he was setting out to persecute them:

"Meanwhile Saul, still breathing threats and murder against the disciples of the Lord, went to the high priest and asked him for letters to the synagogues at Damascus, so that if he found any who belonged to the Way, men or women, he might bring them bound to Jerusalem."[33]

The book of Acts tells us a lot about the People of the Way. In Acts chapter 1, after the descent of the Holy Spirit, Peter and the apostles gathered together and discuss the way that they were going to conduct things in this assembly and as you'll see in this gathering and in all others Peter's name is always mentioned first. This shows that from the very beginning, the leadership of the church was to remain unified and they were to have a decisive leader. Peter was that leader. The first thing they did after was to elect a replacement for Judas. Peter quoted the scriptural basis for this decision in Acts 1:20 – he quoted both Psalm 69:25 and Psalm 109:8. As we will see, this pattern was to be the way that the Church would replace their leaders in the following centuries. The Apostles were to be constantly replaced as they died, so that the original structure would remain in place. In this way the Church will always continue.

---

[32] John 14:6 NSRV
[33] Acts 9:1-3 NSRV

Chapter 2 – The Church

What was Pentecost?

After the descent of the Holy Spirit, Peter went out of the upper room (possibly on a roof of the house of Joseph of Arimathea) to speak to the people that were gathered below from the entire world to tell them about the things that had just happened. We should be aware that there are important things about this very first Christian sermon. The beginning of the speech was to explain to the Jews what just happened during Passover and to mention that they were aware of the strange events that had just taken place. He then told all those assembled that they have brought about their own Messiah's death (which should be something that they were aware of from the prophecies Daniel).

Why were all of those people in Jerusalem again, a mere 50 days after Passover? They were there to celebrate Pentecost, which was the 50th day after the original Passover from Exodus where a pillar of fire came down on the Holy Mountain where Moses was, and the Law was delivered to him there. Does this make it clearer why the events of the New Testament Pentecost took place on that day? The fire of God bringing the Law to Moses on that day during the Exodus has a strong parallel with Jesus delivering tongues of flame to the Apostles as the new Law was written on their hearts. Just as The Mosaic Judaism was born at Pentecost, the New Church of Jesus was established on the new Pentecost.

So that is why all of those people were gathered in Jerusalem – to celebrate the delivery of the Law to Moses. When the crowd had heard all that Peter had to say, they asked what they should do now – the wanted the New Law. Peter's answer is very short, clear and to the point. He said that they must repent and be baptized[34]. This is the basic formula for the early evangelistic phase of the church.

What Did the Earliest Church do?

The Church in Acts began by doing just as all Jews did – they went to Temple on Saturday, they kept the kosher laws, and in all respects they continued to follow Hebrew customs. In addition to

---

[34] Acts 2:38 (NSRV) 'Peter said to them, "Repent, and be baptized every one of you in the name of Jesus Christ so that your sins may be forgiven; and you will receive the gift of the Holy Spirit.'

Chapter 2 – The Church

this, however, they held Sunday to be their meeting day, and they gathered on 'the Lord's Day' to do as the Lord instructed – to break bread together. This gathering was not open to the public, however – it was restricted to the baptized only. In order to become baptized, you had to be catechized (taught about Christianity). The basic requirement to enter the assembly to be baptized was to recite the Lord's Prayer.

So what is the plan for the Church?

What was the plan going forward? We know that there was to be a Church on Earth until His return (Acts Chapter 3), so was He going to run things from Heaven, or did He have an earthly plan for His Church?

The establishment of the Church was done at Caesarea Philippi in Mt 16:20 (we will discuss this in more detail later). The location is important because there is a Huge Rock there, from which the river Jordan begins[35]. The reference to 'Rock' is important because the Messiah is making his establishment of His Church in an obvious parallel to the huge rock there, from the source of the Holy River Jordan: [36]

"And I tell you, you are Peter,[Hebrew: Tsur; Aramaic: Kepha - a huge rock] and on this rock [Hebrew: Tsur; Aramaic: Kepha - the same word] I will build my church, and the gates of Hades [the powers of the infernal region] will not prevail against it [or be strong to its detriment or hold out against it]. I will give you the keys of the kingdom of heaven, and whatever you bind on earth will be bound in heaven, and whatever you loose on earth will be loosed in heaven."[37]

I can almost hear some people murmuring about Greek – the words in Greek were Petros for Peter and Petra for the Rock. Petra is a BIG rock, and Petros is a small one – different words, and different meanings - Right? Yes – you are partially correct – but Jesus was not speaking Greek – he was probably speaking Aramaic or maybe Hebrew, as stated above. There is *no such difference* in Aramaic or Hebrew. You might notice that even in Greek, Peter's name is mentioned to be 'Cephas' in Jn 1:42 – this

---

[35] The Jordan river begins there and from 2 other springs from Mount Hermon
[36] Picture taken by EdoM during august 2005 by a Nikon Camedia 4600 – Public Domain Wikipedia Commons image 2005.
[37] Mt 16:18-20 NSRV

Chapter 2 – The Church

is a Greek version of 'Kepha', which is 'rock' in Aramaic. Again, why are the Greek Language names so different than the original? The problem remains that in Greek, male names <u>never</u> end in vowels, so 'Kepha' is a girl's name. You had to change the names if the Greek speaking audience were to understand that we are talking about men here – so they added to or changed the names to suit. In Peter's case, they added and 's' to the end of his name and called him 'Cephas' in Jn 1:42, and in Mt 13:20 the used the Greek version of the term Rock because the author was trying to deliver the message about rock in Greek – using the 'masculine' name for Peter (Petros) and the original word for rock (Petra). In actuality, Peter was not called Petros at all but Kepha.

The message was *intended* to be clear – on the man Peter, Christ announced that His Church would be built. In the search for an alternative to change the meaning of the text, people look at the Greek to intentionally warp the text. Again, searching for an alternate explanation again leads to some weird conclusions.

A friend of mine was trying to explain Mt 13:20, and although the phrase was clear, he tried using hand gestures to indicate an alternate explanation. He pointed to me saying "You are rock" then pointing to himself, he finished "and on THIS rock I will build my Church." So – hand gestures defy the scriptures now? How many of Christ's important statements could be changed forever in this way? Where His fingers crossed when He forgave the Soldiers from the cross? Was He laughing and slapping His knee during the Last supper, chortling while He explained the significance of the New Covenant in His blood? Clearly, we cannot reasonably expect God to resort to childish deceptions while delivering vital information for His Church.

What can we then understand about the establishment of the Church? When the Church was established, it was **not** established on a book – the assumption that Scripture is the basis for the faith is not only misinformed (there was no Bible until at least 397 AD[38]) but assuming that Scriptures can or *should* run anything is quite contrary to the teachings of Jesus and not at all how His Church operated. Scriptures need to be explained to the

---

[38] The first Canon for the Church was established at the Third Council of Carthage in 397 AD. Before this, Bishops approved their own 'reading lists'. The modem Catholic Bibles are based on this canon from 397 AD.

Chapter 2 – The Church

faithful – they do not explain themselves[39]. Scriptures in themselves <u>are not God's basis for His Church</u> – the Apostles were. That is why so little was written immediately after Christ's ascension – the Church was instructed by word of mouth, not using a book. The Great Commission[40] was: *"Go therefore and make disciples of all nations, baptizing them in the name of the Father and of the Son and of the Holy Spirit. And remember, I am with you always, to the end of the age."* Note that The Savior did not mention writing any Bibles.. or writing anything for that matter. The most prolific writer in the New Testament was Paul, who was not present during the Great Commission. While the Apostles were busy teaching from their experience with Christ, Paul was helping to hunt down and kill Christians!

John preferred to speak in person, as probably did all of the Apostles. In 2 Jn 1:12 he mentions a preference not to write but to relate events to the Church in person, and again he says the same thing in 3 Jn 13-14. Were they instructed not to write? There is no clear indication of that, but there is ample evidence that the followers of Christ in the first years were much more committed to relating events by word of mouth and not by writing. There was never any intention that Christians were to be organized according to a book, but instead on the teachings of Christ *as related through the Church.*

Note that Jesus was never described as writing anything – except in one notable time when He wrote *"with his finger on the ground.*[41]*"*If He wanted to write down His instructions for us to follow, He could have done like Mohammed and Joseph Smith did – written all He wanted to relate in some form. The Ten Commandments were written by the Finger of God Himself, but much of Jesus' teaching was about how even that was corrupted by men.

No, the new covenant was to be written on men's hearts, as prophesized by Jeremiah[42]. It was not to be written in stone or collected in books any more, but the New Covenant is to be found

---

[39] Acts 8:30-31: *"Do you understand what you are reading?" And he said, "Well, how could I, unless someone guides me?"*
[40] MT 28:19 NSRV
[41] The specific word used here is cryptic - γῆ Strong 1093 'gae' - Jesus wrote on the "Earth", "Ground" or the "material from which all things were formed." This is found in Jn 8:6 NSRV, and is amazing – just as man was made from 'gae', Jesus wrote in it..
[42] 2 Cor 3:2, Rom 2:15, Jeremiah 31:33

Chapter 2 – The Church

in the hearts of the Qahal – the leaders of the Church. Specifically, the Law of the eternal New Covenant may be now found in the teachings of Christ's Church – the magisterium of the Holy Catholic and Apostolic Church.

We have Peter's name wrong?

We call St. Peter by that name because of the Greek variant of his actual name – Kepha. In Greek, a rock is Petra, and the male form of that is Petros. Remember that he is also called Cephas as an attempt to transfer his Aramaic name into Greek. As we know, Peter's actual name was Kepha – simply 'Rock' in the common language of the time and place. The Greek form attempted to keep the sound of his name but add the masculine ending when they used the work Cephas in Jn 1:42. In Matthew, however, they used the Greek form of the name, which preserves the intent of the original name – simply the word for rock in Greek. We took the Greek work for rock, in a masculine form, and brought the sound into English: Petros = Peter.

But is that what we should be doing? Peter's name was literally 'Rock' – should we be calling him Rock instead? That would be the proper name for him, as that was what Jesus called him. That would really clear up some of the confusion that the entire name changing has created. The Apostle and leader was named Rock, and that is (perhaps) what we should be calling him. Understanding this might make it easier to understand the important commission in Mt 16:18.

Simon the Rock

How many people did God rename, and why? Five people in the entire Bible were re-named by God[43], and they were renamed because God gave them a specific task to do for Him. These five people were Abram, Sarai, Jacob, Hoshe'a the son of Nun and Simon son of John. These were given a new task to perform in life, and they were named Abraham, Sarah, Israel, Joshua and Peter. These are very important events, and not to be underestimated.

---

[43] Lots of people were given new names or changed their names, but only 5 people had their names specifically changed by God himself (or through a message from an Angel). More were named by God also. Most Christians give themselves new names at confirmation to remind them of their new purpose. Few get new names from God himself.

Chapter 2 – The Church

Peter's preeminent position among the apostles was symbolized at the very beginning of his relationship with Christ. At their first meeting, Christ told Simon that his name would thereafter be Rock, which translates as "Peter" (John 1:42). The startling thing was that—aside from the single time that Abraham is called a "rock" (Hebrew: Tsur; Aramaic: Kepha) in Isaiah 51:1-2—in the Old Testament only God Himself was ever called a 'rock'. The word 'rock' was not used as a proper name in the ancient world. If you were to turn to a companion and say, "From now on your name is Asparagus," people would wonder: Why Asparagus? What is the meaning of it? What does it signify?

Indeed, why call Simon son of John "Rock"? Christ was not given to meaningless gestures, and neither were the Jews as a whole when it came to names. Giving a new name meant that the status of the person was changed, as when Abram's name was changed to Abraham (Gen.17:5), Jacob's to Israel (Gen. 32:28). But no Jew had ever been called "Rock" other than Abraham being referred to as 'Rock' one time in Isaiah. The Jews would give other names taken from nature, such as Deborah ("bee," Gen. 35:8), and Rachel ("ewe," Gen. 29:16), but never "Rock". In the New Testament James and John were nicknamed Boanerges, meaning "Sons of Thunder," by Christ, but that was never regularly used in place of their original names, and it certainly was not given as a new name. But in the case of Simon son of John, his new name Kepha (Greek: Petros) definitely replaced the old.

The only apostle to be renamed was Simon Peter, but one should ask 'why?' What was his special purpose? As it turns out, he had several special purposes, and actually was awarded a new name twice (the only one in the Bible to get this!) When? We are about to find out.

Before we do, it is important to consider the role Peter has, and what a stumbling block it is for non-Catholics. All non-Catholics *have to* deny Peter's role as leader of the Church or they must recognize their own lack of authority to participate in any other Church. Once we accept the obvious and repeated leadership role of Peter, and the fact that he passed this role down to his successors, any other church cannot maintain legitimacy. Was the establishment of Peter as leader an offhand gesture? Was it simply recognizing the fact that he talked more than the others, or was it recognition that God was speaking through him?

Chapter 2 – The Church

Consider the Location

Not only was there significance in Simon being confirmed with a new and unusual name, but the place where Jesus solemnly affirmed it was also important. It happened when *"Jesus came into the district of Caesarea Philippi"* (Matt. 16:13), a city that Philip II built on the site and named in honor of Caesar Augustus, who had died in A.D. 14. This place was again renamed in 61 AD by King Agrippa II to Neronias (in honor of the Emperor Nero). This place is now named Panias or Banias as it was in antiquity, as it was named for the huge temple of the god Pan[44] which still has some ruins there. The city once sat near cascades in the Jordan River and near a gigantic wall of rock, a wall about 200 feet high and 500 feet long, which is part of the southern foothills of Mount Hermon. That city no longer exists, but its ruins are near the small Arab town of Banias; and at the base of the rock wall may be found what is left of one of the springs that fed the Jordan. It was here that Jesus pointed to Simon and said in affirmation of the name: *"You are Peter"* (Matt. 16:18).

This place was far from where Jesus and the apostles were – the site is 25 miles north of the Sea of Galilee, in an area just south of Mount Herman. This would have been not only a long

---

[44] Pan was the god of Fear – hence the term 'Panic'.

Chapter 2 – The Church

distance to travel, but a dangerous one as well, as this area would be popular with bandits. The voyage up to this site, at the base of Mount Herman - the Hebrew name "Hermon", the mighty mountain above Caesarea Philippi, may have been based on the root word Herem (means "out of limits" or "Holy").

The significance of the event must have been clear to the other apostles. As devout Jews they knew at once that the location was meant to emphasize the importance of what was being done. None complained of Simon being singled out for this honor; and in the rest of the New Testament he is called by his new name, while James and John remain just James and John, not Boanerges.

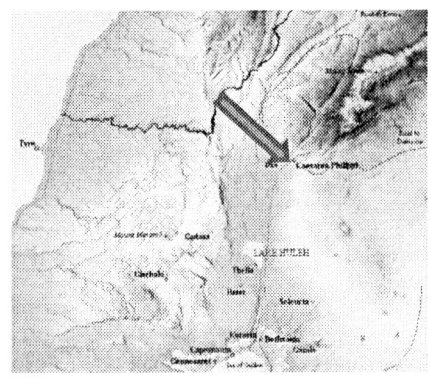

There is ample evidence in the New Testament that Peter was first in authority among the apostles. Whenever they were named, Peter headed the list (Matt. 10:1-4, Mark 3:16-19, Luke 6:14-16, Acts 1:13); sometimes the apostles were referred to as "Peter and those who were with him" (Luke 9:32). Peter was the one who generally spoke for the apostles (Matt. 18:21, Mark 8:29, Luke 12:41, John 6:68-69), and he figured in many of the most dramatic scenes (Matt. 14:28-32, Matt. 17:24-27, Mark 10:23-28). On Pentecost it was Peter who first preached to the crowds (Acts 2:14-40), and he worked the first healing in the Church age (Acts 3:6-7). It is Peter's faith that will strengthen his brethren (Luke 22:32) and Peter is given Christ's flock to shepherd (John 21:17). An angel was sent to announce the resurrection to Peter (Mark 16:7), and the risen Christ first appeared to Peter (Luke 24:34). He headed the meeting that elected Matthias to replace Judas (Acts 1:13-26), and he received the first converts (Acts 2:41). He inflicted the first punishment (Acts 5:1-11), and excommunicated the first heretic (Acts 8:18-23). He led the first council in Jerusalem (Acts 15), and announced the first dogmatic decision (Acts 15:7-11). It was to Peter that the revelation came that Gentiles were to be baptized and accepted as Christians (Acts 10:46-48).

Chapter 2 – The Church

Promises to Peter

When he first saw Simon, "*Jesus looked at him, and said, 'So you are Simon the son of John? You shall be called Cephas [which means Peter]*'" (John 1:42). The word Cephas is merely the attempt to represent the Aramaic Kepha in Greek. Later, after Peter and the other disciples had been with Christ for some time, they went to Caesarea Philippi, where Peter made his profession of faith: "*You are the Christ, the Son of the living God*" (Matt. 16:16). Jesus told him that this truth was specially revealed to him, and then he solemnly reiterated: "*And I tell you, you are Peter*" (Matt. 16:18). To this was added the promise that the Church would be founded, in some way, on Peter (Mt 16:18).

Then two important things were told the apostle. "*Whatever you bind on earth shall be bound in heaven, and whatever you loose on earth shall be loosed in heaven*" (Matt. 16:19). Here Peter was singled out for the authority that provides for the forgiveness of sins and the making of disciplinary rules. Later the apostles as a whole would be given similar power (Matt. 18:18), but here Peter received it in a special sense.

Peter alone was promised something else also: "*I will give you the keys of the kingdom of heaven*" (Matt. 16:19). In ancient times, keys were the hallmark of authority. A walled city might have one great gate; and that gate had one great lock, worked by one great key. To be given the key to the city—an honor that exists even today, though its importance is lost—meant to be given free access to, and authority over, the city. The city to which Peter was given the keys was the heavenly city itself. This symbolism for authority is used elsewhere in the Bible[45].

Finally, after the resurrection, Jesus appeared to his disciples and asked Peter three times, "*Do you love me?*" (John 21:15-17). In repentance for his threefold denial, Peter gave a threefold affirmation of love. Then Christ, the Good Shepherd (John 10:11, 14), gave Peter the authority he earlier had promised: "*Feed my sheep*" (John 21:17). This specifically included the other apostles, since Jesus asked Peter, "*Do you love me more than these?*" (John 21:15), the word "these" referring to the other apostles who were present (John 21:2). In this way Jesus completed the prediction made just before Jesus and his followers went for the last time to the Mount of Olives.

---

[45] Is. 22:22, Rev. 1:18

Chapter 2 – The Church

Immediately before his denials were predicted, Peter was told, "*Simon, Simon, behold, Satan demanded to have you, that he might sift you like wheat, but I have prayed for you that your faith may not fail; and when you have turned again [after the denials], strengthen your brethren*" (Luke 22:31-32). It was Peter who Christ prayed would have faith that would not fail and that would be a guide for the others; and His prayer, being perfectly efficacious, was sure to be fulfilled.

Simon bar Jonah? Why does this mean "Go to Rome"?

In Matthew 16:17, when Jesus is addressing Peter, He calls him '*Simon bar-Jonah*[46].' We know, however, from John 1:42 that Peter's father's name was John, not Jonah[47]. So why this odd statement by Jesus? What is the significance of this new variation to Peter's already new name? Let's look at the statement Jesus is making when this new addition to Peter's name is made:

He said to them, "But who do you say that I am?"

*Simon Peter answered, "You are the Messiah the Son of the living God." And Jesus answered him, "Blessed are you, **Simon son of Jonah**! For flesh and blood has not revealed this to you, but my Father in heaven. And I tell you, you are Peter, and on this rock I will build my church, and the gates of Hades will not prevail against it. I will give you the keys of the kingdom of heaven, and whatever you bind on earth will be bound in heaven, and whatever you loose on earth will be loosed in heaven." Then he sternly ordered the disciples not to tell anyone that he was the Messiah.*[48]

Not only has Peter been renamed 'Rock' since the first time they met, but now (because of this declaration) Peter is given *a new title* – 'Son of Jonah'. This means that Peter is the only one in the Bible to be re-named twice.

'Bar' in Hebrew means 'Son of', like 'Mac' in Scottish Gaelic or 'O'' in Irish Gaelic. So Peter is now *somehow* related to Jonah – so what did Jonah do?

---

[46] Strong's G920 - Barjona= "son of Jonah". Jonah is 'yowna' or Strong's H3123, but Peter's father's name is Ioannes or Strong's G2491 from the Hebrew 'Yowchanan' or Strong H3110 – these are very different names.
[47] 'So you are Simon the son of John? You shall be called Cephas (Peter or rock)'.
[48] Mt 16:16-20 NRSV

Chapter 2 – The Church

Jonah was compelled by God (to the point of being transported by enormous fish) to go to Nineveh to warn them that if they did not turn from their wicked ways, they would be smitten. The God of the Old Testament was known for this sort of thing, and the results were always spectacular. The citizens of Nineveh, being Babylonians, were sworn enemies of the Jews, and you would think that a Jewish prophet would revel in the prospect of going there and informing them of their impending destruction.

Jonah <u>did not</u> want to go there at all. Why?

Jonah knew the message – it was call those people to repent, as is in the Book of Jonah[49]. The text is as shown below:

"Now the word of the Lord[50] came to Jonah son of Amittai, saying "Go at once to Nineveh, that great city, and cry out against it; for their wickedness has come up before me." But Jonah set out to flee to Tarshish from the presence of the Lord. He went down to Joppa and found a ship going to Tarshish; so he paid his fare and went on board, to go with them to Tarshish, away from the presence of the Lord"

Why did Jonah run? It was because Jonah did not want to warn the people of Nineveh! Indeed, when he finally did tell them to repent in Jonah chapter 3, the people repented in such an inspiring way that the LORD let them live. Jonah was furious. Jonah chapter 4 relates Jonah's anger and the Lord's explanation for the action that saved the people of the city.

How does Peter end up in Rome?

Peter knew, when this name was given to him, what his job would be. He would have to bring the Gospel to the Gentiles, no matter how much he might not want to do so. Just as Jonah who was, against his will, sent to preach in Nineveh to convert the pagans there; so Peter was directed to go and convert the pagans in Rome. When he was named "Simon Bar Jonah" the message would have been clear to him and the others. Remember - Jonah was sent to Nineveh, as the capital of Babylon, not to destroy them but to offer them hope of clemency. The Prophet would have delighted in the destruction of the City of Nineveh, as this

---

[49] Jonah 1:1-3 NRSV
[50] Interestingly, this term is often seen in OT writings, and is a term used in the NT to represent Jesus as 'The Word of God made flesh'

Chapter 2 – The Church

would be fair retribution for what they were doing to the Jews. Perhaps this is why Peter packed up and left the land of his birth, and the place his family knew best, and headed to the new Nineveh – Rome.

What were the parallels? The Babylonians conquered Palestine, and dismantled the remains of the Kingdom of Judah, the final part of the Kingdom of Israel. Rome conquered Israel, and at the time of Christ, they were firmly in charge of it. Later, the Romans would destroy the city of Jerusalem (as the Babylonians did) and destroy the Temple (as the Babylonians did), killing and dispersing the people (again, as the Babylonians did). Jonah did not want to follow his instructions, and tried to reject the message – just as Peter would when he denied Christ three times. Regardless, Jonah was compelled to complete the assigned task (delivery by whale) as Jesus had Peter make a threefold confirmation of his dedication to his job as leader of the Church. The parallels are clear once you look at the facts.

Would Peter and the Apostles have understood such a subtle message? Certainly – this was the way Jesus communicated – the messages were deep and complex, intending to convey much information with few words. Naming Peter 'Rock' was a fantastically complex message – showing a new commission and establishment as the new foundation for the faith in a way that the Jews would understand without doubt. It was from Rome that he ran the Church, and it was there that he planted the seed of faith so firmly that the pagan gentiles became the new home for Christ's Church from then until now. Peter was dedicated to remain in Rome – a dangerous place to run a new Church – until he was finally martyred by the Romans. He was immediately replaced by St. Linus in 67 AD. From that time on, up to today with few exceptions, the leader of Christ's Church was firmly established in Rome, and did eventually result in the conversion of the Romans and through them, the conversion of the world. While Jerusalem was destroyed in 70 AD, and that destruction might have heralded the end of Christianity if the Church had been based there, the fact that Peter based the new Church in Rome and not in Jerusalem, as he was instructed, the Church survived and flourished as no one but God Himself could have predicted.

Chapter 2 – The Church

Arguments against Peter as leader of the Church?

Believe it or not, almost none of the 36,000 Christian churches today recognize the authority of Peter or the Church which was built on him. How can they do this in good conscience? Frankly, they *have to* deny his authority, or they cannot invent their own religions, so it becomes a case of grasping at straws. Let's take a closer look at the key verse: "*You are Peter, and on this rock I will build my Church*" (Matt. 16:18). Disputes about this passage have always been related to the meaning of the term "rock." To whom, or to what, does it refer?

Since Simon's new name of 'Peter' itself means rock, the sentence could be rewritten as: "*You are Rock and upon this rock I will build my Church.*" The play on words seems obvious, but commentators wishing to avoid what follows from this—namely the establishment of the papacy—have suggested that the word 'rock' could not refer to Peter but must refer to his profession of faith or to Christ.

From the grammatical point of view, the phrase "*this rock*" must relate back to the closest noun. Peter's profession of faith ("*You are the Christ, the Son of the living God*") is two verses earlier, while his name, a proper noun, is in the immediately preceding clause.

As an analogy, consider this sentence: "*I have a car and a truck, and it is blue.*" Which is blue? The truck is, because that is the noun closest to the pronoun "it." This is all the more clear if the reference to the car is two sentences earlier, as the reference to Peter's profession is two sentences earlier than the term rock. Twisting this simple statement to point to a profession of faith instead of the obvious assignment of Peter as the rock of the Church would be mystifying if it were not so obviously self-serving. Besides, the following statements about the conferral of Keys and power to decide things on earth make no sense if they are not conferred on Peter himself.

Many attempts to avoid the obvious establishment of the papacy and despite the complete acceptance of that role up to the Great Schism around 1,000 AD, people still try to evade the clarity of the scriptures on this subject.

Chapter 2 – The Church

How about Christ as the rock?

The previous arguments also settle the question of whether the word refers to Christ himself, since he is mentioned within the profession of faith. The fact that He is elsewhere, by a different metaphor, called the cornerstone (Eph. 2:20, 1 Pet. 2:4-8) does not disprove that (in this statement) Peter is the foundation. Christ is naturally the principal and, since He will be returning to heaven, the invisible foundation of the Church that He will establish; but Peter is named by Him as the secondary, earthly head of the Church. They will form the visible foundation of the Church on Earth. Peter can be a foundation only *because* Christ is the cornerstone.

In fact, the New Testament contains five different metaphors for the foundation of the Church[51]. One cannot take a single metaphor from a single passage and use it to twist the plain meaning of other passages. Instead, we should respect and harmonize the different passages, for the Church can be described as having different foundations since the word foundation can be used in different senses.

In addition to this, the premise of the argument against Peter being the rock is simply false. In first century Greek the words petros and petra were synonyms. They had previously possessed the meanings of "small stone" and "large rock" in some early Greek poetry, but by the first century this distinction was gone, as Protestant Bible scholars admit (see D. A. Carson's notes on this passage in the Expositor's Bible Commentary).

Some of the effect of Christ's play on words was lost when his statement was translated from the Aramaic into Greek, but that was the best that could be done in Greek. In English, like Aramaic, there is no problem with endings of words; so an English rendition could read: "*You are Rock, and upon this rock I will build my church.*"

Consider another point: If the rock really did refer to Christ (as some claim, based on 1 Cor. 10:4, "*and the Rock was Christ*" though the rock there was a literal, physical rock), why did Matthew leave the passage as it was? In the original Aramaic, and in the English which is a closer parallel to it than is the Greek, the passage is clear enough. Matthew must have realized that his readers would conclude the obvious from "*Rock . . . rock.*"

---

[51] Matt. 16:18, 1 Cor. 3:11, Eph. 2:20, 1 Pet. 2:5-6, Rev. 21:14

Chapter 2 – The Church

If he meant Christ to be understood as the rock, why didn't he say so? Why did he take a chance and leave it up to Paul to write a clarifying text? This presumes, of course, that 1 Corinthians was written after Matthew's Gospel; if it came first, it could not have been written to clarify it.

I apologize if this all seems to be repetitive, but the fact is that there are many subtle attempts to pervert this particular passage by the many millions of people who would prefer not to follow Jesus' instructions to belong to His Church.

What does all of this mean?

The crux of all of this is pretty simple – Jesus came with a plan to save the world from sin, and to make sure that future generations would be able to live the kind of lives God wanted them to. The new Passover Sacrifice of Jesus as the Lamb of God provided the means for the forgiveness of sin, but the process for the delivery of this grace was through the institution of the Church. Baptism was instituted to wash away sin. The Eucharist was instituted to allow us to participate in the new covenant – Christ living through us. Confirmation was instituted to deliver the Holy Spirit to us after Baptism. The institution of Holy Orders was to perpetuate the delivery of the healing Sacraments to the people of God. Confession was instituted to wipe away sins committed after Baptism, as necessary. Marriage was instituted for those who were granted the vocation of the married and family life. Finally Extreme Unction (Sacrament of the sick) was instituted to deliver healing to those in need of healing or who were near death. These all work together to make the Church function in the world as a means to deliver Christ's salvation through the millennia. Without the institution of the Church, which is administrated by men (with all their faults), the mission of Christ falls into chaos and error, as we see throughout the 36,000 broken and separated 'churches', where the mission and message of Christ is destroyed or mangled by well-meaning but ignorant and unauthorized people, who forsake Christ's Church and use the scriptures without understanding.

So is Christ's Church good enough for you? Join the One Holy Catholic and Apostolic Church.

Chapter 3 – Baptism

There are literally hundreds of topics to discuss, and you cannot be prepared for all of them, so the thing to do it to become an expert in a couple of areas – we will prepare for four main areas – Church, Baptism, Salvation and Eucharist. I will fortify these with other topics that may provide the additional details of events that might add hard facts to support the theology.

In Short:

What is Baptism? Do we all agree what it is and what it does? Hardly – there are groups who believe things about Baptism that are very different than the meaning intended and used in scriptures! Today's fundamentalist churches remove the emphasis on Baptism, preferring to place their focus on Faith Alone, in the protestant tradition. Jesus established Baptism for the forgiveness of sin.[52] What else did Christ tell us that we must do to *'gain the kingdom?'* Follow the Commandments and to eat the Body and Blood of Christ to participate in the Covenant. Sounds gruesome? Read on..

Long Version:

There are many references to people being 'saved' in the Bible. Most of the folks today who proclaim themselves 'Saved' are called 'Born Again' Christians. Where did that some from? The term 'Born Again' is not in the Bible[53], so why did some groups latch onto that phrase? All Christians must be baptized, but what about the other sacraments? What did Jesus say must be done to gain His kingdom? He said you must be Baptized, partake in Communion and if you sin, you must confess and get forgiveness from that sin through His Church. Oh, and love God and your neighbor as yourself. Do it all, so you can be 'perfect, therefore, as your heavenly Father is perfect.[54]' Most non-

---

[52] Acts 2:38 NRSV - "Repent, and be baptized every one of you in the name of Jesus Christ so that your sins may be forgiven; and you will receive the gift of the Holy Spirit"
[53] Some Bible versions incorrectly translate 'Annothen' as 'Born Again' instead of 'Born from Above' in Jn 3:7. Although the work can be understood both ways, the use here is consistent with 'being born of the Holy Spirit'.
[54] Mt 5:48 NRSV

Chapter 3 – Baptism

Catholics will tell you that mankind is not able to 'be perfect' as Jesus says – we are all prone to sin, and all sin is the same. This is the Lutheran mindset, and is completely off base. The entire point of the Good News is that sins may be forgiven, and it is possible to now enter the Kingdom of God. No one said it was easy, though. We must each shoulder our cross daily[55], and 'Die to ourselves' as Paul would say[56]. We must reject sin daily to attain the Kingdom. Sounds hard? Yes – yes it is.

Born from Above - Baptism

While Jesus was teaching Nicodemus, He explained that the essential element for salvation was being born from Above by the Holy Spirit and water. Christ did not intend the phrase 'Born from Above' to be understood as 'Born Again' – although a new creation in Christ is to be understood, Nicodemus appeared to misunderstand. Jesus chastised him for his failure to understand the need to be born from above (ἄνωθεν or Annothen) by water and the Holy Spirit through baptism. If you think you have been 'Born Again' by faith alone, you are not doing what Christ instructed – please read and understand.

*"Now there was a Pharisee named Nicodemus, a leader of the Jews. He came to Jesus by night and said to him, "Rabbi, we know that you are a teacher who has come from God; for no one can do these signs that you do apart from the presence of God." Jesus answered him, "Very truly, I tell you, no one can see the kingdom of God without being **born from above**." Nicodemus said to him, "How can anyone be born after having grown old? Can one enter a second time into the mother's womb and be born?" Jesus answered, "Very truly, I tell you, no one can enter the kingdom of God without being born of water and Spirit. What is born of the flesh is flesh, and what is born of the Spirit is spirit. Do not be astonished that I said to you, 'You must be **born from above**.' The wind blows where it chooses, and you hear the sound of it, but you do not know where it comes from or where it goes. So it is with everyone who is born of the Spirit."*

---

[55] Lk 14:27 NRSV: "Whoever does not carry the cross and follow me cannot be my disciple."
[56] 1 Cor 15:31 NRSV:" I die every day! That is as certain, brothers and sisters, as my boasting of you—a boast that I make in Christ Jesus our Lord."

Chapter 3 – Baptism

Nicodemus said to him, "How can these things be?" Jesus answered him, "Are you a teacher of Israel, and yet you do not understand these things?

"Very truly, I tell you, we speak of what we know and testify to what we have seen; yet you do not receive our testimony. If I have told you about earthly things and you do not believe, how can you believe if I tell you about heavenly things? (Jn 3:1-12 NRSV)

The word used in John 3:3-7 is ἄνωθεν or 'An-no-then' in Greek – this means (a) from above, from heaven, (b) from the beginning, from their origin (source), from of old, (c) again, anew. So when Christ said you have to be born 'Annothen' he meant that you have to be born from heaven. Nicodemus appears to have deliberately misunderstood the Messiah, asking how someone could re-enter his mother's womb. So when you use the term 'Born Again' you are quoting Nicodemus, not Christ.

You see, until quite recently (the early 1600s) all Christians believed that Baptism, through a process of the use of Water and the Holy Spirit, allowed someone to be 'Born From Above', as described by the Lord. The cryptic misinterpretation by Nicodemus was always understood to be a double meaning of the term 'Born again'/'Born from above'. This was always the first step in conversion of the Pagan to the Christian – it was the final instruction of Christ to his followers – Baptize all nations in the Name of the Father, and the Son and the Holy Spirit[57]".

Ahh – Baptize only believers? Nope. "Baptize all nations". Households were baptized – Men, Women, Children AND slaves (who were NOT Christians or even Jews).

What does Baptism do?

That is the question, and it is not a simple one. It may be THE question for most people. Why was this 'Ceremonial Washing' so important? More than important – it was considered **Vital** in the early Church. If you are Christian, why did you do it? What is it for?

Let's examine the root of Christianity, and why baptism is so important.

---

[57] MT 28:18-20 NRSV "Go therefore and make disciples of all nations, baptizing them in the name of the Father and of the Son and of the Holy Spirit, and teaching them to obey everything that I have commanded you."

Chapter 3 – Baptism
Who went to Heaven?

Did Jews believe they all went to Heaven? To be clear, did the Jews believe that *anyone* went to Heaven? Sure – 2 or 3 people went to Heaven – Elijah[58], Enoch[59] and probably Moses[60].

No one else[61].

Why not? Because there was no forgiveness of sin. The sin of Adam (Original or Generational sin) carried with it a death sentence. All children of Adam and Eve are doomed to die – and not just physically. Their final resting place was Sheol[62], a shadowy underworld mentioned many times in the Old Testament. This is vital to understand – modern Christians somehow think the forgiveness of sin is a given – if you are sorry, you are forgiven. That is very odd that people think that is the case – **it is not.** No Jews expected their sins to be forgiven, so they worked VERY hard to avoid sin. Think of the stories of the Old Testament – the slightest sin was punished. Why did the Jews wander the desert for 40 years? Not following God's commands. Why was Moses not allowed to enter the Promised Land? The place he performed miracles in the Lord's name to reach? Because he struck a rock twice in defiance of his instructions[63]. That is it – he was told to bring the staff but not to use it. He was instructed to command the water to come out, but hit the rock instead. For us a minor sin – maybe a misunderstanding. For Moses, he never entered the Promised Land. THERE WAS NO FORGIVENESS OF SIN, EXCEPT DIRECTLY FROM THE LORD.

When Jesus forgave someone's sin (Mk 2:7) – the people did not say "OK – that is fine – anyone can do that"? No – they wanted to kill him – only God can forgive sin. Certainly it was

---

[58] 2 Kings 2:11 NASB "there appeared a chariot of fire and horses of fire which separated the two of them. And Elijah went up by a whirlwind to heaven."
[59] Gen 5:24 NASB "Enoch walked with God; and he was not, for God took him."
[60] The book "The Assumption of Moses" was popular in the first century, and many believed Moses to have been assumed into Heaven – it was considered canonical about 800 AD in the Eastern Church
[61] CCC 1026 - By his death and Resurrection, Jesus Christ has opened heaven to us.
[62] Hosea 13:14, Psalm 49:14, 2 Sam 22:6, Proverb 15:24, Proverb 15:11, Job 26:6, Job 11:8, etc. There are about 64 references to Sheol in the Bible.
[63] Numbers 20:11 – the second time Moses was ordered not to strike the rock but did anyway. This is why Moses was not allowed to enter the Promised Land.

Chapter 3 – Baptism

not just a matter of saying "Gosh, I am sorry!" Sins are not forgiven so easily – then or now. Jesus only said 'your sins are forgiven because of your faith' once – to the woman who anointed his feet (Lk 7:50). Several people were healed because of their faith or the faith of their friends, certainly, but sins forgiven due to a personal profession of faith only happened once in the Gospels. The Paralytic had his sins forgiven because of the faith of his friends! [64] This is a lesson indeed.

So what does Baptism do?
Baptism is one of the most basic of Christian Practices, and its purpose is to 'wash away' sin. This should be one of the first six things a Christian learns before going on to learn about more complex things – in Hebrews, Paul[65] is relating that fact (with some frustration) to the Jews:

"Therefore let us go on toward perfection, leaving behind the basic teaching about Christ, and not laying again the foundation: repentance from dead works and faith toward God, instruction about baptisms, laying on of hands, resurrection of the dead, and eternal judgment."[66]

The most basic fundamentals of the faith are:
1) Repentance
2) Faith
3) Baptism
4) the Laying of Hands (Holy Spirit)
5) the resurrection of the dead
6) Eternal judgment

These are the most basic of Christian Beliefs – are they clear to you? If not – you need to drop everything and check what you believe against the teachings of the Early Church, as described in Scripture and the writings of the earliest Christians. If you think you do understand these six essential events in your life, do you know that each of these must happen to you? Are you taught about these as necessary to your salvation? We are only going to

---

[64] Mt 9:2, Mk 2:5, Lk 5:20
[65] Although Hebrews was probably written by St Clement, the 4th Pope.
[66] Heb 6:1-2 NRSV

Chapter 3 – Baptism

cover Baptism in this section, but each of these is vitally important, as understood by the Early Church.

The purpose of the Church is to deliver the sacraments, as established by Jesus, to the world all day every day. The Church also delivers the Good News to all, and by her example, strengthens and guides the people of God towards their heavenly goal.

What Bible passages refer to Baptism? Let's look at the relevant bible passages:

Genesis 1:2 *'the Spirit of God was moving over the face of the waters.'*

In this passage – part of the first statement of Scripture, the Holy Spirit is described bringing about the initial creation events by 'moving over the Face of the Water'. Therefore, God's Holy Spirit and Water together began a new creation.

John 3:5 – *"You must be born from above by water and the Spirit".*

In this passage, the Lord was talking to Nicodemus, and was explaining that a person is 'Born from Above' by Baptism (water and the Holy Spirit), and this was necessary for salvation. Sometimes the Baptism and falling of the Holy Spirit happen in sequence, not always at the same time. By the way, Saint Nicodemus became a leader in the early Church – his commemoration day is July 14th.

Acts 2:38 – *"Repent and be baptized".*

Peter and the Apostles, on Pentecost, went out to speak to the people assembled in Jerusalem. The apostles, having just received the Holy Spirit, spoke in every language and were understood by everyone. Peter made the declaration that the Messiah was just killed, and that he rose from the dead. The people were surprised by this, and they asked what they would have to do to be saved. *"Repent and be baptized, every one of you, in the name of Jesus Christ for the forgiveness of your sins. And you will receive the gift of the Holy Spirit"* Peter said. So

Chapter 3 – Baptism

what does Baptism do? It forgives sin. Then what happens? You will receive the Holy Spirit.

Acts 22:16 *"Get up, be baptized and wash your sins away"*
In this section, Paul is told directly by Ananias to get a move on and immediately be baptized. *"And now what are you waiting for? Get up, **be baptized and wash your sins away**, calling on his name."* There was urgency here, as Paul's life was in danger because he now rejected his old beliefs but was not yet trusted by the Christians. Although Paul clearly believed in the Lord, he had to quickly be baptized.

Acts 19:2-3 – "What Baptism did you receive?"
Here Paul finds that some Christians claimed to be Baptized, but did not yet have the Holy Spirit. He said: *"John's baptism was a baptism of repentance. He told the people to believe in the one coming after him, that is, in Jesus." On hearing this, they were baptized in the name of the Lord Jesus."* At that point they received the Holy Spirit.

Romans 6:3-4 – "Set free from sin"
In this letter to the Romans, Paul explains how baptism allows us to participate in the death and resurrection of the Lord. *".. don't you know that all of us who were baptized into Christ Jesus were baptized into his death? We were therefore buried with him through baptism into death in order that, just as Christ was raised from the dead through the glory of the Father, we too may live a new life. For if we have been united with him in a death like his, we will certainly also be united with him in a resurrection like his. For we know that our old self was crucified with him so that the body ruled by sin might be done away with, that we should no longer be slaves to sin— **because anyone who has died has been set free from sin.**"* In this passage, Paul explains to us how baptism can wipe away all sins – both original sin (sin of Adam) and temporal sins (sins we ourselves have done.) In the process of death and resurrection the person is set free from sin, but that now means that the new person is to avoid sin, and become a 'slave to righteousness'. This makes perfect sense to the Jews, who understood death somewhat differently than we do now. To the Jews of this period, the afterlife was spent in Sheol by all people. Sheol was divided into 4 parts – 2

Chapter 3 – Baptism

for the Jews and 2 for non-Jews (gentiles). The two parts the Jews inhabit was described by Jesus in the story of 'Lazarus at the gate[67]'. The Rich man ended up in the part of Sheol where there is torment for the 'bad' Jews, while Lazarus was in Abraham's Bosom – the place that good Jews went to await the coming of the Messiah. The important part of this relating to Baptism is that (according to Jewish Theology) then you die your sins and commitments died with you, and other than a temporary punishment (up to 7 years in torment for being a 'bad' Jew) your sins and wealth were left behind. In this way, the dead pay their debts due to sin, literally with their life. Remember, Adam's punishment (the one we inherit) was that if he ate from the fruit of Knowledge, he will die. The punishment is quite literally death. The dead have paid that price.

So what Paul is telling us is that through Baptism we die, and are resurrected sinless – just as Adam was created. By the workings of the Holy Spirit, you literally die and then are immediately resurrected into a new life – quite without sin at that point. In that way we all experience death and resurrection at Baptism, and are without sin until we begin to sin (again). Note that this does not prevent future guilt from sins, it just ('Just' – ha ha) wipes away all sins at that time. This is a one-time event – remember – there is ONE baptism for the forgiveness of sins. After that you have to confess your sins and gain absolution through the process instituted by Jesus.

Colossians 2:11-12 – Baptism allows us to participate in the death and resurrection of Christ.

Here Paul is talking about how sin is taken away through the Baptismal death and resurrection, relieving sin. *"Your whole self, ruled by the flesh, was put off when you were circumcised by Christ, **having been buried with him in baptism**, in which you were also raised with him through your faith in the working of God, who raised him from the dead. When you were dead in your sins and in the un-circumcision of your flesh, God made you alive with Christ. **He forgave us all our sins, having canceled the charge of our legal indebtedness, which stood against us and condemned us; he has taken it away, nailing it to the cross.**"*

---

[67] Gospel of Luke 16:19–31

Chapter 3 – Baptism

Titus 3:5 – "Washing of rebirth and renewal"

Here Paul speaks to the Titus about the sin being washed away through Baptism. "**He saved us through the washing of rebirth and renewal by the Holy Spirit**, *whom he poured out on us generously through Jesus Christ our Savior, so that, having been justified by his grace, we might become heirs having the hope of eternal life.*"

1 Peter 3:21 – "this water symbolizes baptism that now saves you also"

Here Peter calls people to be kind and know that, just as Noah was saved through the waters of the flood in his Ark, the faithful are saved from sin by the waters of Baptism. *"God waited patiently in the days of Noah while the ark was being built. In it only a few people, eight in all, were saved through water, and this water symbolizes baptism that now saves you also—not the removal of dirt from the body but the pledge of a clear conscience toward God It is effective because of the resurrection of Jesus Christ."* Just as the Ark saved the 8 people and animals from destruction, Baptism now saves us from sin and destruction. Baptism is not just water to clean us, but it contains the power to 'Save Us' because of the resurrection of Christ.

Acts 10:44 - "Can anyone withhold baptism from these who have received the Holy Spirit?"

Here Peter recognizes that foreigners, who there was some discussion as to if they could become Christian, had received the Holy Spirit, and therefore it was necessary to immediately baptize them. *"Then Peter said, "Surely no one can stand in the way of their being baptized with water. They have received the Holy Spirit just as we have." So he ordered that they be baptized in the name of Jesus Christ."*

All Other references to Baptism in the New Testament:

- **Mt 3:6** *"And when they confessed their sins, he baptized them in the Jordan River."*

- **Mt 3:13-14** *"Then Jesus went from Galilee to the Jordan River to be baptized by John. But John tried to talk him out of it. "I am the one who needs to be baptized by you," he said, "so why are you coming to me?"*

Chapter 3 – Baptism

- **Mt 3:16** *"After His baptism, as Jesus came up out of the water, the heavens were opened and He saw the Spirit of God"*

- **Mk 1:4-5** *"John did baptize in the wilderness, and preach the baptism of repentance for the remission of sins. And there went out unto him all the land of Judaea, and they of Jerusalem, and were all baptized of him in the river of Jordan, confessing their sins." This messenger was John the Baptist. He was in the wilderness and preached that people should be baptized to show that they had repented of their sins and turned to God to be forgiven. This was not the same Baptism as the later Christian Baptism.*

- **Mk 1:9** *"One day Jesus came from Nazareth in Galilee, and John baptized him in the Jordan River."*

- **Mk 10:38-39** *"Are you able to be baptized with the baptism of suffering I must be baptized with?" "Oh yes," they replied, "we are able!" Then Jesus told them, "You will indeed drink from my bitter cup and be baptized with my baptism of suffering.*

- **Mk 16:16** *"Anyone who believes and is baptized will be saved. But anyone who refuses to believe will be condemned."*

- **Lk 3:3** *"Then John went from place to place on both sides of the Jordan River, preaching that people should be baptized to show that they had repented of their sins and turned to God to be forgiven.*

- **Lk 3:7** *"When the crowds came to John for baptism, he said, "You brood of snakes! Who warned you to flee God's coming wrath?"*

- **Lk 3:12-14** *"Even corrupt tax collectors came to be baptized and asked, "Teacher, what should we do?" "Don't collect any more than you are required to," he told them. Then some soldiers asked him, "And what should we do?" He replied,*

Chapter 3 – Baptism

"Don't extort money and don't accuse people falsely--be content with your pay."

- **Lk 3:21** *"One day when the crowds were being baptized, Jesus himself was baptized"*

- **Lk 7:29-30** *"When they heard this, all the people—even the tax collectors—agreed that God's way was right, for they had been baptized by John. But the Pharisees and experts in religious law rejected God's plan for them, for they had refused John's baptism."*

- **Lk 12:50** *"I have a terrible baptism of suffering ahead of me, and I am under a heavy burden until it is accomplished."*

- **Jn 3:23** *"At this time John the Baptist was baptizing at Aenon, near Salim, because there was plenty of water there; and people kept coming to him for baptism."*

- **Acts 1:5** *"John baptized with water, but in just a few days you will be baptized with the Holy Spirit."*

- **Acts 1:21-22** *"So now we must choose a replacement for Judas from among the men who were with us the entire time we were traveling with the Lord Jesus - from the time he was baptized by John until the day he was taken from us. Whoever is chosen will join us as a witness of Jesus' resurrection."*

- **Acts 2:41** *"Those who believed what Peter said were baptized and added to the church that day—about 3,000 in all."*

- **Acts 8:13** *"But now the people believed Philip's message of Good News concerning the Kingdom of God and the name of Jesus Christ. As a result, many men and women were baptized. Then Simon himself believed and was baptized. He began following Philip wherever he went, and he was amazed by the signs and great miracles Philip performed."*

- **Acts 8:36-38** *"As they rode along, they came to some water, and the eunuch said, "Look! There's some water! Why can't I*

Chapter 3 – Baptism

be baptized?" He ordered the carriage to stop, and they went down into the water, and Philip baptized him."

- **Acts 9:18** *"Instantly something like scales fell from Saul's eyes, and he regained his sight. Then he got up and was baptized."*
- **Acts 10:37** *"You know what happened throughout Judea, beginning in Galilee, after John began preaching his message of baptism."*
- **Acts 10:48** *"So he gave orders for them to be baptized in the name of Jesus Christ. Afterward Cornelius asked him to stay with them for several days."*
- **Acts 18:25** *"He had been taught the way of the Lord, and he taught others about Jesus with an enthusiastic spirit and with accuracy. However, he knew only about John's baptism."*
- **Gal 3:27** *"For we died and were buried with Christ by baptism. And just as Christ was raised from the dead by the glorious power of the Father, now we also may live new lives."*
- **Eph 4:5** *"There is one Lord, one faith, one baptism"*
- **Heb 6:2** *"You don't need further instruction about baptisms, the laying on of hands, the resurrection of the dead, and eternal judgment."*
- **1 Jn 5:6** *"And Jesus Christ was revealed as God's Son by his baptism in water and by shedding his blood on the cross—not by water only, but by water and blood."*

John the Baptist was a Levite – remember, his father was the high priest offering incense in the Temple. He would have understood Levitical practices, such as the ceremonial cleaning needed to purify a priest before most rituals in the Temple. It should not be surprising, then, that John's Baptism of Repentance was something the people recognized and thought valid.

Over and over we see that Christ's Baptism is not a hollow ritual – not a ceremonial cleaning at all. It is the very foundation

Chapter 3 – Baptism

of salvation itself – we are saved from sin through the action of the water and Holy Spirit – this works because of the death and resurrection of Christ, and through this process we participate in His death and His resurrection, which allows us to be Born from Above. Is this all we have to do to reach heaven? No, but it is a necessary first step.

How do you attain the Kingdom?

As we see by reading the New Testament, the process of attaining the Kingdom is stated over and over again. There are some variations, but overall the early Church had a set methodology, backed up by the Didache[68]. The set parts are:

1. **Realize that Jesus is the Messiah** (Eph 4:5, many Quotes, if you do not do this the rest doesn't matter)
2. **Repent from ALL SIN** (Acts 2:38, Mt 4:17, Mk 6:12, Lk 11:32, Lk 13:3, Lk 13:5, Lk 15:7, Lk 15:10, Lk 16:30, Lk 24:47, Acts 3:19, Acts 17:30, 2 Tim 2:25, 2 Pet 3:9, Rev 2:5, Rev 2:16-22)
3. **Be Baptized** (Acts 2:38, Acts 19:5, Acts 10:48, Acts 8:36, Acts 8:13)
  a. *Wash away sin* (Acts 22:16, Acts 2:38, Acts 9:18)
  b. *Be saved from sin/Join Church* (Acts 2:41, Mk 16:16, Lk 7:29, Mk 16:16, 1 Pet 3:21)
4. **Receive the Holy Spirit** (Acts 2:38, Acts 10:24, Mt 3:16, Titus 3:5)
5. **Bear Fruit** (Mt 3:8, Lk 3:8, Lk 5:32, James 2)
6. **DO NOT SIN AGAIN** (Rom 6:1-3, Heb 13:4, 1 Cor 6:9, Jn 5:14, 1 Cor 15:34, Lk 17:3-4, Heb 6:1-4, Heb 12:17, Gal 3:27, Rom 6:3)
7. **Judgment** (Mt 5:22, Mt 10:15, Mt 11:22-24, Mt 12:36-42, Mt 25:31, Mt 27:19, Lk 10:14, Lk 11:31, Jn 3:19, Jn 5:22-30, Jn 7:24, Jn 8:16, Jn 9:39, Jn 12:31, Jn 16:8-11, Acts 24:25, Rom 2:1-5, Rom 5:16, Rom 11:33, Rom 12:3, Rom 13:2, Rom 14:3-13, 1 Cor 4:5, 1 Cor 5:3, 1 Cor 7:40, 1 Cor 10:29, 1 Cor 11:29, 2 Cor 5:10, Thes 1:5, 1 Tim 5:24, Heb 6:2, Heb 9:27, Heb 10:27, Jam 2:13, 1 Pet 4:17, 2 Pet 2:4-11, 2 Pet 3:7, 1 Jn 4:17, Jude 1:5-15, Rev 14:7, Rev

---

[68] The Didache (pronounced Did-a-key) is the earliest known Catechism of the Church from the Apostles.

Chapter 3 – Baptism

15:4, Rev 16:7, Rev 17:1, Rev 18:10, Rev 18:20, Rev 19:2, Rev 20:4-15, Rev 21:8, Rev 22:12)

There are many who are aware of these scripture references, but who do not understand that following Christ's instructions and teaching is more than a 'one step process'. The message of Christ is not a single action that must be taken, but in fact it is an entirely new way of life. It begins at Baptism, when validly conducted, but after being 'Born from Above' the new life begins – one entirely in service to God and others, and the rejection of sin. The new Christian is a new creation in Christ, and as such cannot live in sin. Certainly, the earliest Church understood that Christ's message was not an easy one, but it did offer a heavenly reward.

In many respects, the message was quite contrary to the earlier message in these important elements:

- You no longer had to be a descendant of Abraham to take part in the covenants. Anyone can become Christian.
- The Covenant of Moses was being changed in many ways – the Temple and animal sacrifice as outlined in the Law were changed dramatically.
- The Temple was rendered much less important, and the people were warned that it would be destroyed. This prophecy went back to Daniel at least, but the last warning was in the Revelation of John.
- The Commandments of God remained, but were now extended to a new covenant – a covenant in the Messiah's blood. The 10 commandments remained, although the 613 elements of the Law did not.
- Riches and earthly power no longer indicated the Lord's favor. Those who shared wealth and privilege gained greater treasures in Heaven as a result.
- Sin could be wiped away through Baptism, including sins previously irrevocable (generational sin). This is a one-time event, and following Baptism, sin must be avoided at all cost.
- The Holy Days were largely rendered moot. The big days such as Yom Kippur (Day of Atonement) and Passover were now replaced by the Christian weekly celebration of the resurrection of Christ with the

reenactment of the Last Supper on the Lord's Day (Sunday).
- An interior faith was emphasized over the external practices, although many traditional worship methods continued.

What does all of this mean?

As you can see, there are many passages in the New Testament about Baptism. Baptism is the 'new circumcision'[69] for Christians, and indicated participation in the New Covenant. It symbolizes the waters of the 'Red Sea' and 'New Creation' for the new Church, and its effect is to wipe away all sin and allows the indwelling of the Holy Spirit. Baptism is a required sacrament for salvation. Note that there are 3 different elements in the baptismal salvation process: they are related to Justification, Baptism and the Holy Spirit.

Justification (being set right in God's sight) is accomplished by the death and resurrection of the Lord. This is not something that any person can earn or accomplish in themselves – this is the singular accomplishment of the Messiah.

In addition to this, there is one Baptism, which washes away all sin. The Holy Spirit (Paraclete) comes at some point before or after Baptism as a teacher or guide for the Christian. For Jesus, the Holy Spirit descended immediately after Baptism, the Apostles received the Holy Spirit a long time after Baptism, but in Acts 10:44 the un-baptized receive the Holy Spirit, so Peter knew that they must immediately be baptized.

Baptism is not 'an outward expression of an interior change' as some would have us believe, but it is the literal death and resurrection of a Christian into a new life in Christ, cancelling prior sins and giving us strength to practice the Christian life. Despite this gift from God himself, many do not make the efforts necessary to maintain their salvation, and they (through sin) lose it.

Have you been properly baptized and confirmed into Christ's Church?

---

[69] Colossians 2:11-13 ""In Him also you were circumcised having been buried with Him in baptism, in which you also were raised with Him through the faith in the working of God, who raised Him from the dead."

Chapter 4 – What did Jesus say to do to be 'Saved'?

"Saved" is a loaded term today for most English speaking Christians. What they mean by it is very different that the meaning intended and used in scriptures! Forget for a moment the implications of 'Saved' by today's fundamentalist churches, and think about the common use of the word – that was what the Bible writers meant. Being saved from something, specifically Death. How did Christ 'save' us? His sacrifice and establishment of Baptism and Reconciliation for the forgiveness of sin. [70] *Is this what you mean, or are you trying to find out how to get into Heaven? These are very different questions..*

In Short:
There are two conditions described in the New Testament – salvation from sin, and inheriting the Kingdom. The two are related, but are not the same. One must be first saved from sin, and then it is possible to attain the heavenly kingdom. We accomplish this by living according to 'the Way' of Christ so as to pass Judgment. There is no free ticket to Heaven, and although it is possible to have sin removed, avoiding it while living the Christian lifestyle is not intuitive or easy to accomplish. It is only through true commitment to being the New Creation and with help from the Holy Spirit can we do what needs to be done.

To be clear, Baptism saves you from Sin, and Last Judgment evaluates what you have done to determine if you have attained the Kingdom. *Being* Christian is not just a verbal commitment.

Long Version:
What is necessary for Salvation or gaining the Kingdom or Going to Heaven?

That is the Big Question!

Here is an easy answer – straight from Scripture. Follow the message of the Apostles (6 steps – Paul states them in Heb 6:1-3) then at Judgment the Christ will direct you to Heavenly reward or a much less desirable eternal reward.

---

[70] Acts 2:38 - "Repent, and each of you be baptized in the name of Jesus Christ for the forgiveness of your sins"

Chapter 4 – What did Jesus say to do to be 'Saved'?

Can we just do one thing and get 'Saved'? Nope – everyone is subject to Judgment, and that is based on 'What you have done'.[71]

There are many references to people being 'saved' in the Bible. Many of these are listed below:

Hebrew Testament:
- Gen 19:20 – "Let me escape so my life may be SAVED"
- Gen 47:25 – "You have SAVED our lives!"
- Ex 14:30 – "The LORD SAVED Israel.. from the Egyptians"
- Num 10:9 – "You will be SAVED from your enemies"
- Dt 33:29 – "Israel.. a people SAVED by the LORD"
- Jgs 3:31 – "Shamgar.. also SAVED Israel"
- 2Sam 19:5 – "servants.. today SAVED your life"
- 2Sam 19:9 – "The King SAVED us .. from the Philistines"
- 2Sam 22:4 – "I am SAVED from my enemies"
- 2Kgs 14:27 – "He SAVED them by the hand of Jeroboam"
- Etc..

In the Hebrew testament we see, over and over again, that the references to 'saved' are from peril in life, not relating to some afterlife. One important fact here – in the Torah (the basic Hebrew Bible) there is no reference or promise of an afterlife in Heaven! The Hebrew concept of an afterlife centered on Sheol[72], a shadowy afterlife where the faithful get rest in Abraham's Bosom, and the wicked are punished.

Therefore, all references to 'being saved' refer to saving someone from peril or illness or death. This does and has impacted the mindset of the Jews – they often see their faith as a way of life leading to rewards *in this life*, not as a means towards a Heavenly reward in the next. Jews often faithfully observe the Law, while having a weak faith in the afterlife. They do not perform any acts looking for a heavenly reward, but just doing as they are told by their Creator.

---

[71] The two Judgment scenes in Scripture are Mt 25:31-46 and Rev 20:13 specifically say that everyone (other than Martyrs) is judged on their deeds. Rev 22:12 – one of the last statements in the Bible, says that the Christ will give to each "According to what he has done".

[72] Gen 37:35, Gen 42:38, Gen 44:29, Gen 44:31, Num 16:30, Deu 32:22, 1 Sa 2:6, 2 Sa 22:6, 1 Ki 2:6, Job 7:9, Job 11:8, Job 14:13, etc.

Chapter 4 – What did Jesus say to do to be 'Saved'?

Even today in Israel, Orthodox or Observant Jews account for only about 20% of the Jewish population.[73] Over the centuries, there has always been uncertainty about any afterlife in Judaism. At the time of Christ, the Pharisees believed in an afterlife, but the ruling class (Sadducees) did not. As Christians, we often make assumptions in this regard that simply do not match the Hebrew Testament scriptures – specifically the Torah.

What is being saved in the OT?
In the Hebrew Scriptures, we are talking about physical life. Over and over again in the Hebrew Scriptures the reference is not for an afterlife – salvation refers to saving one's life in this world, not the next. Is it different in the Gospels?

Salvation in the New Testament
The Gospels, however, DO teach about an afterlife – quite a lot, actually! Where does the term 'Saved' show up there? Here are all of the references to 'Saved' in the New Testament:

- Mt 10:22 – *"But the one who has endured to the end **will be** SAVED"* – Not now saved; will be saved.
- Mt 19:25 – *"Then who **can be** SAVED?"* Not many are saved..
- Mt 24:13 – *"The one who endures to the end, he will be SAVED"* again – *'will be'* not *'is'* saved.
- Mt 24:22 – *"Unless those days had been cut short, no life **would have been** SAVED"* – saving life.
- Mt 27:42 – *"He SAVED others; He cannot save himself"* Life itself being saved.
- Mk 10:26 – *"Then who **can be** SAVED?"*
- Mk 13:13 – *"the one who endures to the end, he will be SAVED"*
- Mk 13:20 – *"Unless the Lord had shortened those days, no life would have been SAVED"*
- Mk 15:31 – *"He SAVED others; He cannot save Himself."* Saved others from death, can He save himself from death?

---

[73] Rabbi Levi Brackman, "Israel 2010", Ynet 5.18.2010

Chapter 4 – What did Jesus say to do to be 'Saved'?

- Mk 16:16 – *"He who has believed and been baptized **shall be** SAVED"* 'Shall be' not 'Is' saved.
- Lk 7:50 – *"Your faith has SAVED you; go in peace"*
- Lk 8:12 – *"the devil comes and takes away the word from their heart, so that they will not believe and be SAVED."*
- Lk 13:23 – *"Are there just a few who are being SAVED?"*
- Lk 18:26 – *"Then who can be SAVED?"*
- Lk 23:35 – *"He SAVED others; let Him save Himself"*
- Jn 3:17 – *"That the world might be SAVED through Him"*
- Jn 5:34 – *"I say these things that you may be SAVED"*
- Jn 10:9 – *"I am the door; if anyone enters through Me, he will be SAVED"*

The question is (as should be obvious) – what are you being saved from? Why are you are being SAVED? The follow up questions might then be, 'Is there anything that is required after salvation?'

The scriptures use the term 'saved' to describe something that happens before death.

As you can see from all the quotes above, the references never mention anything after death, just references to the immediate or near immediate time. "Being Saved", or "You have been saved" are the terms used in the references above. This indicates that 'being saved' is something that is going on during life, not after death. So if being saved is something that goes on during life, what can it be referring to? Salvation from sin has to take place during your life – this is not something that happens after death. When are you assured that you are going to Heaven?

Only at Judgment are you guaranteed to go to Heaven or Hell, when the Lord tells you that you are to go there[74]. Until then, you are not certain of your final destination.

Let's start with what you are being saved from.

Sin. Death from the Sin of Adam and death from your sins from defying God on a daily basis.

---

[74] Rev 20:13-15, Mt 25:31-46, and many more.

Chapter 4 – What did Jesus say to do to be 'Saved'?

The gift of the Messiah is the forgiveness of sin – something that was impossible before this. When Christ forgave sin, He was rebuked for it – "Only God can forgive sin" was the answer.[75]

Nonetheless, it was in the power of the Christ to forgive sin, and that is how he was saving people – through the forgiveness of sin, as in the examples above. This was truly a unique and powerful function of Christ, and did indeed "Save People from their Sins" as pronounced by Gabriel.[76] Baptism is the first way to have all sin removed[77], so when you are baptized you are 'saved'. Only Mormons believe that one can be baptized after death, but they are not using the Christian Scriptures to determine that.

Therefore, 'Being Saved' in the New Testament context refers to the elimination of sin from the Christian converts through the process of initiation into Christianity[78]. We know this process as Baptism. This process 'saves' the baptized from the ravages of sin, and makes it possible for them to attain the Kingdom after Judgment.

OK – you have been saved – now what?

Let's now separate 'Salvation' from 'Attaining the Kingdom'. Salvation – being saved from sin – is accomplished through Baptism, and then keeping the commandments to the end. Baptism certainly saves you from sin, but what then gets you into Heaven? Did Jesus speak specifically about 'Gaining the Kingdom' or 'Inheriting eternal life'?

What to do for salvation or attaining a heavenly reward?

Did anyone ask Christ the question directly – "What must I do to inherit eternal life?" Yes – quite often, actually. For example:

---

[75] Mark 2:1-12
[76] Luke 1:32
[77] Nicene Creed (325 AD) – "One Baptism for the forgiveness of sin"
[78] Initiation into the Church is through Baptism – CCC 1263

Chapter 4 – What did Jesus say to do to be 'Saved'?

- On one occasion an expert in the law stood up to test Jesus. "Teacher," he asked, "what must I do to inherit eternal life?" <u>"What is written in the Law?"</u> he replied. "How do you read it?"
  He answered: " **'Love the Lord your God with all your heart and with all your soul and with all your strength and with all your mind'; and, 'Love your neighbor as yourself.'"**
  "You have answered correctly," Jesus replied. "Do this and you will live" (Luke 10:25-28).

Unfortunately, in many modern churches, the ministers say, "Simply believe, and have faith." There is an understandable urge to simplify Christianity and try to make it easy in most modern (fundamentalist) churches today. It seems that telling people that they are 'Saved' and promising a heavenly reward for believing fills the pews at church. How about that!

Does everyone who becomes Christian make it to Heaven? That was asked too:

- *"Not everyone who says to me, 'Lord, Lord,' will enter the kingdom of heaven, but only the one who **does the will of my Father** in heaven.* Mt 7:21
- *"Therefore, my beloved, just as you have always obeyed me, not only in my presence, but much more now in my absence, **work out your own salvation with fear and trembling**; for it is God who is at work in you, enabling you both to will and to work for His good pleasure."* Phil 2:12
- Someone asked him, "Lord, will only a few be saved?" He said to them, *"Strive to enter through the narrow door; for **many, I tell you, will try to enter and will not be able**. When once the owner of the house has got up and shut the door, and you begin to stand outside and to knock at the door, saying, 'Lord, open to us,' then in reply he will say to you, 'I do not know where you come from.'"* Luke 13:23-25

So, armed with a laptop computer search engine, I worked my way through the teachings of Jesus to understand what He taught we must do to inherit eternal life. After all, He is "*the way and the truth and the life. No one comes to the Father except through [Him]*" (John 14:6).

Chapter 4 – What did Jesus say to do to be 'Saved'?

One requirement?

Many Christian groups believe that only one thing is required of a Christian – Faith. Faith Alone (Sola Fideles) was the mantra of Luther and his revolution, and this was not accepted in the previous 1,500 years as being the teaching of Christ.

What if Moses had decided that only the First Commandment was required, and did not teach the others? Can a Jew just say that the first commandment is the only requirement to be a Jew? Can anyone ignore the teachings of Jesus in favor of accepting only one of His instructions? What did Jesus teach about being a Christian? It seems odd that a book the size of the Bible just gives one message over and over – surely there is more to Christianity that "Salvation by Faith Alone"? Did Jesus teach us that we must be 'be doers of the word, and not merely hearers who deceive themselves."? (James 1:22)

Faith and . . .

Those who believe today that faith is the only requirement apparently never searched the Scriptures for that phrase. The results are disappointing – there is one result – James 2:24 – *"You see that a man is justified by works and not by faith alone."* Not only does it seem that Faith is not the only requirement, research shows that four times the number of passages deal with putting faith into practice in tangible, practical ways.

John the Baptist implies that both faith and obedience to Christ's teaching are essential for eternal life: "And anyone who believes in God's Son has eternal life. Anyone who doesn't obey the Son will never experience eternal life but remains under God's angry judgment." (John 3:36).

So, please read the following passages carefully and ask yourself, must I go beyond simply faith to experience eternal life. And for those who see a contradiction between "salvation by faith" and "salvation by works," remember that although the First, basic requirement is faith; but that is just the beginning, as Jesus has explained in the Gospels. We are staying in statements attributed directly to Christ from the Gospels alone, because I want to be sure that we are getting instructions directly from Christ.

Before we get started, let us remember that Jesus was (and I assume, still is) a fully Jewish man, a man "born under the Law"

Chapter 4 – What did Jesus say to do to be 'Saved'?

(Gal 4:4). Did Jesus and his followers keep the Laws of Moses? Let's consider these quotes from the NT:

- For all who have sinned without the Law will also perish without the Law, and **all who have sinned under the Law will be judged by the Law (Romans 2:12)**
- Now we know that whatever the Law says, **it speaks to those who are under the Law, so that every mouth may be closed and all the world may become accountable to God** (Romans 3:19)
- to those who are without law, as without law, though not being without the law of God but **under the law of Christ**, so that I might win those who are without law **(1 Cor 9:21)**
- **But if you are led by the Spirit, you are not under the Law.** (Gal 5:18)
- What then? **Shall we sin because we are not under law but under grace**? May it never be! (Rom 6:15)
- For as **many as are of the works of the Law are under a curse**; for it is written, "Cursed is everyone who does not abide by all things written in the book of the law, to perform them." (Gal 3:10)
- But **before faith came, we were kept in custody under the law**, being shut up to the faith which was later to be revealed (Gal 3:23)
- **But we know that the Law is good, if one uses it lawfully**, realizing the fact that **law is not made for a righteous person**, but for those who are lawless and rebellious, for the ungodly and sinners, for the unholy and profane, for those who kill their fathers or mothers, for murderers and immoral men and homosexuals and kidnappers and liars and perjurers, and whatever else is contrary to sound teaching, according to the glorious gospel of the blessed God, with which I have been entrusted.(1 Tim 1:8-11)

What did Jesus say?

- "Don't misunderstand why I have come. **I did not come to abolish the Law of Moses or the writings of the prophets.** No, I came to accomplish their purpose." (Mt 5:17)

Jesus also made several other references to those who kept the Law, and said that that was good enough (Luke 10:25-28, Lk 18:18-21, 1 Jn 2:3-4, etc.)

So what did Jesus say? (WDJS?)

Let's see what you remember from the teachings of Jesus – answer the following questionnaire:

'WDJS' Questionnaire

What Did Jesus Say about salvation? Please answer Yes (He did say that), No (He never said that/someone else did) or Maybe (He said something like that but not *exactly* that).

Did Jesus say:	Yes	No	Maybe
1. To be strong enough to practice your faith or 'lose salvation'?	☐	☐	☐
2. Keep all of the 10 Commandments?	☐	☐	☐
3. Demonstrate your faith with actions, not just rely on faith?	☐	☐	☐
4. Believe Jesus is God incarnate and walk with Him daily, Not just accept Him?	☐	☐	☐
5. Believe and put all of Christ's teachings into action in daily life?	☐	☐	☐
6. To hear the words of Jesus and believe in God the Father?	☐	☐	☐
7. That anyone who does not follow Jesus will face God's wrath?	☐	☐	☐
8. That Jesus will resurrect all of His followers on the last day?	☐	☐	☐
9. That anyone who believes that Jesus is God will never die?	☐	☐	☐
10. To love God with every last ounce of strength?	☐	☐	☐
11. To love every other person exactly as much as you love yourself?	☐	☐	☐
12. To give food and drink to anyone in need?	☐	☐	☐
13. To share your home with strangers?	☐	☐	☐
14. To provide clothes to anyone in need?	☐	☐	☐
15. To look after the sick?	☐	☐	☐
16. To visit those in Prison?	☐	☐	☐
17. To sell of your goods and distribute the money to the poor?	☐	☐	☐
18. To love and pray for your enemies?	☐	☐	☐
19. To step into others' arguments to bring hostility to an end?	☐	☐	☐
20. To eat Jesus' Body and drink His blood?	☐	☐	☐

'WDJS' Questionnaire

What Did Jesus Say about salvation? Please answer Yes (He did say that), No (He never said that/someone else did) or Maybe (He said something like that but not *exactly* that).

Did Jesus say:	Yes	No	Maybe?
21. To become baptized so that you can go to heaven?	☐	☐	☐
22. To do everything that God instructs you to do every day?	☐	☐	☐
23. To keep your heart pure and innocent?	☐	☐	☐
24. To become and act in all righteousness?	☐	☐	☐
25. To do anything possible to avoid any sin?	☐	☐	☐
26. To destroy all things that might lead you to sin?	☐	☐	☐
27. To do good things?	☐	☐	☐
28. To become like a child?	☐	☐	☐
29. To die to yourself daily and carry whatever cross is given to you?	☐	☐	☐
30. To give up all worldly goods?	☐	☐	☐
31. To hate the world and only follow Christ?	☐	☐	☐
32. To use all of the talents that God has given you?	☐	☐	☐
33. To always tell people that you are Christian, especially in hostile company?	☐	☐	☐
34. That you must account for every word that you said on the Day of Judgment?	☐	☐	☐
35. If you are holding a grudge, you should be banned from attending church?	☐	☐	☐
36. To Judge someone else, and say that they are in sin?	☐	☐	☐
37. You do not have to produce any good actions in your life?	☐	☐	☐
38. To repent for all of the bad things you have done?	☐	☐	☐
39. To become baptized for your sins to be forgiven?	☐	☐	☐
40. You must share extra food or clothes with the poor?	☐	☐	☐

'WDJS' Questionnaire

What Did Jesus Say about salvation? Please answer Yes (He did say that), No (He never said that/someone else did) or Maybe (He said something like that but not *exactly* that).

Did Jesus say:	Yes	No	Maybe?
41. That you are to be content with the pay you get?	☐	☐	☐
42. It is ok to demand money or goods that you do not deserve?	☐	☐	☐
43. To constantly pray and reflect what Jesus wants of you?	☐	☐	☐
44. It is expected that you will be hated because you are a Christian?	☐	☐	☐
45. Generally do what Jesus has taught, but to take a break sometimes?	☐	☐	☐
46. That you can be a Christian without following every command Jesus gave?	☐	☐	☐
47. That if someone is living in sin, should you tell them the right thing to do?	☐	☐	☐
48. That it is Ok to have 'naughty thoughts' about someone else?	☐	☐	☐
49. That anyone can be rich and easily enter Heaven?	☐	☐	☐
50. To leave everything – including family and all possessions – to be Christian?	☐	☐	☐
51. That you can love money and love God?	☐	☐	☐
52. To practice Righteousness?	☐	☐	☐
53. You are saved by Grace alone?	☐	☐	☐
54. To do as the Pharisees taught?	☐	☐	☐
55. We are to baptize the world in the name of the Father, Son and Holy Spirit?	☐	☐	☐
56. We are to rely on Grace for salvation instead of works?	☐	☐	☐
57. Salvation comes from Faith alone?	☐	☐	☐
58. It is OK to angrily call a person a "Fool!"?	☐	☐	☐
59. I can never ever swear to do anything: I can just say "yes" or "no"?	☐	☐	☐
60. To pray or give to the poor secretly	☐	☐	☐

'WDJS' Questionnaire

Answers:

1. Yes - Jn 15:1-6, Lk 18:18-22
2. Yes - Jn 15:1-6, Mt 5:17-19, Mt 19:16-18, Mt 10:32-33, Mk 8:38, Lk 9:26
3. Yes - Jn 15:1-6, Mt 7:24-27, Lk 7:50, Jn 8:11, Mt 10:32-33, Mk 8:38, Lk 9:26
4. Yes - Jn 8:24
5. Yes - Jn 12:25-26, Mt 28:19-20, Jn 8:51
6. Yes - Jn 1:12, Jn 17:3
7. Yes - Jn 3:36, Mk 16:15-18
8. Yes - Jn 6:47
9. Yes - Jn 3:14-15, Jn 5:24, Jn 11:25-26
10. Yes - Jn 3:16-18, Jn 17:3, Lk 10:25-28
11. Yes - Jn 15:12-14, Mt 5:44-45
12. Yes - Mt 25:34-46
13. Yes - Mt 25:34-46
14. Yes - Mt 25:34-46
15. Yes - Mt 25:34-46
16. Yes - Mt 25:34-46
17. Yes - Lk 18:18-22
18. Yes - Mt 5:44-45
19. Yes - Mt 5:9
20. Yes - Jn 6:53-54, Mt 26:27-28, Mk 14:23-25, Lk 22:19
21. Yes - Jn 3:5-8, Mk 16:15-18
22. Yes - Jn 8:51
23. Yes - Mt 5:8, Mt 5:43-48
24. Yes - Mt 5:20, Jn 8:51, Mt 25:34-46
25. Yes - Mt 13:41-43
26. Yes - Mt 5:29-30, Mt 18:8-9, Mk 9:43-48
27. Yes - Mt 13:47-50, Jn 5:29
28. Yes - Mt 18:3, Mk 10:15, Lk 18:17
29. Yes - Mt 16:14-27, also Mk 8:34-35, Jn 8:51
30. Yes - Lk 14:33
31. Yes - Jn 15:12-19
32. Yes - Mt 25:21-30, Mt 21:43, Jn 15:1-6
33. Yes - Mt 10:32-33, Mk 8:38, Lk 9:26, Lk 12:8, Mt 12:36-37
34. Yes - Mt 12:36-37
35. Yes - Mk 11:25, Lk 6:37
36. Yes - Mk 11:25, Lk 6:37
37. No - Lk 3:1-20, Mt 28:16-20
38. Yes - Lk 7:50, Jn 8:11
39. Yes - Mk 16:15-18
40. Yes - Mt 25:34-46
41. Yes – Lk 3:14
42. No – Lk 3:14
43. Yes – Lk 21:19
44. Yes - Mt 10:32-33, Mk 8:38, Lk 9:26, Lk 12:8, Mt 5:44-45
45. No - Mt 10:22
46. No - Mt 28:19-20, Mt 28:16-20
47. Yes - Mt 7:1-5
48. No - Mt 5:27-30
49. No - Mk 10:21, Mt 19:21, Lk 18:22
50. Yes – Mt 13:44
51. No - Mt 6:24, Lk 16:13
52. Yes - Mt 3:8, Lk 3:8, Mt 28:16-20
53. No - Lk 21:19
54. Yes - Matt 23:2-3
55. Yes - Jn 3:5-8, Mk 16:15-18
56. No – The word 'Grace' is not mentioned by Jesus
57. No – Mt 5:17-19, (James 2)
58. No - Mt 5:21-22
59. Yes - Mk 3:28-30, Mt 5:33-37, Lk 12:10-12
60. Yes - Mt 6:1-6

What Did the Savior Say?

The answers listed are by no means the only ones to the questions posed, but just some of them. There are many, many more directly or indirectly related to those questions. Let's look at 60+ quotes from Jesus. Note that I am only quoting Jesus from the Gospels, and no other writings. After all, we must read what the Messiah said if we are to understand His message, right?

To make this more organized, and perhaps shed some light on the subject, I am grouping the quotes into categories.

Believe in God

- *"Yet to all who received him, to those who believed in his name, he gave the right to become children of God"* (**Jn 1:12**). Q6
- *"Just as Moses lifted up the snake in the desert, so the Son of Man must be lifted up, that everyone who believes on him may have eternal life"* (**Jn 3:14-15**). Q9
- *"For God so loved the world that he gave his one and only Son, that whoever believes on him shall not perish but have eternal life. For God did not send his Son into the world to condemn the world, but to save the world through him. Whoever believes on him is not condemned, but whoever does not believe stands condemned already because he has not believed in the name of God's one and only Son"* (**Jn 3:16-18**). Q9, Q10
- *"Whoever believes on the Son has eternal life, but whoever rejects the Son will not see life, for God's wrath remains on him"* (**Jn 3:36**). Q7
- *"I tell you the truth, whoever hears my word and believes him who sent me has eternal life and will not be condemned; he has crossed over from death to life"* (**Jn 5:24**). Q9
- *"For my Father's will is that everyone who looks to the Son and believes on him shall have eternal life, and I will raise him up at the last day"* (**Jn 6:40**). Q8
- *"I tell you the truth, he who believes has everlasting life"* (**Jn 6:47**). Q8
- *"I told you that you would die in your sins; if you do not believe that I am the one I claim to be, you will indeed die in your sins"* (**Jn 8:24**). Q4

Chapter 4 - What did Jesus say to do to be 'Saved'?

- *"I am the resurrection and the life. He who believes on me will live, even though he dies; and whoever lives and believes in me will never die"* (**Jn 11:25-26**). Q9
- *And he said: "I tell you the truth, unless you change and become like little children, you will never enter the kingdom of heaven"* (**Mt 18:3, also Mk 10:15, Lk 18:17**).Q28
- *"I tell you the truth, anyone who will not receive the kingdom of God like a little child will never enter it"* (**Lk 18:17**).Q28
- *"All men will hate you because of me, but he who stands firm to the end will be saved"* (**Mt 10:22**). Q45
- *"By standing firm you will save yourself"* (**Lk 21:19**).Q53, Q43
- *Jesus looked at him, he felt love for him and said, "You lack one thing. Go, sell whatever you have and give the money to the poor, and you will have treasure in heaven. Then come, follow me."* (**Mk 10:21,Mt 19:21,Lk18:22**) Q49,Q50
- *Then Jesus looked around and said to his disciples, "How hard it is for the rich to enter the kingdom of God!" The disciples were astonished at these words. But again Jesus said to them, "Children, how hard it is to enter the kingdom of God!" They were even more astonished and said to one another, "Then who can be saved?" "It is easier for a camel to go through the eye of a needle than for a rich person to enter the kingdom of God." Jesus looked at them and replied, "This is impossible for mere humans, but not for God; all things are possible for God." Peter began to speak to him, "See, we have left everything to follow you!" Jesus said, "Truly, I say to you, there is no one who has left house or brothers or sisters or mother or father or children or lands, for my sake and for the gospel, who will not receive a hundredfold now in this time, houses and brothers and sisters and mothers and children and lands, with persecutions, and in the age to come eternal life."* (**Mk 10:23-29, Lk 18:24-28, MT 19:23-28**) Q49, Q50
- *"No one can serve two masters. Either you will hate the one and love the other, or you will be devoted to the one and despise the other. You cannot serve both God and money."* **Mt 6:24, Lk 16:13** Q51
- *"This is eternal life, that they may know You, the only true God, and Jesus Christ whom You have sent."* (**Jn 17:3**)Q6, Q10

Chapter 4 - What did Jesus say to do to be 'Saved'?

- *[To the servant who had wisely used his talent] "His master replied, 'Well done, good and faithful servant! You have been faithful with a few things; I will put you in charge of many things. Come and share your master's happiness!'"* (**Mt 25:21**). Q32
- *[To the servant who buried his talent] "'And throw that worthless servant outside, into the darkness, where there will be weeping and gnashing of teeth'"* (**Mt 25:30**). Q32

Keep Commandments
- *Therefore I tell you that the kingdom of God will be taken away from you and given to a people who will produce its fruit* (**Mt 21:43**). Q32
- *"I am the true vine, and my Father is the gardener. He cuts off every branch in me that bears no fruit, while every branch that does bear fruit he prunes[a] so that it will be even more fruitful. You are already clean because of the word I have spoken to you. Remain in me, and I will remain in you. No branch can bear fruit by itself; it must remain in the vine. Neither can you bear fruit unless you remain in me. I am the vine; you are the branches. If a man remains in me and I in him, he will bear much fruit; apart from me you can do nothing. If anyone does not remain in me, he is like a branch that is thrown away and withers; such branches are picked up, thrown into the fire and burned"* (**Jn 15:1-6**). Q1, Q2, Q3, Q32,
- *A ruler questioned Him, saying, "Good Teacher, what shall I do to inherit eternal life?" And Jesus said to him, "Why do you call Me good? No one is good except God alone. You know the commandments, 'Do not commit adultery, do not murder, do not steal, do not bear false witness, honor your father and mother.'" And he said, "All these things I have kept from my youth." When Jesus heard this, He said to him, "One thing you still lack; sell all that you possess and distribute it to the poor, and you shall have treasure in heaven; and come, follow Me"* (**Lk 18:18-22**). Q1, Q17
- *"Do not judge, or you too will be judged. For in the same way you judge others, you will be judged, and with the measure you use, it will be measured to you. "Why do you look at the speck of sawdust in your brother's eye and pay no attention to the plank in your own eye? How can you say to*

Chapter 4 - What did Jesus say to do to be 'Saved'?

your brother, 'Let me take the speck out of your eye,' when all the time there is a plank in your own eye? You hypocrite, first take the plank out of your own eye, and then you will see clearly to remove the speck from your brother's eye." (**Mt 7:1-5**) Q47

- *"Blessed are the pure in heart, for they will see God"* (**Mt 5:8**). Q23
- *"Do not think that I have come to abolish the Law or the Prophets; I have not come to abolish them but to fulfill their purpose. For truly I tell you, until heaven and earth disappear, not the smallest letter, not the least stroke of a pen, will by any means disappear from the Law until everything is accomplished. Therefore anyone who sets aside one of the least of these commands and teaches others accordingly will be called least in the kingdom of heaven, but whoever practices and teaches these commands will be called great in the kingdom of heaven."* (**Mt 5:17-19**) Q2, Q57
- *"For I tell you that unless your righteousness surpasses that of the Pharisees and the teachers of the law, you will certainly not enter the kingdom of heaven."* (**Mt 5:20**) Q24
- *"If your right eye causes you to sin, gouge it out and throw it away. It is better for you to lose one part of your body than for your whole body to be thrown into hell. And if your right hand causes you to sin, cut it off and throw it away. It is better for you to lose one part of your body than for your whole body to go into hell."* (**Mt 5:29-30, also Mt 18:8-9 and Mk 9:43-48**). Q26
- *"The Son of Man will send out his angels, and they will weed out of his kingdom everything that causes sin and all who do evil. They will throw them into the fiery furnace, where there will be weeping and gnashing of teeth. Then the righteous will shine like the sun in the kingdom of their Father. He who has ears, let him hear. The kingdom of heaven is like treasure hidden in a field. When a man found it, he hid it again, and then in his joy went and sold all he had and bought that field."* (**Mt 13:41-44**). Q25, Q50
- *"Once again, the kingdom of heaven is like a net that was let down into the lake and caught all kinds of fish. When it was full, the fishermen pulled it up on the shore. Then they sat down and collected the good fish in baskets, but threw the bad away. This is how it will be at the end of the age. The*

Chapter 4 - What did Jesus say to do to be 'Saved'?

angels will come and separate the wicked from the righteous and throw them into the fiery furnace, where there will be weeping and gnashing of teeth" (**Mt 13:47-50**). Q27
- *"Those who have done good will rise to live, and those who have done evil will rise to be condemned"* (**Jn 5:29**). Q27
- *"Therefore bear fruits in keeping with repentance, and do not begin to say to yourselves, 'We have Abraham for our father,' for I say to you that from these stones God is able to raise up children to Abraham. Indeed the axe is already laid at the root of the trees; so every tree that does not bear good fruit is cut down and thrown into the fire."* (**Lk 3:1-20**) Q37
- *Then Jesus said to his disciples, "If anyone would come after me, he must deny himself and take up his cross and follow me. For whoever wants to save his life will lose it, but whoever loses his life for me will find it. What good will it be for a man if he gains the whole world, yet forfeits his soul? Or what can a man give in exchange for his soul? For the Son of Man is going to come in his Father's glory with his angels, and then he will reward each person according to what he has done"* (**Mt 16:14-27, also Mk 8:34-35**). Q29
- *". . . any of you who does not give up everything he has cannot be my disciple"* (**Lk 14:33**) Q30
- *"The man who loves his life will lose it, while the man who hates his life in this world will keep it for eternal life. Whoever serves me must follow me; and where I am, my servant also will be. My Father will honor the one who serves me"* (**Jn 12:25-26**). Q5
- *"Therefore everyone who hears these words of mine and puts them into practice is like a wise man who built his house on the rock. The rain came down, the streams rose, and the winds blew and beat against that house; yet it did not fall, because it had its foundation on the rock. But everyone who hears these words of mine and does not put them into practice is like a foolish man who built his house on sand. The rain came down, the streams rose, and the winds blew and beat against that house, and it fell with a great crash"* (**Mt 7:24-27**). Q3
- *"Therefore go and make disciples of all nations, baptizing them in the name of the Father and of the Son and of the Holy Spirit, and teaching them to obey everything I have*

Chapter 4 - What did Jesus say to do to be 'Saved'?

- *commanded you. And surely I am with you always, to the very end of the age."* (**Mt 28:19-20**) Q3, Q5, Q46
- *"You did not choose Me but I chose you, and appointed you that you would go and bear fruit, and that your fruit would remain, so that whatever you ask of the Father in My name He may give to you. "This I command you, that you love one another. "If the world hates you, you know that it has hated Me before it hated you. "If you were of the world, the world would love its own; but because you are not of the world, but I chose you out of the world, because of this the world hates you."* (**Jn 15:12-19**) Q11, Q31
- *"Not everyone who says to me, "Lord, Lord," will enter the kingdom of heaven, but only he who does the will of my Father who is in heaven"* (**Mt 7:21**). Q1, Q3
- *Now a man came up to Jesus and asked, "Teacher, what good thing must I do to get eternal life?" "Why do you ask me about what is good?" Jesus replied. "There is only One who is good. If you want to enter life, obey the commandments"* (**Mt 19:16-17**). Q2
- *"If a man keeps my word, he will never see death"* (**Jn 8:51**). Q1, Q3, Q5, Q22, Q24, Q29
- *Then Jesus spoke to the crowds and to His disciples, saying: "The scribes and the Pharisees have seated themselves in the chair of Moses; therefore all that they tell you, do and observe, but do not do according to their deeds; for they say things and do not do them."* **Matt 23:2-3** Q54

Do not blaspheme
- *"Truly, I say to you, all sins will be forgiven the sons of men, and whatever blasphemies they utter; but whoever blasphemes against the Holy Spirit never has forgiveness, but is guilty of an eternal sin"— for they had said, "He has an unclean spirit."* (**Mk 3:28-30**) Q59
- *"Again, you have heard that it was said to the people long ago, 'Do not break your oath, but fulfill to the Lord the vows you have made.' But I tell you, do not swear an oath at all: either by heaven, for it is God's throne; or by the earth, for it is his footstool; or by Jerusalem, for it is the city of the Great King. And do not swear by your head, for you cannot make even one hair white or black. All you need to say is simply*

Chapter 4 - What did Jesus say to do to be 'Saved'?

'Yes' or 'No'; anything beyond this comes from the evil one." **(Mt 5:33-37)** Q59

- *"I tell you, whoever publicly acknowledges me before others, the Son of Man will also acknowledge before the angels of God. But whoever disowns me before others will be disowned before the angels of God. And everyone who speaks a word against the Son of Man will be forgiven, but anyone who blasphemes against the Holy Spirit will not be forgiven."* **(Lk 12:10-12)** Q59

Observe the Sabbath day

- *On one occasion an expert in the law stood up to test Jesus. "Teacher," he asked, "what must I do to inherit eternal life?" "What is written in the Law?" he replied. "How do you read it?"*
  He answered: " 'Love the Lord your God with all your heart and with all your soul and with all your strength and with your entire mind'; and, 'Love your neighbor as yourself.'"
  "You have answered correctly," Jesus replied. "Do this and you will live" **(Lk 10:25-28)**. Q2, Q10

Do not Murder

- *"You have heard that it was said to the people long ago, 'You shall not murder, and anyone who murders will be subject to judgment.' But I tell you that anyone who is angry with a brother or sister will be subject to judgment. Again, anyone who says to a brother or sister, 'Raca,' is answerable to the court. And anyone who says, 'You fool!' will be in danger of the fire of hell."* **(MT 5:21-22)** Q58

Honor your Father and Mother

- *And someone came to Him and said, "Teacher, what good thing shall I do that I may obtain eternal life?" And He said to him, "Why are you asking Me about what is good? There is only One who is good; but if you wish to enter into life, keep the commandments." Then he said to Him, "Which ones?" And Jesus said, "You shall not commit murder; You shall not commit adultery; You shall not steal; You shall not bear false witness; Honor your father and mother; and You shall love your neighbor as yourself."* **(Mt 19:16-18)** Q2

Chapter 4 - What did Jesus say to do to be 'Saved'?

You shall not commit adultery

- *"Jesus said to the woman [who had washed His feet], "Your faith has saved you; go in peace"* (**Lk 7:50**). Q3, Q38
- *She said, "No one, Lord." And Jesus said, "I do not condemn you, either. Go. From now on sin no more."* (**Jn 8:11**) Q3, Q38
- *"You have heard that it was said, 'You shall not commit adultery.' But I tell you that anyone who looks at a woman lustfully has already committed adultery with her in his heart. If your right eye causes you to stumble, gouge it out and throw it away. It is better for you to lose one part of your body than for your whole body to be thrown into hell. And if your right hand causes you to stumble, cut it off and throw it away. It is better for you to lose one part of your body than for your whole body to go into hell.* (**Mt 5:27-30**) Q48

You shall not steal (or fail to be generous)

- *[To those who showed compassion] "Then the King will say to those on his right, 'Come, you who are blessed by my Father; take your inheritance, the kingdom prepared for you since the creation of the world. For I was hungry and you gave me something to eat, I was thirsty and you gave me something to drink, I was a stranger and you invited me in, I needed clothes and you clothed me, I was sick and you looked after me, I was in prison and you came to visit me.'*
"*Then the righteous will answer him, 'Lord, when did we see you hungry and feed you, or thirsty and give you something to drink? When did we see you a stranger and invite you in, or needing clothes and clothe you? When did we see you sick or in prison and go to visit you?'*
"*The King will reply, 'I tell you the truth, whatever you did for one of the least of these brothers of mine, you did for me.'"* (**Mt 25:34-46**). Q12, Q13, Q14, Q15, Q16, Q24, Q40
- *[To those who showed no compassion] "Then he will say to those on his left, 'Depart from me, you evil doers, into the eternal fire prepared for the devil and his angels. For I was hungry and you gave me nothing to eat, I was thirsty and you gave me nothing to drink, I was a stranger and you did not invite me in, I needed clothes and you did not clothe me, I was sick and in prison and you did not look after me.'*

Chapter 4 - What did Jesus say to do to be 'Saved'?

> *"They also will answer, 'Lord, when did we see you hungry or thirsty or a stranger or needing clothes or sick or in prison, and did not help you?'*
> *"He will reply, 'I tell you the truth, whatever you did not do for one of the least of these, you did not do for me.'*
> *"Then they will go away to eternal punishment, but the righteous to eternal life"* (**Mt 25:34-46**). Q12, Q13, Q14, Q15, Q16, Q24

- *"Beware of practicing your righteousness before other people in order to be seen by them, for then you will have no reward from your Father who is in heaven. "Thus, when you give to the needy, sound no trumpet before you, as the hypocrites do in the synagogues and in the streets, that they may be praised by others. Truly, I say to you, they have received their reward. But when you give to the needy, do not let your left hand know what your right hand is doing, so that your giving may be in secret. And your Father who sees in secret will reward you. "And when you pray, you must not be like the hypocrites. For they love to stand and pray in the synagogues and at the street corners, that they may be seen by others. Truly, I say to you, they have received their reward"* (**Mt 6:1-6**) Q60

You shall bear True Witness

- *"Whoever acknowledges me before men, I will also acknowledge him before my Father in heaven. But whoever disowns me before men, I will disown him before my Father in heaven"* (**Mt 10:32-33, also Mk 8:38, Lk 9:26, Lk 12:8**). Q33, Q2, Q3, Q44
- *"But I tell you that men will have to give account on the Day of Judgment for every careless word they have spoken. For by your words you will be acquitted, and by your words you will be condemned."* (**Mt 12:36-37**). Q33, Q34
- *"And when you stand praying, if you hold anything against anyone, forgive him, so that your Father in heaven may forgive you your sins"* (**Mk 11:25**). Q35, Q36
- *"Do not judge, and you will not be judged. Do not condemn, and you will not be condemned. Forgive, and you will be forgiven"* (**Lk 6:37**). Q35, Q36

Chapter 4 - What did Jesus say to do to be 'Saved'?

- *"But I tell you: Love your enemies and pray for those who persecute you, that you may be sons of your Father in heaven"* (**Mt 5:44-45**). Q11, Q18, Q44
- *"Blessed are the peacemakers, for they will be called sons of God"* (**Mt 5:9**). Q19
- *"Therefore bear fruits in keeping with repentance, and do not begin to say to yourselves, 'We have Abraham for our father,' for I say to you that from these stones God is able to raise up children to Abraham. Indeed the axe is already laid at the root of the trees; so every tree that does not bear good fruit is cut down and thrown into the fire."* (**Mt 3:8, Lk 3:8**) Q52

You shall not covet anything that is your neighbor's
- *"You have heard that it was said, 'Love your neighbor and hate your enemy.' But I tell you, love your enemies and pray for those who persecute you, that you may be children of your Father in heaven. He causes his sun to rise on the evil and the good, and sends rain on the righteous and the unrighteous. If you love those who love you, what reward will you get? Are not even the tax collectors doing that? And if you greet only your own people, what are you doing more than others? Do not even pagans do that?* **Be perfect, therefore, as your heavenly Father is perfect.***"* (**Mt 5:43-48**) Q23

Communion
- *Jesus said to them, "I tell you the truth, unless you eat the flesh of the Son of Man and drink his blood, you have no life in you. Whoever eats my flesh and drinks my blood has eternal life, and I will raise him up at the last day."* (**Jn 6:53-54**). Q20
- *And when He had taken a cup and given thanks, He gave it to them, saying, "Drink from it, all of you; for this is My blood of the covenant, which is poured out for many for forgiveness of sins."* (**Mt 26:27-28**) Q20
- *And when He had taken a cup and given thanks, He gave it to them, and they all drank from it. And He said to them, "This is My blood of the covenant, which is poured out for many."* (**Mk 14:23-25**) Q20
- *And when He had taken some bread and given thanks, He broke it and gave it to them, saying, "This is My body which*

Chapter 4 - What did Jesus say to do to be 'Saved'?

is given for you; do this in remembrance of Me." And in the same way He took the cup after they had eaten, saying, "This cup which is poured out for you is the new covenant in My blood." (**Lk 22:19-20**) Q20

Baptism

- *Jesus answered, "Very truly I tell you, no one can enter the kingdom of God unless they are born of water and the Spirit. Flesh gives birth to flesh, but the Spirit gives birth to spirit. You should not be surprised at my saying, 'You must be born from above.'* "(**Jn 3:5-8**) Q21 Q55
- *And he said to them, "Go into the entire world and preach the gospel to the whole creation. He who believes and is baptized will be saved; but he who does not believe will be condemned. And these signs will accompany those who believe: in my name they will cast out demons; they will speak in new tongues; they will pick up serpents, and if they drink any deadly thing, it will not hurt them; they will lay their hands on the sick, and they will recover."* (**Mk 16:15-18**) Q5, Q7, Q21, Q39, Q55
- *But the eleven disciples proceeded to Galilee, to the mountain which Jesus had designated. When they saw Him, they worshiped Him; but some were doubtful. And Jesus came up and spoke to them, saying, "All authority has been given to Me in heaven and on earth. "Go therefore and make disciples of all the nations, baptizing them in the name of the Father and the Son and the Holy Spirit, teaching them to observe all that I commanded you; and lo, I am with you always, even to the end of the age."* (**Mt 28:16-20**) Q55, Q37, Q46, Q52

Other Answers

- Q41 – Lk 3:14 *"Soldiers also asked him, "And we, what should we do?" He said to them, "Do not extort money from anyone by threats or false accusation, and be satisfied with your wages."*
- Q53/56 – Jesus never mentions the word 'Grace' in the New Testament. Others do, but Jesus does not.
- Q57 – one mention of 'Faith Alone' in the Bible - James 2:24 – **"You see that a man is justified by works and not by faith alone."** Jesus **does not say** that anyone is 'saved by faith

alone'. In Lk 7:50 a woman has her sins forgiven by her faith, but this is not 'Salvation' is it due to faith *alone*. In this single case, the woman had to be very persistent to get the blessing. This is the only example, and hardly the entire basis for a movement like Protestantism!

What does all of this mean?
If you find yourself asking that question, you are not alone. When the Lord speaks directly and clearly saying *"you have to serve Him and live the commandments, abandoning everything else"*[79] and the first thing on your mind is **"How do I get out of this and still do God's will?"** then you are missing the point. There is no avoidance – only Truth and Evading the Truth. At least be honest with *yourself* – if you are like almost all modern 'Christians', you are not doing as we were all instructed.

BTW – count me in too – I am a miserable sinner despite my best efforts. I do not want to brag, but in case you think I am a Holy Roller, nothing could be farther from the truth! I am just a pitiful an excuse for a Christian as you *may* be. Perhaps the difference is that I know I am pathetic, and I am making a sincere effort to reform and to do as I have been instructed. I am a 'Practicing Christian', and one day I hope to get it right. How about you? You hope to claim ignorance? Are you thinking 'I do the best I can?' Are you sure you are not just doing as much as you *want to do*? Are you planning to tell the judge that you are a 'victim of circumstance'? You did not understand? The Scriptures are well translated into most languages so all I can say is: **good luck with that.**

What do you have to do? We have listed 50+ specific examples of what must be done – you must do all of them. Not 40, or 33. Not sure what they all mean?

It is all there for you, and there are many examples to refer to. If your name is that of a Saint (as it should be) start by reading about your saint(s). Follow their examples.

Work on it, or get used to high temperatures.

---

[79] Deuteronomy 10:12-13, Joshua 22:5, Exodus 20:2-17, etc.

Chapter 5 – The Last Supper

Do you know why Jesus had to die on a cross? Really – are you sure? How about the 'Cup' which He did not want to drink from in the Garden? Why did He say that He would not drink from the fruit of the vine, but the last act before death was to drink wine? To find the answers, read on...

In Short:

Again, the story of salvation was not an accident – over and over again God reveals His plan, in detail, with prophecy and showing the same events over and over. The life and death of Jesus was planned since Genesis 5 (in scripture), and the elements all come together to culminate in the exact events carried out the way that they did. Jesus was the final sacrifice for remediation of Adam's sin, offered as the ultimate Passover offering for sin. Jesus was tried according to prophecy, dies when and where exactly He had to, and placed in the tomb as foreseen. After the three days that He was in Sheol, he liberated the captives there and returned to restore His Church leaders. Every element exactly as foretold by the Prophets.

Long Version:

The Last supper was one of the most important events in history, and (as with most of Scripture) there is an enormous amount of information packed into a relatively short section of each of the Gospels. The Synoptic Gospels line up pretty closely with each other, and their message is complex. Let's take a look at one of these accounts, and look for not only what is said, but possibly as important, what is not said. Remember – this was the night before he was crucified, and they were all in Jerusalem for the Passover feast. What is wrong with this picture, and why?

When the hour came, he took his place at the table, and the apostles with him. He said to them, "I have eagerly desired to eat this Passover with you before I suffer; for I tell you, I will not eat it until it is fulfilled in the kingdom of God." Then he took a cup, and after giving thanks he said, "Take this and divide it among yourselves; for I tell you that from now on I will not drink of the fruit of the vine until the kingdom of God comes."

Chapter 5 – The Last Supper

Then he took a loaf of bread, and when he had given thanks, he broke it and gave it to them, saying, "This is my body, which is given for you. Do this in remembrance of me." And he did the same with the cup after supper, saying, "This cup that is poured out for you is the new covenant in my blood.[80]

This is one of the passages where Jesus clearly says that the last supper was a Passover meal, and clearly there are many similarities between the events there and the Passover Meal practiced by the Jews in the first century – but there were differences as well. Some of the questions you might ask are:
- Why did they eat this meal on Thursday – the day before Passover?
- Why was there no Lamb served?
- Why did the meal end before the 4th cup was drunk?
- Why did Jesus say that he would "not drink of the fruit of the vine until the kingdom of God comes"?
- Why did the group walk out of the Dinner and off to the Garden of Gethsemane?
- In the Garden, why did Jesus asks that the "Cup be taken" from him – what cup?
- What did the timing of the meal and the following events have to do with the Preparation day for Passover?

---
[80] Lk 22:14-20 NRSV

Chapter 5 – The Last Supper

- How did the Crucifixion match up with the traditional slaughter of the Lambs?
- When did Jesus have the last drink of wine?

When you look at the accounts of the last supper, we see that in the Synoptic gospels, all 3 relate that it was the regular Passover meal (Nisan 14), but just without mentioning the Lamb. John, on the other hand, says that it was on Thursday/Friday, and that the events of the Crucifixion took place on the day of Passover (Nisan 13). How can the Last Supper happen both on the Passover day and the day before? How could it be the Passover meal and a day early? Also, we will find out **which Cup** Jesus did not want to drink from in the Garden.

Let's consider what Jesus did on the week of Passover in 33 AD and what the usual process for observing Passover was at that time, so we may better understand what was going on during the Last Supper. Most people do not understand that that week was the culmination of Prophecy and Theology that culminated in the greatest event in History – the Crucifixion. This was not a random series of events, but a carefully designed series of events to fulfill the promises of the Old Covenant so as to establish the new and everlasting covenant of Christ.

What did Jesus do Passover week?

1. **Monday – Nisan 10** – Jesus Triumphal Entry (Mt 21:1-9, Mk 11:1-10, Lk 19:28-40, John 12:12-19). He visited the Temple that day (Mt 21:10-11, Mk 11:11) then He returned to Bethany.
2. **Tuesday – Nisan 11** – Jesus cursed the Fig tree (Mt 21:18-19, Mk 11:12-14) then he cleansed the Temple (Mt 21:12-13, Mk 11:15-17, Lk 19:45-46). Jewish leaders plotted against Him, and He returned to Bethany (Mk 11:18-19, Lk 19:47-48)
3. **Wednesday – Nisan 12** – Disciples see withered fig tree (Mt 21:20-22, Mk 11:20-26). At the Temple, Jesus argued with Temple leaders (Mt 21:23 – 23:39, Mk 11:27-12:44, Luke 20:1 – 21:4). In the afternoon, He delivered the Olivet Discourse (Mt 24:1-25:46, Mk 13:1-37, Lk 21:5-36). Jesus predicted his crucifixion (Mt 26:1-5, Mk 14:1-2, Lk 22:1-2) and Judas Planned betrayal (Mt 26:14-16, Mk 14:10, Lk 22:3-6)
4. **Thursday – Nisan 13** – Passover meal (Mt 26:20-30, Mk 14:17-26, Lk 22:14-30, Jn 13:1-14:31). Leaving the upper room, Jesus offered prayers for the disciples (Mt 26:30-35, Mk 14:26-31, Lk

Chapter 5 – The Last Supper

22:31-39, Jn 15:1-18:1). They then arrived at the Garden of Gethsemane (Mt 26:36-46, Mk 14:32-42, Lk 22:39-46, Jn 18:1). Jesus betrayed that night and arrested (Mt 26:47-56, Mk 14:43-52, Lk 22:47-53, Jn 18:2-12) During the night, Jesus is tried by Annas and then by Caiaphas (Mt 25:57-75, Mk 14:53-72, Lk 22:54-65, Jn 18:13-27)

5. **Friday – Nissan 14** – Early Jesus is tried by Sanhedrin, Pilate, Herod Antipas and Pilate again (Mt 27:1-30, Mk 15:1-19, Luke 22:66-23:25 and Jn 18:28-19:16). Jesus was crucified at 9:00 am and died at 3:00 pm, to be buried late that day (Mt 27:31-60, Mk 15:20-46, Lk 23:26-54, Jn 19:16-42).
6. **Saturday – Nisan 15** – Jesus lying in the Tomb during the Sabbath, and Pharisees secured a Roman Guard to watch the tomb (Mt 27:61-66, Mark 15:47, Luke 23:55-56).
7. **Sunday – Nisan 16** – Christ resurrected from the dead (Mt 28:1-15, Mk 16:1-8, Lk 24:1-35). He is a type of the offering of the first fruits that was offered the first day after the Sabbath (Lev 23:9-14, 1 Cor 15:23).

The Passover (Seder) Meal

Before we can understand the Last supper, we need to understand the Passover meal as it was practiced in the first century.

Overall, the meal is organized to follow a specific pattern – in fact, 'Seder' means 'Order' in Hebrew. This meal was organized and scripted to follow an exact sequence of events, just as Moses instructed during the Exodus. The preparation of the Food, Drink and Conversation had to follow a specific sequence, as outlined below:

Modern Seder Plate

Preparation –

The lamb for the sacrifice had to be bought and examined – typically on Nisan 10, the date of Jesus' entry into Jerusalem.

Chapter 5 – The Last Supper

This was a process lasting days, as the lamb is located, examined (typically for 4 days) then paid for and delivered. The lamb should be as perfect as possible, free from blemish or disfigurement.

The lamb is brought with a representation of the group (the Passover should be shared between at least 10 people) to the Temple at or just before the 9th to 12th hour (3-6 PM) on the day before Passover – 14 Nisan. Remember, Jews consider days to begin at nightfall, so Passover was 15 Nisan. (Lev. 23)

All of the lambs are quickly slaughtered during the 3 hours, and their blood drained and some given to the family, the rest offered as sacrifice. According to Josephus, over 256,500 such offerings take place during this time (Antiquities of the Jews 3.10.5 248-251)

How was the Lamb sacrificed? *'Each division (group of Jews allowed in the Temple Court at one time) must consist of not less than thirty persons (3x10, the symbolic number of the Divine and of completeness). Immediately the massive gates were closed behind them. The priests drew a threefold blast from their silver trumpets when the Passover lamb was slain. Altogether the scene was most impressive. All along the Court up to the altar of burnt-offering priests stood in two rows, the one holding the golden, the other, silver bowls. In these the blood of the Paschal lambs, which each Israelite slew for himself (as representative of his company at the Paschal Supper), was caught up by a priest, who handed it to his colleague, receiving back an empty bowl, and so the bowls with the blood were passed up to the priest at the altar, who jerked it in one jet at the base of the altar. while this was going on, a most solemn hymn of praise was raised, the Levites leading in song, and the offerers either repeating after them or merely responding..... This service of song consisted of the so-called Hallel, which comprises Psalms 113 to 118.....Next, the sacrifices were hung up on hooks along the court, or laid on staves which rested on the shoulders of two men (on Sabbath they were not laid on staves), then flayed, the entrails taken out and cleansed, and the inside fat separated, put in a dish, salted, and placed on the fire of the altar of burnt-offering. This completed the sacrifice.....the service being in each case conducted in precisely the same manner'*[81].

---

[81] Alfred Edersheim - The Temple, Its Ministry and Services' - London 1874, pp. 191-193

Chapter 5 – The Last Supper

The lambs are quickly and simply prepared to be roasted – all that is done is removing the skin/wool, gutting and bleeding it and trussing it to a cross. Literally, the lamb is tied to a roasting spit along the backbone, and the 4 legs are tied to a crosspiece that sits across the middle back, holding the legs up as though the lamb were resting on the ground. It is not spiced or the head removed, just quickly roasted whole.

The Lamb could not have any bones broken during sacrifice or preparation. All of the Lamb had to be consumed that evening; any leftovers had to be burnt before sunrise.

The unleavened bread is prepared for the meal, and the sauces are prepared as well.

The special red wine is procured, and prepared for the four or more cups to be consumed during the meal. The wine is 'the blood of the grape' and dark red wine represents the blood of the lamb in this context. The lamb's blood was to be used to mark the doorways to the Jews to protect them from the Angel of Death, and as they did not do that in following Passovers, the consumption of the dark red wine signified their personal 'marking with the blood of the lamb'.

On the day of Passover, shortly before nightfall, family and guests gather around a large table. Everyone must be dressed as though ready to take a long journey, with loins girded and sandals on their feet and walking sticks next to them as they eat.

Traditional meal components:
- Charoseth,
- Parsley,
- Horseradish,
- Matzah Bread,
- Roasted Lamb,
- Red Wine (4 Cups)

Charoseth represents the mortar that the Jews used to cement bricks together, the Matzah (unleavened) bread represented the bricks, the parsley represents the hope of the promised land, the Horseradish (bitter herbs) represents the bitterness of slavery in Egypt, the lamb is the sacrifice to God and the wine is its blood symbolized.

Chapter 5 – The Last Supper

The order of the Passover meal:
1. **First Cup – Introductory Rites**
   a. Preparation of the wine – the *Kiddush* cup (sanctification)
      i. The cups of wine were prepared by mixing red wine with water
      ii. Each step is marked by this ceremonial 'mingling' of water and wine
   b. Blessing "Blessed are you, O Lord our God, King of the Universe, who created the fruit of the vine" (Mishnah, *Berakoth* 6:1)
   c. Food brought to the table and arranged as prescribed
   d. At least 4 basic elements must be represented: Unleavened Bread, Bitter Herbs, haroseth sauce and specially roasted and sacrificed Passover lamb.
   e. Father breaks bread and dips pieces in haroseth sauce, and distributes them
2. **Second Cup – Proclamation of Scripture**
   a. Preparation of the wine – the *Haggadah* cup (proclamation)
   b. "Then they mix him (the father) the second cup of wine. And here the son asks the father.. "Why is this night different from other nights? For on other nights we eat seasoned food once, but this night twice; on other nights we eat leavened or unleavened bread, but this night all is unleavened; *on other nights we eat flesh (of the Lamb) roast, stewed or cooked, but this night all is roast.*" And according to the understanding of the son his father instructs him. He begins with disgrace and ends with the glory; he expounds from "Then you must affirm before the Lord your God, "A wandering Aramean was my ancestor, and he went down to Egypt and lived there as a foreigner with a household few in number, but there he became a great, powerful, and numerous people. But the Egyptians mistreated and oppressed us, forcing us to do burdensome labor. So we cried out to the Lord, the God of our ancestors, and he heard us and saw our humiliation, toil, and oppression. Therefore the Lord brought us out of Egypt with tremendous strength and power, as well as with great awe-inspiring signs and wonders. Then he brought us to this place and gave us

Chapter 5 – The Last Supper

    this land, a land flowing with milk and honey. So now, look! I have brought the first of the ground's produce that you, Lord, have given me." Then you must set it down before the Lord your God and worship before him. You will celebrate all the good things that the Lord your God has given you and your family, along with the Levites and the resident foreigners among you." (Deut 26:5) until he finishes the whole section." (Mishnah, *Pesahim* 10:4)

  c. The Father explains the significance of the parts of the meal – "Rabbi Gamaliel used to say: Whosoever has not said (the verses concerning) these three things at Passover has not fulfilled his obligation. And these are they: Passover, unleavened bread and the bitter herbs: 'Passover" – because God passed over the houses of our fathers in Egypt; "unleavened bread" – because our fathers were ransomed from Egypt; "Bitter Herbs" because the Egyptians embittered the lives of our fathers in Egypt. In every generation a man must so regard himself as if he came forth himself out of Egypt, for it is written:" And you shall tell your son in that day, saying, 'It is because of that which the Lord did for me when I came out of Egypt.' (Exodus 13:8)

  d. In response to the proclamation of Scripture, all Passover participants were bound to give thanks – it was recommended to sing Psalms 113-114 (Mishnah, *Pesahim* 10:6). This with Psalms 115-118 were considered the *Hallel* Psalms, and were sung throughout the Passover meal.

3. **Third Cup – the eating of the Meal**
   a. The third cup is mixed – the *Berakah* cup (Blessing)
   b. Blessing over bread – "Blessed are you, Lord God, who brings forth bread from the earth" (Mishnah *Berakoth* 6:1)
   c. An appetizer is served – small pieces of the bread dipped in sauces.
   d. Then the main meal is served – Bread and roasted lamb meat
   e. The father says another blessing and everyone drinks the third cup of wine

Chapter 5 – The Last Supper

4. **Fourth Cup – conclusion Rites**
    a. It is forbidden to drink any wine between the 3rd and 4th cup (*Pesahim* 10:7) just as Jesus says in Mt 26:29.
    b. The *Hallel* Psalms were completed (Psalms 115-118) – the *Great Hallel*
    c. At the end of the song, all that remains is to drink the fourth cup of wine.
    d. "It is Finished" – everyone abruptly gets up and goes home.

Did any of this seem interesting to you?

    The normal Passover proves should have rung quite a few bells for you – from the preparation of the lamb with no bones broken, skin flayed off and tied to a cross. How about the cups of wine – what they represent and when they are consumed? These were the normal events – Jesus would have done this every year. He knew every nuance of this process, and understood the deep meaning behind it. He probably knew that one day he would have to play a different role in this feast – that of the Lamb of God who will take away the sins of the world.

Chapter 5 — The Last Supper

How did Jesus do it?
This is the traditional version of how the Passover meal is conducted — we only have the Mishnah to tell the details, but the general order is aligned with Exodus. It is interesting to note that the Seder traditions practiced by modern Jews is somewhat different that the meal in the first century. These differences are:
- No Elijah cup or egg in first century
- Current Seder does not have lamb meat, only burnt bone
- Current Seder leaves out the last verse of the question/answer concerning the Lamb (Section 2b)

How did the Last Supper compare to the Passover Meal?
Let's review and consider the odd things about Jesus' Last Supper, from the Passover perspective:

When was it?
The Synoptic Gospels all say it was on the day of Passover or Nisan 14 (Mt 26:19, Mk 14:16, Lk 22:13) but John says it was the day before Passover or Nisan 13 (Jn 13:1). The accounts of the Crucifixion in John clearly indicate that Jesus was crucified on the day before Passover (Nisan 13), when the Lambs are prepared for the feast. This was the 'Day of Preparation' before the feast.

In what way was it Passover by the descriptions?
- Over and over the meal was described as Passover in the Synoptic gospels.
- The meal was at night, according to custom (typically Jews did not eat at night but in the evening).
- It was in a room that Jesus procured specifically for Passover. In fact, the disciples stay in the upper room until Pentecost.
- The room was in the city of Jerusalem, a hard place to get space at that time, so it had to be for a special purpose. Passover was that occasion.
- After the Last Supper, they went to the Garden of Gethsemane, still technically in Jerusalem, to stay there. Why sleep in a garden? Because you had to spend Passover in Jerusalem, and it was cooler in a Garden than in a room.
- They seemed to follow the general Seder meal schedule, with the prayers, cups and Psalms as required.

Chapter 5 – The Last Supper

In what ways wasn't it Passover?
- It was a day early – the Lambs were not slaughtered until the next day.
- In 33 AD, Passover was on Friday (Nisan 14). Jesus is reported to have been crucified on Friday, and the probable year of Crucifixion was 33 AD, in line with prophecy of Daniel and other reported events.
- John clearly says it was the day before Passover. (Jn 13:1)
- Luke says that Jesus died on the cross at 3pm – the time the lambs began to be slaughtered for the Passover meal. (Lk 23:44, Mk 15:33, Mt 27:45)
- Jesus did not drink the final cup of wine of Passover – specifically saying that he would not until He came into his kingdom. (Mt 26:29, Mk 14:25)
- There was no lamb at the meal – it was a requirement to have one!

Anything else odd about the event?
- Jesus says he will not drink wine again until he comes into his kingdom. (Mt 26:29, Mk 14:25)
- In the Garden after this meal, Jesus asks that the "Cup be taken" from him – what cup? (Lk 22:42)
- During the Crucifixion, Jesus refuses wine until immediately before death (Lk 23:36, Mk 15:23 and Mt 27:34) then finally takes it (Mk 15:36, Mt 27:48 and Jn 19:28-30). Note that in Proverbs it is recommended to offer a condemned man wine mixed with gall (Myrrh) to dull the pain. (Pr 31:6)
- Jesus had his skin removed by whipping before crucifixion – just as the lambs do at Passover.
- Jesus had no bones broken during crucifixion - again like the Lambs.

Why the differences?
Scholars have long been confused by the inconsistencies here – the questions are not easily understood. Why did this meal seem to be a day early? Why did Jesus say that He would not drink again from the fruit of the vine until he came into his kingdom if He drank immediately before his death? What is the cup he earnestly prayed 'Be taken from" Him? (Lk 22:42, etc.)

Chapter 5 – The Last Supper

Which Cup is which?

Luke 22 describes the Last supper as shown below:

Now when the hour came, Jesus took his place at the table and the apostles joined him. And he said to them, "I have earnestly desired to eat this Passover with you before I suffer. For I tell you, I will not eat it again until it is fulfilled in the kingdom of God." Then he took a cup, and after giving thanks he said, "Take this and divide it among yourselves. For I tell you that from now on I will not drink of the fruit of the vine until the kingdom of God comes." Then he took bread, and after giving thanks he broke it and gave it to them, saying, "This is my body which is given for you. Do this in remembrance of me." And in the same way he took the cup after they had eaten, saying, "This cup that is poured out for you is the new covenant in my blood.

In Lk 22:20 the second cup of wine is described as the cup "After Supper", which makes it the 3rd cup of wine. That implies that the earlier cup is either the first or second cup of wine. How do we know that this was not the final cup of wine? Matthew and Mark end the Passover meal with singing the Hallel:

Matt 26:30 *After singing a hymn, they went out to the Mount of Olives.*

The meal ends with the 4th cup of wine, which is preceded by singing the Hallel. Not drunk before the song.

So, what is the big deal? They drank the cup then sang the Hallel – does it matter? Maybe they drank the last cup but did not put it in the account anywhere? What does it matter? Why should we care?

Let's compare the events in Passover with the Events in the Gospels. The events are listed to the right.

Event in Passover	Event in Gospels
1. First cup	
2. Preparation of Kiddush Cup	
3. Blessing of Wine	
4. Breaking of the Bread	
5. Second cup - Proclamation	Lk 22:17
6. Preparation of Haggadah cup	
7. Scriptures (Deut 26:5)	
8. Explains meal (Exodus 13:8)	Lk 22:19
9. Sing Psalms 113-114	
10. Third Cup - Blessings	
11. Third Cup - Berakah cup	
12. Blessing over Bread	Lk 22:19
13. Appetizer served	
14. Main Meal - Lamb and Bread	
15. Blessing and third cup	Lk 22:20; 1 Cor 11:16
16. Fourth Cup - Conclusion Rite	
17. The Hallel - Psalms 115-118	Mt 26:30; Mk 14:26
18. Drink fourth cup	Did not happen: Mt 26:30, Mk 14:24. Did Happen: Mk 15:36, Mt 27:48 and Jn 19:28-30
19. It is finished	Jn 19:30

Chapter 5 – The Last Supper

There are several important points here:

First, the process is very organized; in fact it is called 'Order'. Not doing this properly is a grave problem for the first century Jew – it meant that his coming year would, essentially, be cursed by his failure to participate in the Passover meal.

Second, the following events point to a cup that Jesus did not want to drink – what cup is this? The reference to a 'Cup' for an event is not common in the Bible – nowhere is that term used other than here, so there is every reason to believe that Jesus is referring to a literal 'Cup' here.

Third, Jesus avoids the attempts to get Him to drink wine after this – the people offered Him wine with gall on Golgotha (Mk 15:23 and Mt 27:34), the Roman soldiers offered him sour wine (Luke 23:36) which He refused. It was not until He was on the verge of death that He finally accepted the Wine (Mk 15:36, Mt 27:48 and Jn 19:28-30).

My God, why have you forsaken me?

Before the 4th cup was offered and accepted while Jesus was on the Cross, Jesus makes an odd statement:

"At three o'clock, Jesus cried out in a loud voice, 'Eloi, Eloi, lema sabachthani?' which is translated, 'My God, my God, why have you forsaken me?'"[82]

Why did He say this? Well, He was quoting Scripture – specifically Psalm 22:1:

"My God, my God, why have you forsaken me? Why are you so far from saving me, so far from my cries of anguish?"

This is a Psalm of David, which begins with the complaint that David feels persecuted by his enemies – the end of this Psalm is the important message, though:

"You who fear the LORD, praise Him; all you descendants of Jacob, glorify Him, and stand in awe of Him, all you descendants of Israel.

For He has not despised nor abhorred the affliction of the afflicted; nor has He hidden His face from him; But when he cried to Him for help, He heard.

From You comes my praise in the great assembly; I shall pay my vows before those who fear Him.

---

[82] Mark 15:34; Matthew 27:46

Chapter 5 – The Last Supper

The afflicted will eat and be satisfied; those who seek Him will praise the LORD.
Let your heart live forever!
All the ends of the earth will remember and turn to the LORD, and all the families of the nations will worship before You.
For the kingdom is the LORD'S and He rules over the nations.
All the prosperous of the earth will eat and worship,
All those who go down to the dust will bow before Him,
Even he who cannot keep his soul alive.
Posterity will serve Him; it will be told of the Lord to the coming generation.
They will come and will declare His righteousness to a people who will be born, that He has performed it.

This Psalm is about the coming savior – that although he must suffer, the final result will be a restoration of God's Kingdom where the faithful will be rewarded and the wicked will be punished. This is a Psalm of thanksgiving, not of despair.

Many people do not understand this statement, and in fact have very odd interpretations of it – like "God at this point cannot bear to look at Jesus because He is carrying the sins of the world". How can two persons of the Trinity not look at each other? Why is God 'unable' to look on sin – He does it all the time! (With us around, He can hardly avoid it). Whereas, understanding the meaning of the statement 'Eloi, Eloi, lema sabachthani?' as a reference to the coming of God's Kingdom and the triumph of the Cross is vitally important.

When did Jesus drink the 4th cup of the Passover?

As we can see from the Gospels, the 4th cup was offered and accepted while Jesus was on the Cross – in John the events are clearly shown:

After this Jesus, realizing that by this time everything was completed, said (in order to fulfill the scripture), "I am thirsty!" A jar full of sour wine was there, so they put a sponge soaked in sour wine on a branch of hyssop[83] and lifted it to his mouth. When

---

[83] A Hyssop branch is used for purification: Exodus 12:24, Lev. 14:4-7, Lev. 14:49-51, Ps. 51:7, 1 Kings 4:33 - it was used to put the lamb blood around the door at Passover.

Chapter 5 – The Last Supper

*he had received the sour wine, Jesus said, "It is completed!"
Then he bowed his head and gave up his spirit.*

Here are the questions and answers:
In verses 28 and 30 the word 'Completed' is used – what was just completed? The short answer is: The Passover Sacrifice

Why did He have to extend the Passover feast by a day?
Because the Passover feast included the sacrifice of the lamb as a sin offering – this was accomplished within the Passover meal as prescribed in the Law. In this way, the new Passover completes the old Passover, where sin was 'covered' for a year – now the sin is wiped away by this new sacrifice.

Conclusions
The timing and execution of the Last Supper as the New Passover meal is critical to the foundations and traditions of the New Church.

Remember, as Jesus approached Jerusalem, He Wept (Lk 19:41). He was weeping for the City – the very core of the Jewish Faith. He knew that the people would not accept their Messiah, and that would mean the destruction of Jerusalem and the Temple. Soon, the Temple would be destroyed, and without a Temple, the Law as prescribed in Leviticus could not be fulfilled. The Passover meal would no longer be possible. As we know, without the lamb sacrificed at the temple, there was no Passover meal possible. No Passover = no relief from sins (not even the temporary one offered at Passover). In short, the prophecy of Daniel (Dan 9:24-27) was coming to fruition – Judaism as prescribed by Moses was coming to an end, so Jesus wept. It was the end of their world.

The New Covenant Passover

Chapter 5 – The Last Supper

Then what could take its place?

Given that the 'world was coming to an end', and the Temple would be destroyed – how could the people of God do their required Passover observances? There was a new Passover – one where Jesus is the Lamb sacrificed. The Jews believed that their participation in Passover made them true participants in the original events, not just a hollow feast of remembrance. Just as Passover was an eternal re-experience of the Exodus, Jesus asked that the Last Supper be done 'In Remembrance' of Him and His Sacrifice. Just as the Jews remembered and re-lived their rescue from slavery in Egypt, to escape through the waters of the Red Sea, Christians now would remember and re-live how the New and Final Sacrifice on the Cross would rescue us from the slavery of Sin, and through the waters of Baptism we can now escape to the new promised land - Heaven.

What does all of this mean?

As we have seen before, there was a plan, and Jesus acted on it. The actions during the Triduum (the 3 days leading up to Easter Sunday) were carefully planned to redeem mankind – this plan had been in place since the fall of man in Genesis! Jesus, as the new Adam, brought about the means for redemption and the new way that people can live without sin – but you have to do what He tells you to. The events of Holy Week resulted in the completion of the Ultimate Passover. The original Passover was the yearly event where sins are just covered for a year, and the people saved from the visit of the Angel of Death. The new Passover instead offers a way to wash away original (generational) sin and then have Christ live through you. When Jesus promised to be 'with you always' He was not talking figuratively. Just as the God of Abraham resided with the Children of Israel on the Ark of the Covenant and the Temple, the New Covenant provided that God now resides within each faithful Christian. Participation in the New Covenant (the Covenant in His blood) is done through this New Passover.

Do you participate in the New Covenant in the Blood of Christ at Eucharist? It is something you must do..

Chapter 6 – Judgment Day?

Judgment is coming – for everyone. It is better to know what is expected of you, and how it will be measured than to be surprised. The Messiah went into quite explicit detail about judgment, both before and after resurrection. This is probably the most important section in the book, because if you think you are exempt from judgment you are mistaken... unless, of course, you are already dead as a martyr.

In Short:

How can God punish someone who *tried* to do His will? How could He punish someone who did not know right from wrong? Really? Have you read the Bible? Name an unrepentant sinner- or an ignorant sinner - in the Bible who is not punished? Was Sodom wiped out entirely because 'they knew better?' What about the children there – were they to blame for the sin of their elders? Yes. How about those who are outstanding followers of God, but who get punishment anyway? Job for example. How about Abraham, and Moses? The Jews tried time and again, but always ended up being smitten in one way or the other by God. You think you are exempt? Are you a greater servant of God than Abraham or Moses? It is possible to make it through Judgment Day, but it is not 'easy or simple'. You should "work out your salvation with fear and trembling[84]." How? Follow the instructions of Christ, and live for God and Others above your own needs, following the examples of the saints.

Long Version:

How can Jesus, who loves us, punish those who once believed but then fall away? Remember, Jesus, the Holy Spirit and God the Father are One God in three persons – Jesus is, in fact, the same God who wiped out the entire earthly population (Other than Noah and his boat of survivors) for their sinfulness; the same God who wiped out Sodom for their perversions, who forbade Moses from entering the Promised land after all he did for the Lord because of a (minor) failure to follow instructions. The same God who wanted to wipe out the entire children of Israel after the 'Golden Calf' incident, but did not only after

---

[84] Phil 2:12

Chapter 6 – Judgment Day

Moses pleaded for their lives? Jesus is not a new God of some kind – He is God Incarnate – <u>the same God of Abraham,</u> and He is not lenient or forgiving for those who reject the New Covenant. In fact, He shows up in the last days as the "Final Reaper":

Then I looked, and there was a white cloud, and seated on the cloud was one like the Son of Man, with a golden crown on his head, and a sharp sickle in his hand! Another angel came out of the temple, calling with a loud voice to the one who sat on the cloud, "Use your sickle and reap, for the hour to reap has come, because the harvest of the earth is fully ripe." So the one who sat on the cloud swung his sickle over the earth, and the earth was reaped.

Then another angel came out of the temple in heaven, and he too had a sharp sickle. Then another angel came out from the altar, the angel who has authority over fire, and he called with a loud voice to him who had the sharp sickle, "Use your sharp sickle and gather the clusters of the vine of the earth, for its grapes are ripe." So the angel swung his sickle over the earth and gathered the vintage of the earth, and he threw it into the great wine press of the wrath of God. And the wine press was trodden outside the city, and blood flowed from the wine press, as high as a horse's bridle, for a distance of about two hundred miles."[85]

Here Jesus starts the final clearing of all living creatures on the Earth – all people are killed, and their blood is as deep as a Horse's bridle for about 200 miles.

Again, Jesus is described in Rev 19:

Then I saw heaven opened, and there was a white horse! Its rider is called Faithful and True, and in righteousness he judges and makes war. His eyes are like a flame of fire, and on his head are many diadems; and he has a name inscribed that no one knows but himself. He is clothed in a robe dipped in blood, and his name is called The Word of God. And the armies of heaven, wearing fine linen, white and pure, were following him on white horses. From his mouth comes a sharp sword with which to strike down the nations, and he will rule them with a rod of iron;

---

[85] Rev 14:14-20 NRSV – in verse 16 Jesus (the Son of Man) reaps the Earth

Chapter 6 – Judgment Day

he will tread the wine press of the fury of the wrath of God the Almighty. On his robe and on his thigh he has a name inscribed, "King of kings and Lord of lords."

Then I saw an angel standing in the sun, and with a loud voice he called to all the birds that fly in midheaven, "Come, gather for the great supper of God, to eat the flesh of kings, the flesh of captains, the flesh of the mighty, the flesh of horses and their riders—flesh of all, both free and slave, both small and great."[86]

Not a kind, forgiving figure, but the instrument of Justice. He brings wrath to those who do not do His will. How are the good separated from the wicked?

The judgment scene follows, and is broken into 2 parts – the martyrs (Rev 20:4-6) and the general judgment followed (the second judgment for those who were not martyrs – those killed specifically for their faith in Christ). Judgment is rendered to each *'According to his deeds'* in Rev 20:12, and *'by what they had done'* in Rev 20:13, and finally again in Rev 22:12 *"I will give to each person according to what they have done."* Please note that in this people are not judged based on their faith or what they *wanted to do* – they were solely judged to be either 1) a martyr or 2) on what they have done.

There is no judgment scene in the Bible where anyone is judged on their faith or their 'heart'. If you have some reference to judgment based on faith alone, I would love to see it – again, in the entire Bible the only reference to "Faith Alone" is in James 2:24 which says: *"You see that a person is considered righteous by* ***what they do*** *and not by faith alone."* Over and over we see that people will be judged on what they do, not what they say that they believe.

So, when we look at the question of 'falling away' or 'backsliding', it is clear that what you have done is what you are judged by, not your 'heart' or 'Faith'. If you are not acting in righteousness and living as instructed by Christ, you will be cut off from the Body of Christ and be burned, as He said.

If you want to help your brothers and sisters in Christ, you have to do what will save them – teach them what Jesus taught his followers – Repent from your sins, and never sin again,

---

[86] Rev 19:11-18 NRSV

Chapter 6 – Judgment Day

because if you do, you cannot enter the Kingdom of God. If one has committed a Mortal Sin[87], one has to repent and confess it using the Sacrament of Reconciliation. Of course, the Judge (Jesus) can choose to forgive anyone of anything, but His way to handle sin after baptism is through this process of reconciliation.

Mortal sin? Are all sins the same?

Many non-Catholics believe that all sins are the same – probably from James where he writes "Whoever fails in one sin is guilty of breaking all of the Law." (Jas. 2:10)

Mortal Sin[88] is described in the first letter of John as:

*"If any one sees his brother committing what is not **a mortal sin**, he will ask, and God will give him life for those **whose sin is not mortal**. There is **sin which is mortal**; I do not say that one is to pray for that. **All wrongdoing is sin, but there is a sin which is not mortal**."*

James also talks about deadly sin in James 1:14-15:

"But one is tempted by one's own desire, being lured and enticed by it; then, when that desire has conceived, it gives birth to sin, and that sin, when it is fully grown, gives birth to death."

In Catholic teaching, in order to commit a grave, or mortal sin, where one ceases to be in a state of grace and is literally in real danger of hellfire, three requirements are necessary: 1) it must be a very serious matter, 2) the sinner has to have sufficiently reflected on, or had adequate knowledge of the sin, and 3) he must have fully consented in his will.

Scripture provides many indications of this difference in seriousness of sin, and in subjective guiltiness for it:

Luke 12:47-48: *"And that servant who knew his master's will, but did not make ready or act according to his will, shall receive a severe beating. But he who did not know, and did what deserved a beating, shall receive a light beating. Everyone to whom much is given, of him will much be required; and of him to whom men commit much they will demand the more."* (cf. Lev. 5:17, Lk. 23:34)

---

[87] Mortal and Venial sins referred to in 1 John 5:16-17, 1 Cor. 6:9-10; Gal. 1:8; Eph. 5:5; Heb. 12:16; Rev. 22:15
[88] Mortal and Venial sins referred to in 1 John 5:16-17 RSV

Chapter 6 – Judgment Day

Different sins result in different culpability, based on the seriousness of the sins committed.

John 19:11: "'. . . he who delivered me to you has the **greater sin**.'"

1 Timothy 1:13: *"though I formerly blasphemed and persecuted and insulted him; but I received mercy because I had acted **ignorantly** in unbelief."*

Hebrews 10:26: *"For if we sin **deliberately** after receiving the knowledge of the truth, there no longer remains a sacrifice for sins,"*

Cardinal Newman spoke on this subject:

"This distinction in the character of sins, viz. that some argue absence of faith and involve the loss of God's favor, and that others do not, is a very important one to insist upon, even though we cannot in all cases draw the line and say what sins imply the want of faith, and what do not; because, if we know that there are sins which do throw us out of grace, though we do not know which they are, this knowledge, limited as it is, will, through God's mercy, put us on our guard against acts of sin of any kind; both from the dread we shall feel lest these in particular, whatever they are, may be of that fearful nature, and next, from knowing that at least they tend that way. The common mode of reasoning adopted by the religion of the day is this: some sins are compatible with true faith, viz. sins of infirmity; therefore, willful transgression, or what the text calls "departing" from God, is compatible with it also. Men do not, and say they cannot, draw the line; and thus, from putting up with small sins, they go on to a sufferance of greater sins. Well, I would take the reverse way, and begin at the other end. I would force upon men's notice that there are sins which do forfeit grace; and then if, as is objected, that we cannot draw the line between one kind of sin and another, this very circumstance will make us shrink not only from transgressions, but also from infirmities. From hatred and

Chapter 6 – Judgment Day

abhorrence of large sins, we shall, please God, go on to hate and abhor the small."[89]

So how does the faithful Christian wipe away sin? The Catechism of the Catholic Church says that, "Christ instituted the sacrament of Penance for all sinful members of his Church: above all for those who, since Baptism, have fallen into grave sin, and have thus lost their baptismal grace and wounded ecclesial communion. It is to them that the sacrament of Penance offers a new possibility to convert and to recover the grace of justification. The Fathers of the Church present this sacrament as "the second plank [of salvation] after the shipwreck which is the loss of grace.""[90]

How many will attain the Kingdom?

Let's look at the passages where Jesus is clearly talking about Heaven, and see what can be deduced from the passages.

"Enter through the narrow gate; for the gate is wide and the road is easy that leads to destruction, and there are many who take it."[91]

This is related to the question "Will many enter the Kingdom?" in Luke 13:23 – *"Many will seek to enter, but few will be strong enough."* We read that *many* will try – not everyone, not most, 'many' will try. Are all of those who try to enter all Christians? We do not know… but few will be strong enough. Again, not a couple, not most, not many – but how many is that? Repentance is necessary, complete with STOPPING the sins, and confessing them for forgiveness. Just being 'sorry' is not enough. Repentance requires rejecting the sin, and turning away from them. Continuing to sin shows a failure to repent.

Can Unrepentant Sinners come into the Kingdom?

Also related is Galatians 5:21 – those who practice Envy, Drunkenness, orgies and similar sins will not inherit the kingdom.

Only the righteous will inherit the kingdom of God – *"Do not be misled. Neither fornicators, nor idolaters, nor adulterers, nor men kept for unnatural purposes, nor men who lie with men, nor*

---

[89] Parochial and Plain Sermons, Vol. 5, Sermon 14: "Transgressions and Infirmities" - from Newman's Anglican period: 1840)
[90] CCC paragraph 1446
[91] Mt 7:13 NRSV

Chapter 6 – Judgment Day

thieves, nor greedy persons, nor drunkards, nor revilers, nor extortionists will inherit God's kingdom."[92]

Not only must we do good things, we cannot do evil things – there are many examples, but here are two:

*"I never knew you: depart from me, you **evildoers**."*[93] People who acted as Christians, and even Prophets and Exorcists, are rejected because they did **evil deeds**.

*"Those who have done good will rise to live, and those who have **done evil** will rise to be condemned."*[94]

Judgment by Faith?

Judgment scene in Mt 25:31-46 – judgment is based on actions, not faith – in fact there are about fifty references to judgment by actions in the Bible.[95] There are none referencing judgment by Faith apart from actions.

*"Look, I am coming soon! My reward is with me, and I will give to each person according to **what they have done**"*[96]

Judgment is based on Actions, not faith in Revelation 20 also.

The Angels will purge anything impure from the Kingdom in Mt 13:41-43 – only the righteous will enter. Nothing is said about those who have faith alone except the one passage in the Bible dedicated to faith alone – James 2:24.

How are the Righteous rewarded?

One recurring theme in the passages on judgment refers to giving 'Just Recompense' to each according to their deeds. Some examples of this are:

*"For all of us must appear before the judgment seat of Christ, so that each may **receive recompense for what has been done** in the body, whether good or evil."* (2 Cor 5:10)

---

[92] 1 Cor 6:9-11
[93] Mt 7:22
[94] Jn 5:29
[95] Some are: 1 Samuel 28:15-19, 2 Kings 22:13 (cf. 2 Chron 34:21), Psalm 7:8-10, Ecclesiastes 12:14, Matthew 5:22, Matthew 7:16-27, Matthew 10:22 (cf. Mt 24:13; Mk 13:13), Matthew 16:27, Matthew 18:8-9 (cf. Mk 9:43,47), Matthew 25:14-30, Matthew 25:31-46, Luke 3:9 (+ Mt 3:10; 7:19), Luke 14:13-14, Luke 21:34-36, Luke 21:34-36, John 5:26-29, Romans 2:5-13 etc.
[96] Revelation 22:12

Chapter 6 – Judgment Day

> *"For the Son of man is to come with his angels in the glory of his Father, and then he will **repay every man for what he has done**."* (Mt 16:27)
>
> *"You will be repaid at the resurrection of the just."* (Lk 14:13-14)
>
> *"He who plants and he who waters are equal, and each shall receive his wages according to his labor"* (1 Cor 3:8-9)
>
> *"…who judges each one impartially according to his deeds"* (1 Pet 1:17)
>
> *"I am he who searches mind and heart, and I will give to each of you as your works deserve."* (Rev 2:23)
>
> *"Behold, I am coming soon, bringing my recompense, to repay every one for what he has done."* (Rev 22:12)

Over and over again, the ideas of 'Assured Salvation' or 'Salvation by Faith Alone' are invalidated by Scriptures, and have never been acceptable to the Church. It would be nice to believe that merely acknowledging Christ would be enough, but clearly it was not considered nearly enough.

Another proof of this was by the understanding of the Apostles and the early church – there was no doubt that all of them except John were martyred. If faith alone was enough, why did any of them risk their lives? All of the early Church clearly understood that deeds were required, and following the commands of Christ demonstrated their faithfulness to His message.

Is God a Just God?

Yes – certainly – but that is not good news for you and I unless we work very hard. Will He condemn those who insist on being ignorant of the Gospel or those who fail to do as they are expected to do to an eternal punishment?

Yes on all counts. Why?

Nothing imperfect enters Heaven (Rev 21:27 – *'nothing unclean, and no one who practices abomination and lying, shall ever come into it'*).

Jesus teaches that several specific items must be accomplished to inherit the Kingdom:
- Born from Above – Jn 3:5
- Baptism - Acts 2:38
- Believe in Him – Jn 3:16

Chapter 6 – Judgment Day

- Eat His Body and Drink His Blood – Jn 6:43-58
- Keep the Law – Lk 18:18
- Be like Children - Mt 18:3, also Mk 10:15, Lk 18:17
- Be Righteous - Mt 5:20
- Etc..

Pretty tough goals to reach? Have courage – there are tools to help us on the way. Confession, the Graces given by God to strengthen us when we fail and finally the gift of Purgatory to clean up whatever failures we may have remaining if we show enough commitment on Judgment day to 'make the cut' to Purgatory. The desire of God is that everyone will love Him – and love all others. This is the sum of the Law: to Love God and Love others as yourself. If you do not want to do this, or will not do it, you would not be happy in Heaven.

If you want to be in Heaven, you must start act that way NOW – you are currently living in Eternity, as Death will mark a transition - not an end - of life. If you are not living NOW to preparation to be suitable for Heaven, when do you plan to start? If you live your life and shape yourself to be without God, why should you radically change after death?

In many religions, entrance to Heaven is conditional on having lived a "good life" (within the terms of the spiritual system) or "accepting God into your heart".

In the "sola fide" belief of many mainstream Protestant Christians, one does not *have to* live a "good life", but one must accept (believe and put faith in) Jesus Christ as one's savior, and then Jesus Christ will assume the guilt of one's sins; believers are considered to be forgiven regardless of any good or bad "works" they have participated in. This is called 'Imputed Righteousness'.

Catholic Christians also speak of heaven as unattainable by even heroic human effort and having been "opened" instead by the death and resurrection of Jesus (Catechism of the Catholic Church, CCC 1026). They see heaven as "God eternal reward for good works accomplished with the grace of Christ" and giving rise to no strict merit on the part of human beings (CCC 1821), while "the works of the flesh" are excluded from heaven. That statement means that works alone cannot provide enough merit for anyone to get into Heaven, but instead that works of mercy

Chapter 6 – Judgment Day

with the Grace of God can provide the means for an eternal reward in Heaven for a job well done.

For the Orthodox faith too, "free will and our cooperation with God is always understood to be an act of grace". This essentially also means that works alone does nothing to merit salvation, but works in conjunction with the Grace provided by God can give the eternal reward that we are looking for.

Christian Universalism, on the other hand, holds that, because of divine love and mercy, <u>all will</u> ultimately be reconciled to God, regardless of present faith or good deeds. Well, that pretty much removes all value from Christianity, doesn't it?

What does all of this mean?

Ultimately, Jesus is the Judge, and how He decides is entirely in His hands. I do recommend studying what He said was required for salvation, and not relying on anyone else to provide that information for you. When the moment comes (and it will) neither your Pastor nor anyone else will take responsibility for *your failure* to be aware of the Teachings of Christ and His Church. You will be judged according to <u>your</u> works. This is probably something you should do something about now!

What have you done for Him lately?

Chapter 7 – What hard proof exists?

Chapter 7 – What Hard Proof Exists?

There is a ton of proof provided over the centuries, but again, many do not like this section for some reason. Perhaps being faced with the facts removes doubt, and makes obedience less of a choice but a necessity.

In Short:

From the Shroud that Christ was buried in to the appearances of Mary over the centuries to the Incorruptible dead, there have been thousands of well documented, scientifically investigated and undeniable miracles supporting the reality of Christ. Eucharistic miracles have always provided stunning proof of the power of God. These are given to us to point us to Christ – please look at them!

Long Version:

In his life, Christ showed many signs of his power, and demonstrated the reality of His Good News. Why do people have such a hard time with recent examples of the miraculous? Let's consider, with an open mind, but a desire to find the truth, about some examples of modern miracles and some ancient miracles that are being proved by modern science.

Shroud of Turin/Sudarium
Shroud of Turin:

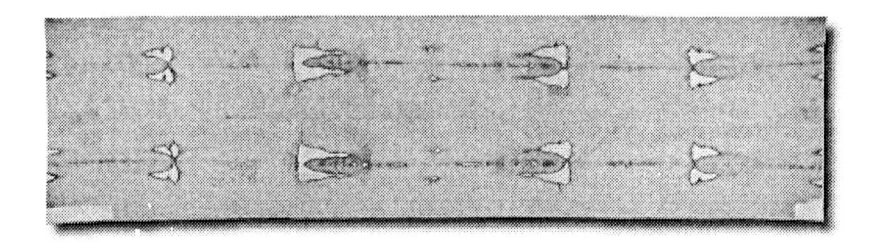

What is the Shroud of Turin? This is reputed to be the burial cloth of Christ. The Shroud is a 14½ foot long, 3½ foot wide linen cloth that bears the ventral and dorsal image of a scourged, crucified man. The blood on the cloth are typical for a Jew, but rare for most ethnic groups – blood group AB. Owned by the Dukes of Savoy (former ruling family of Italy) until the late 1980's and now the property of the Catholic Church, it has been

Chapter 7 – What hard proof exists?

permanently kept in Turin, Italy, since 1578. It is stored in a special reliquary in a chapel behind the altar in the Cathedral of St. John the Baptist. The cathedral was erected specifically to house the Shroud and was built adjoining the Royal Palace (the King's former residence) in Turin.

This cloth has been the subject of much controversy for over 1,000 years, and despite intensive scrutiny of the cloth in 1988 recent discoveries again seem to make the object appear completely authentic. There are many aspects to this item, and I cannot hope to thoroughly cover them all, but I will present a short summary of the main points with references for further study for those items that may interest you.

Why do we think the Shroud and Sudarium are in any way linked to the Christ?

Officially, and absolutely, there is no way to prove that anything about these pieces of cloth are related to Christ. Even if the Shroud had a note in Aramaic saying "Jesus was Here" we still would have no proof positive that after 2,000 years anything is undeniably connected to Christ. The fact is that no matter what evidence we may pull together, there will always be some doubt about anything that important. We have some DNA evidence, but we cannot be sure who originated the DNA after so long. Witnesses are long gone, and their writings could have been faked. The image is essentially a photograph, but a photo of who?

On the other hand, the circumstantial evidence is quite astonishing. For the sake of argument, let us consider the possibility that the Shroud and Sudarium are, in fact, the burial cloths of Christ, to see how the evidence lines up.

How old is the shroud of Turin?

A huge and well known project in 1988 set about to discover the true origins of the Shroud, and at that time the findings were almost entirely in favor of the authenticity of the Shroud as the possible burial cloth of Christ, with one notable exception – the age of the material was found to be about 700 years old, not 2,000 years old as was expected.[97] Despite this finding, another series of

---

[97] In 1988 carbon-14 dating of scraps of the cloth carried out by labs in Oxford, Zurich and Arizona that dated it from 1260 to 1390

Chapter 7 – What hard proof exists?

tests were done on the original samples from 1988, and these tests seem to make the object appear completely authentic[98]. The reason for the disagreement was related to the fire in 1532 in the chapel in Chambery, France. This fire was known to have damaged the cloth – burning part of it and scorching more, leaving carbon residue in the material itself. Scientists state that this was the reason for the date range of the original 1988 study by the 3 labs, all 3 of which specified the date range of 1260 to 1390 AD for the manufacture date of the cloth.

In the most recent tests, the carbon ash was removed from the test materials, and the results were between 300 BC and 400 AD. This newest date range puts the cloth in the correct time to be the burial cloth of Christ.

Was the Shroud in Palestine in the First Century?

Spore analysis was conducted on the cloth to determine if it had been in the area of Jerusalem in the first century AD. These results were published by Zurich pathologist Max Frei, who was a botanist (Ph.D.) and a recognized authority on Mediterranean flora, studied pollen samples that had been tape-lifted from the Shroud surface (1973, 1978); and under various kinds of microscopes he identified 57 pollen species, microscopic grains that can last for millions of years. Many of these pollens are found in the area of Jerusalem (45), with a lesser number found around Edessa (15) and Constantinople (13), cities where the Shroud had been, or elsewhere in the Mediterranean area. Frei found only 17 pollen species that grew in France or Italy, while nearly all of the rest had a non-European origin or grew in the Jerusalem area. Zugibe[99] considers this "strong evidence" that the Shroud originally came from Jerusalem.[100] Different species of plant pollens can be identified under a microscope by their diverse shapes and surface features. Frei spent the last nine years of his life identifying these pollens, making seven trips to the Middle East in different floral seasons.[101] This makes it clear that the Shroud has a history outside of and predating France and Italy. However, some botanists have complained

---

[98] In March 2013 the University of Padua dated the shroud to between 300 BC and 400 AD using the same samples used in 1988
[99] Zugibe 2005, pp. 283–285, and for pollen photo see Figure 17–1 on p. 28.
[100] Zugibe 2005, p. 288; Frei, pp. 3–7; Wilson 2010, pp. 62–64.
[101] Antonacci, pp. 109–110.

Chapter 7 – What hard proof exists?

that Frei did not confirm his identifications by using a scanning electron microscope—which was because he wanted to preserve these samples for future research.[102]

What formed the Image on the Shroud?

Paul Vignon, the assistant to the first photographer (Yves Delage) was the first to discover the negative photographic qualities of the Shroud, and he said "No such impression on a winding-sheet has ever been found in any [other] tomb, and we may add that it is materially impossible that such a thing should be found."[103] How could a 'simple' image be so surprising? Surely we are used to photographic images appearing on things these days – why is this different?

[104]First, this image appears only on the very surface of the cloth – it is a discoloration of the fibers themselves, similar to what might happen if cloth is left out in the sun. Adler[105] found that a single thread of the shroud cloth was made up of many very small (10 to 15 microns in diameter) linen fibers. The width of one of these fibers is much smaller than a human hair. Only the TOPMOST fibers of the thread were yellowed. These yellowed fibers, composed of cellulose, were found only on the image side of the cloth and were responsible for the image. The fibers on the bottom side of the threads were NOT yellowed.

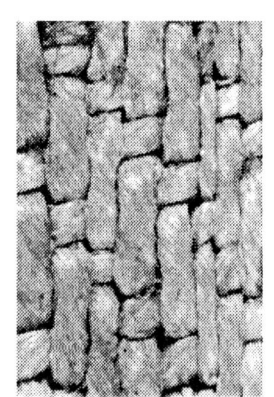

Micrograph taken at the image area of the right eye at 32x magnification

Adler finally concluded that the yellowing of the shroud image fibers was produced by dehydration, or an oxidative process that affected the fiber (cellulose) structure itself and caused it to yellow. Therefore, this process is a degradation of the fibers themselves and is identical to the aging of linen, causing linen to turn from white to yellow.

---

[102] Zugibe 2005, pp. 288–289, Wilson 2010, p. 65.
[103] Vignon, Paul. *The Shroud of Christ.* New York: E. P. Dutton, (translated from the French), 1902., p. 44.
[104] Vern Miller, one of the official professional photographers for the American scientific team has a micrograph (a slide) that was taken at 64x magnification. It was taken at the image area of the nose, which happens to be the darkest portion of the entire shroud image.
[105] Dr. Alan Adler, a professor of chemistry from western Connecticut State University

Chapter 7 – What hard proof exists?

What is peculiar about the image on the Shroud?

Probably the oddest feature of the Shroud image is its 3 dimensionally encoded information – unlike anything but the most modern and purpose – made images. The Space Program created this technology to examine images of the Moon's Surface, and NASA scientists were astonished that their image technology rendered the Shroud image in 3D. Dr. John Jackson, who is a physicist, placed a photograph of the shroud image under a VP8 image analyzer[106]. This electronic device is "…ideally suited for determining whether a given image contains distance information because it converts image shading into relief." Jackson found that the frontal image of the shroud has a three-dimensional quality. Photographs of people do not exhibit this quality. Much later, in 1992, Dr. Alan Whanger discovered another quality about the image. He found "X-ray-like images of internal body structures, such as bones of the face and hands.

The ventral image of the Shroud of Turin as it appears on the screen of a VP-8 Image Analyzer

This is a unique and complex image that one may say is more than a photograph: it seems to possess some characteristics of an X-ray, and carries with it information that gives it a three-dimensional quality.

When input to a VP-8, a normal photograph does not result in a properly formed dimensional image but in a rather distorted jumble of light and dark "shapes." That is because the lights and darks of a normal photograph result solely from the amount of light reflected by the subject onto the film. The image densities do not depend on the distance the subject was from the film. Yet the image on the Shroud of Turin yields a very accurate dimensional relief of a human form. This seems to show that the

---

[106] http://shroudnm.com/docs/SEAM-VP8-Presentation.pdf

Chapter 7 – What hard proof exists?

image density on the cloth is directly proportionate to the distance it was from the body it covered. The closer the cloth was to the body (tip of nose, cheekbone, etc.), the darker the image, and the further away (eye sockets, neck, etc.), the fainter the image. This spatial data encoded into the image actually eliminates photography and painting as the possible mechanism for its creation and allows us to conclude that the image was formed while the cloth was draped over an actual human body. So the VP-8 Image Analyzer not only revealed a previously unknown and very important characteristic of the Shroud image, but historically it also provided the actual motivation to form the team that would ultimately go and investigate it. Interestingly, only sixty VP-8 Image Analyzers were ever constructed and only two remain functional today.

How was an image of this sort created? Many efforts for hundreds of years (literally) have failed to re-create the image. No one to date has come close, despite their best efforts. Encoding the information into an image created by apparent radiation interaction with the surface of fibers borders on the impossible or, perhaps, the miraculous?

Why would the man in the image seem to be Christ?

If the Cloth is from the right time (around 33 AD), and **if** it comes from the right place (Jerusalem), and the image is of a crucified person, how can we be sure in any way that this crucified person was the *one and only* Messiah, Jesus of Nazareth? Many people were executed in that time and at that place, so why should we jump to the conclusion that this particular person is the Christ? Let's consider the possible reasons:

- The unusual nature of the image – no other similar image exists from antiquity.
- The Crucified man was brutally beaten, in line with the Gospel writers' accounts before crucifixion. This would be very unusual indeed.
- The Cloth has been considered to be Christ's image for as long as records exist.
- The crucified man wore a band of thorns around his head – again, recorded in the Gospels but very unusual indeed.

Chapter 7 – What hard proof exists?

- The image is of an upright man despite the fact that he is clearly deceased – the hair and muscles are in a position that naturally connotes an **upright posture.**

Where did the burial shroud of Christ come from?

There are theories that the burial cloth, which was provided by Joseph of Arimathea[107], was actually the tablecloth from the table used by Christ at the last supper. Was this the case?

To get a clear picture of Jewish life and practice during the first two centuries C.E. we must rely on the primary Tannaitic sources, namely the Mishnah, the Tosefta and the other Tannaitic passages dispersed throughout the Talmud of Babylon (Bavli) and of the Land of Israel (Yerushalim).[108]

During this period, a table was used for meals... We find no evidence that the Jewish people used different tables for the Sabbath and festivals, including Passover, than they ordinarily used; although they probably subjected it to a thorough cleaning, same as the rest of the house, to clear away the leaven immediately before Passover. (Mishnah, Pesahim, Ch.1 et passim)

What did the last supper table look like?

It had a square top (sometimes also a square bottom), usually made of wood, (Mishnah Kelim 16:1), pottery (Mishnah Kelim 2:3); overlaid with marble (ibid 22:1). It usually had three legs (ibid 22:2), and could accommodate three or four people. For larger groups, such as weddings, long boards were used (called dahavanot) (Tosefta Kelim, Baba Metzia, 5:3).

Food was ordinarily eaten off the bare table top (Bavli, Baba Batra 57b), and only the intellectual elite seem to have used a cloth to cover part of the small table for use as napkins to wipe their lips after eating (ibid). According to Maimonides, the Mishnah refers to a leather table covering (skortia), probably designed to protect the table from the elements (Mishnah Kelim 16:4). The only explicit reference to "a cover for tables" (Mishnah Makshirin 5:8) is explained as a sheet spread over the food (not

---

[107] Mt 27:59
[108] This information comes from British Society for the Turin Shroud (BSTS) Newsletter #35, Aug/Sept 1993, pages 10-11.

Chapter 7 – What hard proof exists?

the bare table) to protect it from flies and other insects. (M. Jastrow, Dictionary, vol. II, p.1396, col.1, bot. sub Kesiyah, Cf. P. Blackman, Mishnah VI, 682).

The theory that the Shroud was actually a tablecloth was advanced by Dr. John Jackson[109] and his wife Rebecca. The idea that this was a cloth that was quickly and easily available, given the surprising circumstances of Christ's death, and that it was an appropriate size makes some sense. In addition, there are apparently some remaining markings on the edge of the shroud that may indicate thirteen place settings – a cloth that size could easily serve as a tablecloth for a party of that size. If you are interested in their explanation in depth, I recommend visiting their web site.

---

[109] The couple has a website dedicated to the Shroud at www.ShroudOfTurin.com and a facility in Colorado.

Chapter 7 – What hard proof exists?
The Sudarium:

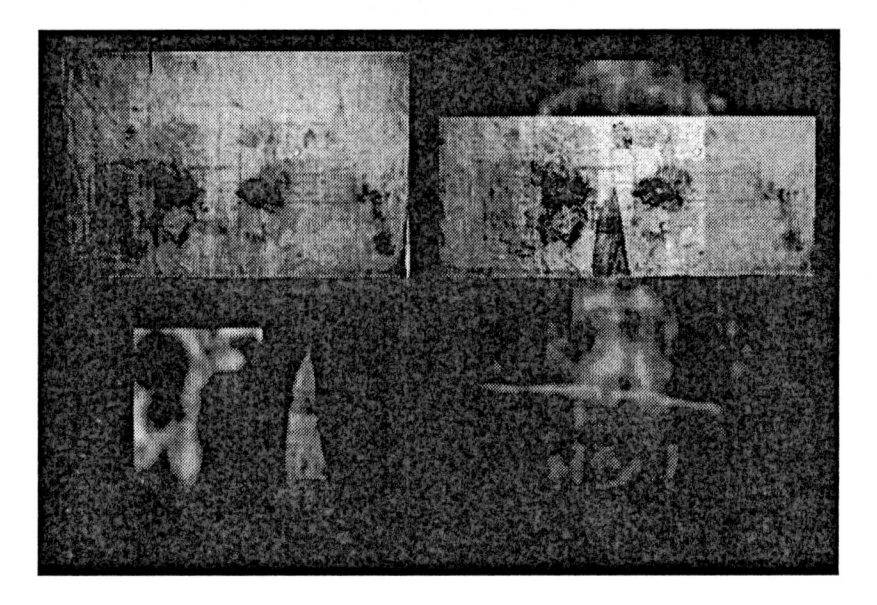

The History of the Cloth

One of the relics held by the cathedral in the town of Oviedo, in the north of Spain, is a piece of cloth measuring approximately 84 x 53 cm. There is no image on this cloth. Only stains are visible to the naked eye, although more is visible under the microscope. The remarkable thing about this cloth is that both tradition and scientific studies claim that the cloth was used to cover and clean the face of Jesus after the crucifixion. Let's look at the facts and consider these claims.

This cloth is known to have existed from the gospel of John 20:6-7. These verses read as follows, *"Simon Peter, following him, also came up, went into the tomb, saw the linen cloth lying on the ground, **and also the cloth that had been over his head;** this was not with the linen cloth but rolled up in a place by itself."* John clearly differentiates between this smaller face cloth, the sudarium, and the larger linen that had wrapped the body.

The history of the sudarium is well documented, and much more direct than that of the Shroud. Most of the information comes from the twelfth century bishop of Oviedo, Pelagius, whose historical works are the Book of the Testaments of Oviedo, and the Chronicon Regum Legionensium. According to this

Chapter 7 – What hard proof exists?

history, the sudarium was in Palestine until shortly before the year 614, and has been carefully tracked ever since.

All the credit for the investigations carried out on the sudarium must go to the Investigation Team of the Spanish Centre for Sindonology, under the leadership of Guillermo Heras. The medical part of the investigation was done by Dr. José Villalaín.

The stains on the sudarium show that when the cloth was placed on the dead man's face, it was folded over. Counting both sides of the cloth, there is therefore a fourfold stain in a logical order of decreasing intensity.

From the composition of the main stains, it is apparent that the man whose face the sudarium covered died in an upright position. The stains consist of one part blood and six parts fluid from a pleural oedema. This liquid collects in the lungs when a crucified person dies of asphyxiation, and if the body subsequently suffers jolting movements, can come out through the nostrils. These are in fact the main stains visible on the sudarium.

These stains in the nasal area are also superimposed on each other, with the different outlines clearly visible. This means that the first stain had already dried when the second stain was formed, and so on.

Dr. Villalaín had a specially modeled head made to reconstruct the process of staining and drying, and was thus able to calculate the time that elapsed between the formations of each stain.

The cloth was not wrapped entirely round the head because the right cheek was almost touching the right shoulder. This suggests that the sudarium was put into place while the body was still on the cross. The second stain was made about an hour later, when the body was taken down. The third stain was made when the body was lifted from the ground about forty five minutes later. The body was lying at the foot of the cross for about forty-five minutes before being buried. The marks (not fingerprints) of the fingers that held the cloth to the nose are also visible.

Chapter 7 – What hard proof exists?

How the sudarium was wrapped around the head[110]:

The experiments with the model head and the study of the stains also show that when the man died his head was tilted seventy degrees forward and twenty degrees to the right. This position further suggests that the man whose face the sudarium covered died crucified.

There are smaller bloodstains at the side of the main group. It would appear that the sudarium was pinned to the back of the dead man's head, and that these spots of blood were from small sharp objects, which would logically be the thorns that caused this type of injury all over Jesus' head.

The medical studies are not the only ones that have been carried out on the sudarium. Dr. Max Frei analyzed pollen samples taken from the cloth, and found species typical of Oviedo, Toledo, North Africa and Jerusalem. This confirms the historical route described earlier. There was nothing relating the cloth to Constantinople, France, Italy or any other country in Europe.

An international congress was held in Oviedo in 1994, where various papers were presented about the sudarium. Dr. Frei's work with pollen was confirmed, and enlarged on. Species of pollen called "quercus caliprimus" were found, both of which are limited to the area of Palestine.

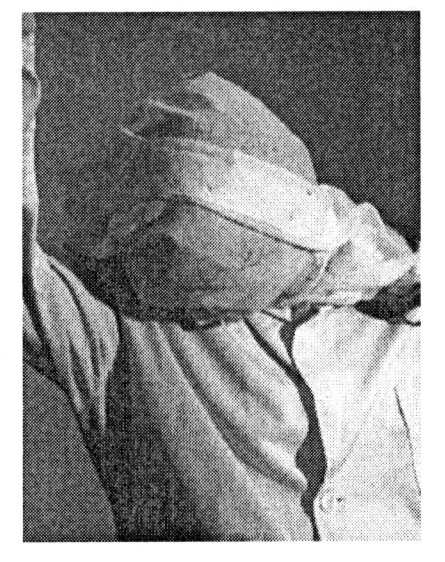

Residues of what is most probably myrrh and aloe have also been discovered, mentioned directly in the gospel of John 19:39-40, *"Nicodemus came as well...and he brought a mixture of myrrh and aloes...They took the body of Jesus and bound it in linen cloths with the spices, following the Jewish burial custom."*

---

[110] Photo © Jorge Manuel Rodríguez & the Centro Español de Sindonología – used with permission.

Chapter 7 – What hard proof exists?

The stains were also studied from the point of view of anthropology. The conclusion was that the face that had been in contact with the sudarium had typically Jewish features, a prominent nose and pronounced cheekbones.

Comparison with the Shroud

The sudarium alone has revealed enough information to suggest that it was in contact with the face of Jesus after the crucifixion. However, the really fascinating evidence comes to light when this cloth is compared to the Shroud of Turin.

The first and most obvious coincidence is that the blood on both cloths belongs to the same group, namely AB. This blood type is found in other miraculous Eucharistic events.

The length of the nose through which the pleural oedema fluid came onto the sudarium has been calculated at eight centimeters, just over three inches. This is exactly the same length as the nose on the image of the Shroud.

If the face of the image on the Shroud is placed over the stains on the sudarium, perhaps the most obvious coincidence is the exact fit of the stains with the beard on the face. As the sudarium was used to clean the man's face, it appears that it was simply placed on the face to absorb all the blood, but not used in any kind of wiping movement.

A small stain is also visible proceeding from the right hand side of the man's mouth. This stain is hardly visible on the Shroud, but Dr. John Jackson, using the VP-8 and photo enhancements has confirmed its presence.

The thorn wounds on the nape of the neck also coincide perfectly with the bloodstains on the Shroud.

Dr. Alan Whanger applied the Polarized Image Overlay Technique to the sudarium, comparing it to the image and bloodstains on the Shroud. The frontal stains on the sudarium show seventy points of coincidence with the Shroud, and the rear side shows fifty. The only possible conclusion is that the Oviedo sudarium covered the same face as the Turin Shroud.

The Sudarium and the Shroud

The sudarium has no image and none of the facial stains of dried or drying blood visible on the Shroud, especially the stain on the forehead in the shape of an inverted three. The stains on the sudarium were made by a less viscous mixture.

Chapter 7 – What hard proof exists?

This, together with the fact that the fingers which held the sudarium to Jesus' nose have left their mark, point to a short temporal use of the cloth and eliminate the possibility of its contact with the body after burial.

Jewish tradition demands that if the face of a dead person was in any way disfigured, it should be covered with a cloth. This would certainly have been the case with Jesus, whose face was covered in blood from the injuries produced by the crown of thorns and swollen from falling and being struck.

It seems that the sudarium was first used before the dead body was taken down from the cross and kept with the body when it was buried.

This fits in with what we learn from John's gospel, which tells us that the sudarium was rolled up in a place by itself.

What does this mean?

The studies on the sudarium and the comparison of this cloth with the Shroud are just one of the many branches of science which point to both having covered the dead body of Jesus. The history of the Oviedo cloth is well documented, and the conclusions of this for the dating of the Shroud seem obvious. These cloths were clearly used in the burial of Jesus, and were in contact or close to the body at resurrection. This is incredibly important information, but more than that, it does fit into a whole series of other miraculous events. Consider how the Shroud, Sudarium and Eucharistic miracles all fit together.

Chapter 7 – What hard proof exists?

Eucharistic Miracles

There are literally hundreds of these over the centuries, but four recent examples that seem well linked are:

1. The Shroud of Turin
    a. Blood type (AB) analysis on the cloth, and the fluid analysis of the spot where the wound on the side was, show a crucified man with the same blood type as the other 3 sources.
    b. Many resources, but recent carbon 14 testing indicates that the cloth is from the correct time period [111]
    c. Blood marks match up with Sudarium
2. The Sudarium – facecloth of Jesus
    a. Many websites provide information[112]
    b. Blood type (AB) match those of the Shroud [113]
    c. Holes and Marks consistent with crucified person with crown of thorns who was dead wearing the cloth for a short period.
3. The Eucharistic Miracle at Lanciano
    a. Early Eucharistic Miracle (700 AD)[114]
    b. Investigations since 1574
    c. Material exhaustively investigated [115]
    d. Scientific study done in 1971/1981[116]
    e. Flesh and Blood still existent - Defies explanation – should be dust after 1,300 years!
    f. Blood type AB
    g. Flesh is from the Myocardium
4. Eucharistic Miracle in Buenos Ares
    a. One of the investigators has a video for a starting point[117]
    b. Investigations currently going on – recent event[118]
    c. On October 5, 1999, Dr. Castañón removed tissue samples bloodied and sent to New York for further analysis – it was found to be living Myocardium.

---

[111] http://www.usatoday.com/story/news/world/2013/03/30/shroud-turin-display/2038295/
[112] http://www.shroud.com/guscin.htm
[113] http://www.shroud.com/guscin.htm
[114] http://en.wikipedia.org/wiki/Miracle_of_Lanciano
[115] http://www.zenit.org/en/articles/physician-tells-of-eucharistic-miracle-of-lanciano
[116] http://www.therealpresence.org/eucharst/mir/lanciano.html
[117] http://www.youtube.com/watch?v=APzl v8ozl ms
[118] http://www.bubblews.com/news/428870-eucharistic-miracle-in-buenos-aires

Chapter 7 – What hard proof exists?

    d. Five years later (2004), Dr. Gomez contacted Dr. Frederick Zugibe and asked to evaluate a test sample – same results with several witnesses at a different lab.

    e. Blood type was found to be AB

Some points about these Eucharistic Miracles:
- Some are very recent – 1991
- Some are extremely old – 700 AD and earlier with less physical evidence
- These are not specifically to oppose a Protestant doubt in the Eucharist, as most happened before there was any doubt about the transubstantiation of the Eucharist
- First group to reject True Presence in Eucharist was in Jn 6:66 – the Jews refused to accept the doctrine.
- Luther denied Transubstantiation, but offered Consubstantiation instead – it remained bread/wine but was ALSO the Body and Blood.
- Anglicans accepted Transubstantiation, and then moved to Consubstantiation after Henry VIII, then more recently to True Presence.
- First rejection of True Presence/Trans/Consubstantiation was radical groups like Huldrych Zwingli in the 1500's.

There are, of course, many other Eucharistic miracles, but many are too long ago to get accurate scientific data. Some of the approved Eucharistic Miracles are[119] in appendix 5.

As you can see, these are numerous and well documented events. The phenomenon of Eucharistic Miracles is unmistakable, and the official record above is a tiny subset of the reported miraculous events of this nature.

---

[119] Details for these can be found on http://www.therealpresence.org

Chapter 7 – What hard proof exists?

Marian Apparitions

Zeitun Egypt – April 2, 1968-1971

Probably the most astounding of the modern Marian Apparitions was this one in Zeitun - an estimated 40 million people saw this unexplainable event. Our Lady reportedly appeared in Zeitun, Egypt hovering above Saint Mark's Coptic Church for a span of three years. The Church is dedicated to the Holy Family, which according to tradition rested in that place during their stay in Egypt.

For about three years Our Lady appeared on many occasions especially at night, and sometimes she was accompanied by white doves that would fly around her. The first two years she appeared about two to three times a week.

These apparitions attracted large crowds by night, sometimes up to 250,000 people. Christians, Jews, Moslems, and unbelievers gathered to view the sight. The apparitions were photographed, filmed and broadcast on Egyptian TV.

Anba Kyrillos VI, Pope of Alexandria, delegated a commission of priests to research and investigate the phenomenon. They stayed there for several nights enquiring and investigating until they saw with their own eyes the blessed Virgin's apparition in the full form moving on the domes and

Chapter 7 – What hard proof exists?

blessing the multitudes in front of the church.

Kyrillos VI's official statement was:

"The Blessed Virgin Mary has appeared several times on the Coptic Orthodox Church named after her at Zeitun in Cairo."

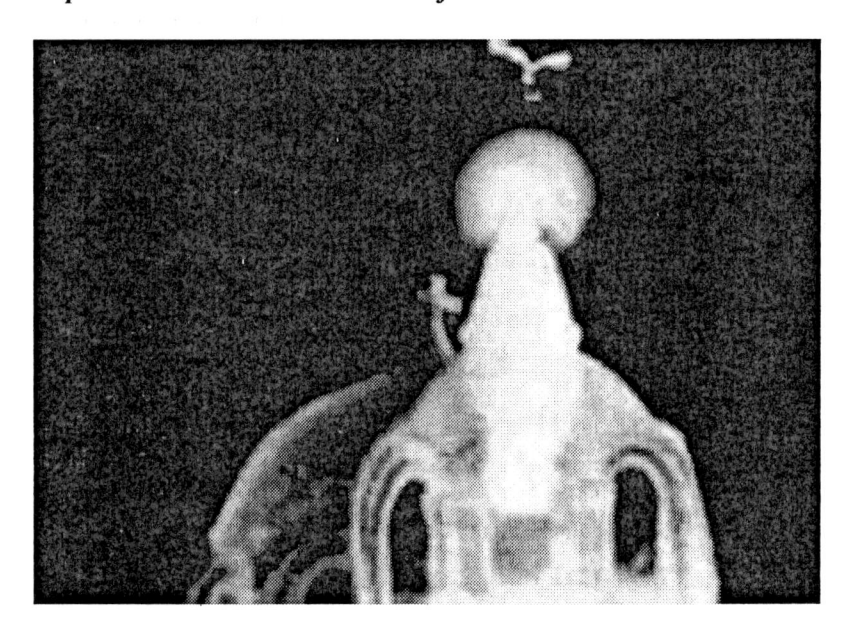

The apparitions were also confirmed by the Jesuit Father Dr. Henry Ayrout. Nuns of the Society of the Sacred Heart also witnessed the phenomenon and sent a detailed report to the Vatican, resulting in the arrival of an envoy on April 28, 1968, who also saw the apparitions and sent a report to Pope Paul VI.

This event was witnessed and photographed thousands of times, with literally millions of people witnessing them.

There are several thousand Marian Apparitions over the centuries, many having a permanent effect on the world. The apparitions in Fatima predicted the fall of Russia into Communism, World War I and the eventual collapse of communism in Russia! Lourdes is an international site where healings occur daily.

Why are there Marian Apparitions? Mary remains present to us and points to her Son, Jesus. Her visitations always ask for repentance and obedience to Jesus, which is the message of the Church.

Chapter 7 – What hard proof exists?

Why Mary? Why not Jesus Himself? What about someone else – Moses or Abraham, for example? The answer is simple enough, and in the Scriptures – Mary is described as 'Full of Grace[120]' (khä-rē-to'-ō). She was given special grace by God, so that she could perform her duty as mother of Jesus. Read more about Mary in a later chapter. Her job is to reveal her Son to us, as she did at His birth, and to continue to point us towards Him.

There are many, many Marian apparitions, so I will not attempt to give details on all of them, but instead I recommend going into one of the many supporting books on the following major approved Marian apparitions:

Catholic Approved Marian Apparitions, (except where noted)
- Guadalupe – 1531
- Laus – 1664
- Salette - 1846
- Lourdes – 1858
- Pontmain – 1871
- Fatima 1917
- Knock – 1879
- Beauraing – 1932
- Banneaux – 1930
- Assiut – 2000-1 (Orthodox)
- Walsingham – 1921 (Anglican)
- Yankalilla – 1994 (Anglican)

---
[120] Luke 1:28

Chapter 7 – What hard proof exists?

Incorruptibles

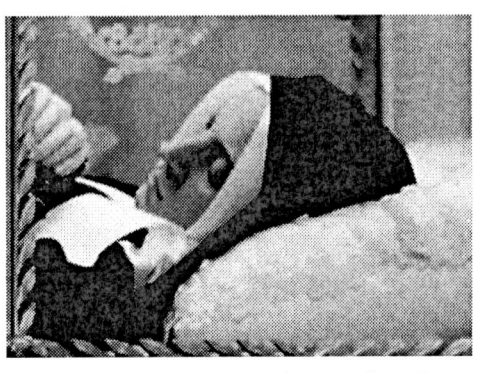

Since the earliest days, there have been examples of the 'Incorruptibles' – the saints who, because of their holy lives, remain much as they were in life – their bodies not decomposing. An example to the right is the incorrupt body of St. Bernadette of Lourdes (shown above).

These saints, whose bodies are miraculously preserved after death, defy the normal process of decomposition. St. Cecilia is probably the first saint known to be incorrupt, but the bodies of these saints can be found in many places throughout the world. These bodies are not like mummies, because their skin is soft and their limbs pliable, nothing at all like the dry, skeletal remains of mummies. Under normal circumstances, nothing at all has been done to preserve the bodies of these saints. In fact, some of them have been covered in quicklime, which should have easily destroyed any human remains, yet it has no effect of these saints. Many of them also give off a sweet, unearthly odor, and others produce blood or oils that defy any scientific explanation. St. Bernadette is an example of this sweet, rose-like smell.

Many modern scientists consider the Incorruptibles to be mummies, pretending they understands and can comfortably categorize these saints. How then do the scientists explain the fact that a year and a half after the death of St. Francis Xavier, a medical examiner placed a finger into one of the saint's wounds and found fresh blood on his finger when he withdrew it? Or that when a finger was amputated from St. John of the Cross several months after his death, it was immediately observed that blood began to flow from the wound? Or the case of St. Nicholas

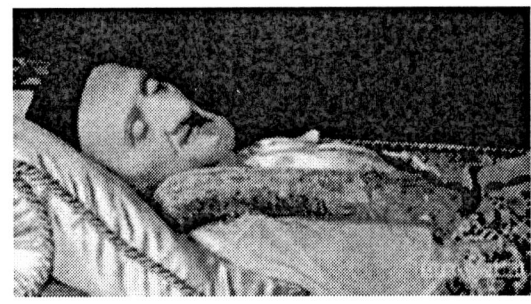

St. Vincent De Paul – died 1660 – incorrupt.

132 | Page

Chapter 7 – What hard proof exists?

of Tolentino, whose arms have bled occasionally over the last 400 years?

These saints are not mummies – mummies were carefully prepared and (typically) dried out for preservation. Even though incorruptibility does not automatically confer sainthood upon the subject, it is still properly appreciated by the Church as a supernatural occurrence. Part of the canonization process is to exhume the body and examine it. This is how many of the Incorruptibles were discovered. The truth is that these occurrences cannot be understood outside of Divine intervention on behalf of these saints, as the laws of nature have been suspended on their behalf. Perhaps it is that God is visibly showing us his pleasure with these saints? Still, it is a physical manifestation of God's love, and the incorruptible saints console us by their presence, seeming to plead with us to likewise make ourselves pleasing to God in all ways.

A list of approved Incorruptibles in included in Appendix 6.

Why are there Incorruptibles?

It is understood that some saints have incorrupt bodies to remind the rest of us that one day we will all be restored to our bodies for judgment. The body is not something that we leave behind forever at death – the resurrection of the body is a fundamental part of the Christian faith, and therefore the Church has always instructed the faithful to preserve, as much as is appropriate, the body for resurrection. The pagans practiced incineration of the body for hygienic reasons, which was strictly against the beliefs of the Church throughout the centuries. Romans outlawed the burial of bodies in their cities, which was why Christians used the Catacombs to bury their dead in the earliest days of the Church in Rome.

What do these things mean?

Honestly, I could easily fill a book with these events – there are literally thousands of impossible events associated with Christ's Church, all pointing to the greater reality beyond this life. I pointed to the Eucharistic miracles, which are astonishingly impossible but none the less scientifically provable. The Marian Apparitions have had tens of millions of people witness them – including video and photographs. The Incorruptibles are likewise impossible, but true. Time and time again the facts of the

Chapter 7 – What hard proof exists?

teachings of the Church are confirmed by the miraculous. People do not want facts, though, and generally the 'uncommitted' dislike the evidence. Proving the veracity of the Church means you have to obey it, and people do not want to be obedient.

Share these Miracles, and help others to decide to become faithful Christians.

Chapter 8 – Where did our Bible come from?

Where did our Bible come from? The roots of our modern Bible are very likely completely different that you think. Since the discovery of the Dead Sea Scrolls, the world of Scripture has erupted in controversy, and the 'Good Old Days' where the carefully preserved scriptures being delivered to us as one original source document is now only a distant and convenient memory. The truth is much more complex, but it makes perfect sense..

In Short:

The Scriptures were collected over thousands of years – the events were repeated over and over orally before being written down. This does not imply that the accounts are inaccurate, but that generally they were not written down at the time that the events occurred. The events in Genesis, of course, were not written until much later – we know that Moses wrote the book of Genesis, and clearly Moses was not there at the time of Creation. This is typical of ancient writings – events were remembered and memorized to keep them safe for the Generations to come, and those events were carefully passed down until they were collected and written down. This does not imply inaccuracy or invalidity, but it does cause variations in the reporting of events. There are many versions available, but which is the 'best' version? A simple answer would be the oldest version, but that is not entirely true either. What are our Bibles based on? Most are based on the MT version, which is relatively new (finished c.800 AD) and heavily edited by the Masorites. What did Jesus use? He never mentions the word 'Bible' and with good reason – there were none! For more details and explanations, read on..

Long Version:

Many people think that the Bible is the only basis for Christianity. Where does the Scripture say that? Well, it does not. The closest it gets in in **2 Tim 3:15-16**:

"All Scripture is inspired by God and profitable for teaching, for reproof, for correction, for training in righteousness."

Scripture is profitable – not necessary. Is the term 'Scripture' a reference to the Bible? Not hardly – when this letter was written, the only scriptures he could have been talking about was the Septuagint or the Hebrew Scriptures, which contained many (but not all) of the books of the Old Testament. The earliest 'Bible' would not be decided upon for another 350 years.. So who determines what scripture is?

Chapter 8 – Where did out Bible come from?

The Catechism states that *"The inspired books teach the truth. Since therefore all that the inspired authors or sacred writers should be regarded as affirmed by the Holy Spirit, we must acknowledge that the books of Scripture firmly, faithfully, and without error teach that truth which God, for the sake of our salvation, wished to see confided to the Sacred Scriptures."*[121]

How did we get the scriptures we have today? Why do we have scriptures at all?

Brief History of Written Hebrew - עברית (Ivrit)

Ivrit (עברית) – Hebrew – is a Semitic (Northwest Semitic) language and one of the world's oldest languages. The name Ivrit is derived from Ever (עבר), the son of Shem. Ever means "a region across or beyond" and is derived from Avar (עבר) which means "to cross over". It is taught by the rabbis that Ivrit was the original language given to Adam and remained the only language until the time of the Tower of Babel.

Genesis 11:7-9: *[7] Come, let us descends and confuses their language, so that one will not understand the language of his companion." [8] And the Lord scattered them from there upon the face of the entire earth, and they ceased building the city. [9] Therefore, He named it Babel, for there the Lord confused the language of the entire earth, and from there the Lord scattered them upon the face of the entire earth.*

Written Hebrew had no written vowels or punctuation in its earliest forms. If we were to simulate the Early Hebrew text in English, it might look like this:

nthbgnnnggdcrtdthhvnsndthrthnwthrthwsfrmlssndmptydrknss wsvrthsrfcfthdpndthsprtfgdwshvrngvrthwtrsndgdsdltthrblghtndthr wslghtgdswthtthlghtwsgdndhsprtdthlghtfrmthdrknssgdclldthlghtdy ndthdrknsshclldnghtndthrwsvnngndthrwsmrnngthfrstdy

Can you read it? It is Genesis 1:1.
If you can read it, why? Try again – it starts with: "**In the beginning, God created the heavens and the earth.**" What does this

---

[121] CCC (Vatican City: Libreria Editrice Vaticana, 1997), par. 107.

Chapter 8 – Where did out Bible come from?

say about the depth of knowledge the Jews had to have to be able to read the Scriptures..?

How did Ivrit develop over the centuries?

Ivrit is divided into four basic periods by scholars.
1. Biblical/Classical Hebrew is the form of Ivrit in which the Tanakh was written.
2. Mishnaic/Rabbinic Hebrew is the form of Ivrit in which the Talmud and Midrash were written.
3. Medieval Hebrew is the form of Ivrit that was used by Maimonides and other medieval scholars to translate Arabic works into Ivrit.
4. Modern Hebrew is the form of Ivrit that was developed in the nineteenth century as an attempt to bring Ivrit back into the modern-day usage of the Jews.

Proto-Sinaitic /Proto-Canaanite

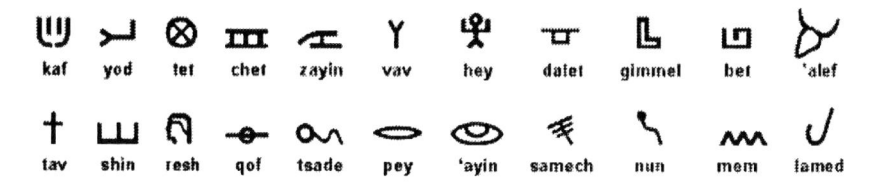

kaf	yod	tet	chet	zayin	vav	hey	dalet	gimmel	bet	'alef

tav	shin	resh	qof	tsade	pey	'ayin	samech	nun	mem	lamed

Like many other languages, Ivrit began as a pictographic script. Proto-Sinaitic Script is the stage of the alphabet at the end of the Middle Bronze Age. During the Late Bronze Age, the script splits into the South Arabian and the Canaanite groups.

The script became well-known from a series of inscriptions from c.1700 BC in turquoise mines at Serabit al-Khadim in Sinai. Other examples were found in Shechem, Gezer, and Lachish. The discovered texts are in West Semitic Canaanite which means the origin of the script was in a Semitic area. This script was inspired by the Egyptian hieroglyphs based upon "similarities of signs and the basic acrophonic principle". The Semitic word for the object of the original pictograph is the starting point and the first letter of that word is the value of the sign. For example, house is "beit" so the pictograph for house was used for the consonant "b".

Chapter 8 – Where did out Bible come from?
Phoenician Alphabet

ḥēt	zayin	wāw	hē	dālet	gīmel	bēt	'ālef
ḥ	z	w	h	d	g	b	'
sāmek	nun	mēm	lāmed	kaf	yōd	ṭēt	
s	n	m	l	k	y	ṭ	
tāw	śin/šin	rēš	qōf	ṣādē	pē	'ayin	
t	š	r	q	ṣ	p	'	

There are many Semitic languages, thought to be related to the ancient Hebrew written language Ivrit. One of the most striking is the Phoenician written language, as you can see compared to Proto-Hebrew – there is a close relationship.

Proto-Hebrew/Aramaic

kāph	yudh	ṭēth	ḥēth	zain	waw	hē	dālath	gāmal	bēth	ālaph
k	y	ṭ	ḥ	z	v	h	d	g	b	'
tau	shin	rēsh	qoph	ṣādhē	pē	'ē	semkath	nun	mim	lāmadh
t	sh	r	q	ṣ	p	'	s	n	m	l

The Proto-Hebrew alphabet developed during the late tenth or early ninth century BC, replacing cuneiform as the main writing system in the Assyrian Empire. At the end of the sixth century BC, the Proto-Hebrew alphabet was replaced by the Hebrew square script (also known as the Aramaic alphabet).

The earliest known inscription in Paleo-Hebrew was discovered in 2005 on a 38-pound limestone boulder embedded in a wall at Tel Zayit (located in the Beth Guvrin Valley). The inscription was determined to be an abecedary – letters of the alphabet written out in sequence. This raises the possibility of formal scribal training at Tel Zayit in the late tenth century BC.

The Gezer Calendar, discovered in 1908, is an engraved limestone tablet written in Paleo-Hebrew. The script dates to the tenth century BC

Chapter 8 – Where did out Bible come from?

and describes an annual cycle of agricultural activities that begin in the Hebrew month of Tishri.

The Torah documents found in the Dead Sea were mostly written in this older form of Hebrew writing. It seems that the Torah was specifically written in this older 'First Temple' period writing in and prior to the First Century.

Samaritan Alphabet

kaf	yod	tet	chet	zayin	vav	he	dalet	gimel	bet	alef
k	y	t	h	z	w	h	d	g	b	'

tav	shin	resh	kof	tzadi	pe	ayin	samech	nun	mem	lamed
t	sh	r	k	tz	p	'	s	n	m	l

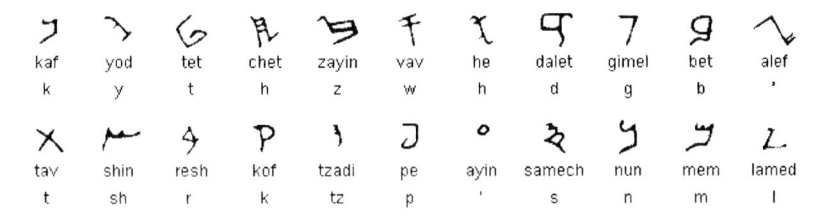

The Samaritan alphabet – which is used to this day – was derived from the Proto-Hebrew alphabet.

Aramaic/Hebrew Block Script

א ב ג ד ה ו ז ח ט י כ ך ל מ ם

| Mem | Mem | Lamed | Khaf | Khaf | Yod | Teit | Cheit | Zayin | Vav | He | Dalet | Gimel | Beit | Aleph |

נ ן ס ע פ ף צ ץ ק ר ש ת

| Tav | Shin | Reish | Qof | Tzadi | Tzadi | Peh | Peh | Ayin | Samekh | Nun | Nun |

After the sixth century BC Babylonian captivity, the Jews adopted the now Classic Hebrew script. The Aramaic characters were chosen as the official script for the Sefer Torah by the Jews who were captive in Babylon.

Chapter 8 – Where did out Bible come from?
Standardized Masoretic Script

The Masorites developed a new version of Ivrit script after the destruction of the Temple in 70 AD, which added a complete vowel and pronunciation system for Hebrew writing – the example is from the MT (Masorite Text) version of the Bible as exemplified by the Aleppo Codex that was produced in the 8th century AD. For the first time this script included vowel representation.

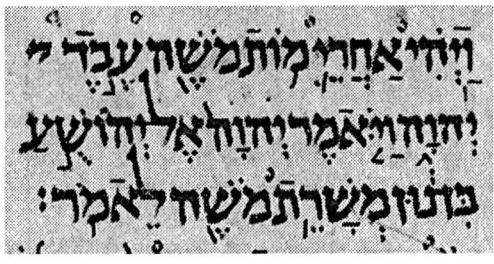

STAM

STAM is a stylized version of the Hebrew block letters used specifically for writing Sefer Torah, Tefillin, and Mezuzah. It is a modification of the earlier Masoretic script. As you can see, it is a more artistic representation of Ivrit.

Rashi Script

| kaf | yod | tet | chet | zayin | vav | he | dalet | gimel | bet | alef |

| tav | shin/sin | resh | kof | tzadi(k) | pe | ayin | samech | nun | mem | lamed |

Rashi script is used in commentaries to Jewish texts – especially the Talmud. It is named after Rabbi Shlomo Yitzchaki (Rashi) who was a medieval Jewish scholar and Biblical commentator.

Chapter 8 – Where did out Bible come from?
Hebrew Cursive

כּ	כ	׳	ט	ח	ז	ו	ה	ג	ג	ב	א
kaf		yod	tet	chet	zayin	vav	he	dalet	gimel	bet	alef

ת	ש	ר	ק	צ 3	פ ּ	ע	ס	ן נ	ם מ	ל
tav	shin/sin	resh	kof	tzadi(k)	pe	ayin	samech	nun	mem	lamed

The Modern Hebrew cursive script derives from Ashkenazi Jews. This is the form of Hebrew writing used today.

What does this mean?

The image below is a good example of the Dead Sea Scrolls text might be this section of the scroll of Leviticus (11Q1-11qpaleoLevi) – this is written in the First Temple style script which is Proto-Hebrew, and is one of the oldest examples of Torah writing still existent. It appears that the Torah was written in the earliest form of Hebrew – not in the much later Babylonian block lettering common after the Babylonian captivity.

This shows that the scriptures, before the Babylonian captivity, were written in an older form of Hebrew as we described above, and in fact pre-date the Babylonian captivity, despite the opinions of many modern bible scholars. The ancient Hebrew writings were translated into Greek after the Bablyonian captivity so that the scriptures could be read by Greek speaking Jews living both in the mediterannean and Roman held areas, therefore spreading the Scriptures across a much larger area, and allowing a person to read them without memorizing them first.

The idea that Hebrew was the very first written and spoken language is deeply rooted in Judaism. The legend was that Adam was the first to write in Hebrew, and that his children could read it, but could not write

Chapter 8 – Where did out Bible come from?

it. To us that makes no sence, unless you realize that (without vowels) you can only read what you already know, so although someone could write without vowels, there was no point unless you were relating things that the reader already knew to the point of having the words memorized.

Enoch – the 'Scribe of Reighteousness' was reputed to be the second Patriarch to write, and his writings were popular at the time of Christ. The letter of Jude referred to the Book of Enoch (Jude 1:14-15) and quotes his writings (1 Enoch 1:9). These writings were found in the collection of the Dead Sea Scrolls, and were found in both Hebrew and Greek.

Written Hebrew (Ivrit) is certainly an ancient language, and understanding some of the basic elements of it helps us to understand that the Scriptures were never intended to be understood in a vaccuum, but in the light of a community who understands not just the words, but the meaning and intent of the writings.

Appendix 3 contains a list of the earliest Christian writings, for your reference. You can see there that there were many writings in this early period – not everything was proclaimed to be Scripture – nor should it! On the other hand, it is important to know that many people considered these writings important and informative. There were not merely a couple of writings in this period, that were all collected together to form the Bible – there were literally hundreds, not all of which are still existant. The Church decided, over the years up to 397 AD, which writings were truly 'scripture' and which were not.

The New Testament - the Christian Canon

In the year 397 the third Council of Carthage published a list of books to be read in all of the churches. This list was to become the blueprint for our Bible. In this list was included all 73 of the books we have in our Bibles (including those regarded as 'Apocrypha' or 'Deuterocanonical'). Other such lists had been published by others, as early as the year 170, although they did not all agree. How did the men who published these lists decide which books should be called Scripture? The Bishops of the Church pulled together the important writings and between them discussed what should be considered Scripture and what should not. We are able to prove this by examining the surviving works of Irenaeus (born 130), who lived in days before anyone felt it was necessary to list the approved books. The process of defining what writings were sacred, and which were not, was a lengthy and carefully evaluated process.

Chapter 8 – Where did out Bible come from?

Bishops in the Church, as governors of groups of churches, conferred and met to discuss what was *truly scripture* and what was less than scriptural. This process of developing the Canon was not an evaluation of whether or not a writing was reliable or not – it was based on the question of theological significance – is this writing important to the Church for the education of the faithful? The epistle of Hebrews, for example, was almost not included in the canon because it was thought to be written by St. Clement, and not St. Paul, but despite the uncertain author, the epistle was finally included due to its theological content.

It is clear that the Bishops had each approved certain writings and rejected others as they became available, although there is certainly much evidence of uncertainly about many of the books that later were added or dropped from the canon. The approved books were probably set in the western Church at the Synod of Hippo Regius in North Africa (393); although the records of this Council are lost, shortly after this council, St. Augustine referred to the canon as having been set. A list of approved books was again published at the Third Council of Carthage in 397 AD. This collection of scriptures was then called the "canon" of Scripture, "canon" being a Greek word meaning "rod" or "ruler." It included 73 Books now considered scripture by the Catholic Church, but not just 66 books recognized by most Protestant Churches.

There are many canons (lists of books considered to be Scripture) from many groups over the centuries. For example, the Hebrew Bible is compiled based on the Hebrew canon. The Catholic Bibles are composed of writings as specified by the Catholic Canon. Note that these lists <u>do not include</u> the specific texts of the writings, but the general titles of the writings. For example, the Canon from 170 AD (the Muratorian Fragment) specified the Gospels of Luke and John, but not the specific approved text. In fact, there are variants of the texts themselves, which results in the same canon having quite different texts in the final document.

Some of the early known canons are:
- *The Muratorian Fragment*   *(c. 170 AD)*
- *Melito*   *(c. 170 AD)*
- *Origen*   *(c. 240 AD)*
- *Eusebius of Caesarea*   *(c. 324 AD)*
- *Cyril of Jerusalem*   *(c. 350 AD)*
- *Hilary of Poitiers*   *(c. 360 AD)*
- *The Cheltenham List*   *(c. 360 AD)*
- *Council of Laodiocia*   *(c. 363 AD)*
- *Letter of Ananasius*   *(367 AD)*

Chapter 8 – Where did out Bible come from?

- Gregory of Nazianzus (c. 380 AD)
- Amphilochius of Iconium (c. 380 AD)
- Apostolic Canons (c. 380 AD)
- Epiphanius of Salamis (c. 385 AD)
- St. Jerome (c. 390 AD)
- St. Augustine (c. 397 AD)
- **Third Council of Carthage** **(c. 397 AD)**
- Codex Claromontanus (c. 400 AD)
- Rufinus of Aquileia (c. 400 AD)
- Innocent I (c. 405 AD)
- Decree of Gelasius (c. 550 AD)
- Sixty Canonical Books (c. 7th Cent. AD)
- Stichometery of Nicephorus (810 AD)

As the needs of the Church grew, the need to consolidate and specify the 'approved' books grew. It was not simply good enough that books be historically accurate, but that they contain Truths that can be relied on without doubt. There was certainly useful and important information in the Acts of Peter or the Acts of Paul, such as 'How was Peter crucified?" We know the answer – he was crucified upside down. How do we know this? We learned it from the non-canonical book of the Acts of Peter.

'Non-canonical' does not mean 'heretical' or 'inaccurate'. It simply means that it is not deemed necessary for the faith, and perhaps not reliable as a basis for the teachings of the Church. The events may or may not be accurate – this is not an evaluation of accuracy. The writings of Tacitus or Josephus are not canonical, but we accept them as accurate. Historical events can come from many sources – not just the Bible.

Canon(s)?

In Appendix 4, we have a list of the books that were all mentioned in the earliest canon lists from various sources within the Catholic Church – you will see many books that did not make it to the final canon, or became more valued as time went on and were finally added to the canon.

The lists of the Hebrew Testament, however, stayed quite static. In the early years, the Christians adopted the Septuagint, referred to in later Jewish writings as 'The Christian Book' (as described by the 'Council' of Jamnia[122] c. 90 AD) and therefore was distained by the Rabbinic

---

[122] Or the Council of Yavne first proposed by Heinrich Graetz in 1871. Rabbi Yohanan ben Zakkai relocated to the city of Yavne/Jamnia, where he received permission from the Romans to found a school of Halakha (Jewish law) before 70 AD.

Chapter 8 – Where did out Bible come from?

writers, who relied on the 'Hebrew Only' books. Indeed, this was the root of the problem that would eventually result in a reduced number of books in the Hebrew and Protestant Bibles. Books not originally written in Hebrew were excluded in the Hebrew Bible produced by the Masorites, and finally completed by the Ben Asher family and published as the Aleppo Codex (10th Century AD) and the Leningrad Codex (1008 AD). Over the 1,000 years, the Masorite Rabbis collected and refined all variants of the scriptures to produce a single 'perfect' version of the Hebrew Bible, which removed all of the parts that were not considered 'pure text'. This final version was largely adopted by the West, although the Eastern Church retained its Greek Septuagint – this and many other factors led to the Great Schism (1053) where the Eastern Church and Western Church separated.

Although the Western Church adopted the text of the Masorite Text Bible (MT for short), the canon remained the same – so they had the canon from the Septuagint (c. 300 BC) with the text from the MT Bible (c. 800 AD) together – with the official Bible remaining St. Jerome's Vulgate (405)! Confused? That is just the beginning.

When Luther came on the scene, he decided (for self-serving reasons) to choose the MT bible as his Hebrew Testament, dropping the other traditional books from the canon, and added the New Testament, except for the Book of James (which he did not like). This is where we get the Protestant Bible.

I have put together a collection of the historic canons, with their original texts and the circumstances in which they were developed in my book 'The Foundations of the Bible, The Early Church Leaders, Volume 2.'[123]

So then, given the variety of scripture collections over time, what were the major collections and what should we know about them? A summary of the canons and what they prescribed is included in the tables below – the most notable is the canon from the Third Council of Carthage, which established the first universal list for the entire Christian Church.

What does this all mean?

Let's take some examples.
- If you were a Rich Christian in the year 45 AD, your collection of scriptures would probably be the Septuagint, with the books only

---

[123] 978-1500101459, to be published in 2015.

Chapter 8 – Where did out Bible come from?

from the Hebrew (Old) Testament, as listed in the Septuagint – the books in that collection match the list used by the Catholic Bible, not the Protestant one. No books of the New Testament had been written yet, although the men teaching in the Churches were Apostles who walked with Christ.

- If you lived in 170 AD you would recognize the books listed by Melito and the Muratorian Fragment. The Apocalypse of Peter was recognized, and the Shepherd of Hermas was recommended reading as well. The Book of Hebrews was not recognized, neither was James or the letters of Peter.
- If you lived in 400 AD you would recognize the usual books but also the Shepherd of Hermas, Barnabas, the Acts of Paul, the Apocalypse of Peter but not the Book of James!

Today, there are several canons of scripture – in Ethiopia their Coptic tradition includes the Books of Jubilees and Enoch, which have ancient roots but the Western Churches do not accept as Scripture.

So then, given the variety of scripture collections over time, what were the major collections and what should we know about them? A couple of the popular canons and what they prescribed is included in the tables below. A quick summary of the versions is:

- **The Hebrew Bible** is one that was accepted by the Jews, specifically the Masorites, which resulted in the MT version of the bible as exemplified by the Aleppo Codex and the Leningrad Codex which were compiled between 800 and 1000 AD.

- **The Greek Septuagint** was initially translated by 72 Jews which were sponsored by Ptolemy II in the 3rd Century BC for use by the many Alexandrian Jews who were not fluent in Hebrew but fluent in Koine Greek. This translation began as the Torah alone, but over the centuries expanded to include many important works, as listed in the table below.

- **The Latin Vulgate** was composed by Jerome in 405 AD, and was based on the Canon of that time, that of the Third Council of Carthage, and is the standard Bible of the Catholic Church.

- **The Protestant Canon** is really the current collection of books recognized by many of the Protestant churches, and is largely based on the opinions of Luther, the Anglican church, with support from various other denominations. Luther's version (1534) had many changes in it, including the relocation of the books of Jude, Revelation, Hebrews and James to an end section, as he did not consider them to be authoritative. Luther also chose to place the Biblical 'Apocrypha' between the Old and New Testaments. These books of Biblical canon of the Old Testament are found in the ancient Greek Septuagint but not in the Hebrew Masoretic text – for this reason Luther and most of the reformers refused to continue to recognize them, but they remained in the Catholic canon.

Chapter 8 – Where did out Bible come from?

The Old Testament Canon

Hebrew Bible	Greek Septuagint	Latin Vulgate	Protestant Canon
THE LAW	Genesis	Genesis	Genesis
Genesis	Exodus	Exodus	Exodus
Exodus	Leviticus	Leviticus	Leviticus
Leviticus	Numbers	Numbers	Numbers
Numbers	Deuteronomy	Deuteronomy	Deuteronomy
Deuteronomy	Joshua	Joshua	Joshua
	Judges	Judges	Judges
	Ruth	Ruth	Ruth
THE PROPHETS	1 Samuel	1 Samuel	1 Samuel
Joshua	2 Samuel	2 Samuel	2 Samuel
Judges	1 Kings	1 Kings	1 Kings
1 Samuel	2 Kings	2 Kings	2 Kings
2 Samuel	1 Chronicles	1 Chronicles	1 Chronicles
1 Kings	2 Chronicles	2 Chronicles	2 Chronicles
2 Kings	[Prayer of Manasseh]	Prayer of Manasseh	
Isaiah	1 Esdras	1 Esdras	
Jeremiah	Ezra	2 Esdras	
Ezekiel	Tobit	Ezra	Ezra
Hosea	Judith	Tobit	
Joel	Esther (with insertions)*	Judith	
Amos	1 Maccabees	Esther (with insertions)*	Esther (Hebrew)*
Obadiah	2 Maccabees	1 Maccabees	
Jonah	[3 Maccabees]	2 Maccabees	
Micah	[4 Maccabees]		
Nahum	Job	Job	Job
Habakkuk	Psalms	Psalms	Psalms
Zephaniah	[Psalm no. 151]		
Haggai	[Odes]		
Zechariah	Proverbs	Proverbs	Proverbs
Malachi	Ecclesiastes	Ecclesiastes	Ecclesiastes
	Song of Songs	Song of Songs	Song of Songs
	Wisdom of Solomon	Wisdom of Solomon	
	Ecclesiasticus	Ecclesiasticus	
	[Psalms of Solomon]		
	Isaiah	Isaiah	Isaiah
THE WRITINGS	Jeremiah	Jeremiah	Jeremiah
Psalms	Lamentations	Lamentations	Lamentations
Proverbs	Baruch	Baruch	
Job	Epistle of Jeremiah	Epistle of Jeremiah	
Song of Songs	Ezekiel	Ezekiel	Ezekiel
Ruth	Daniel (with insertions)**	Daniel (Full version)**	Daniel (Hebrew)**
Lamentations	Hosea	Hosea	Hosea
Ecclesiastes	Joel	Joel	Joel
Esther	Amos	Amos	Amos
Daniel	Obadiah	Obadiah	Obadiah
Ezra	Jonah	Jonah	Jonah
Nehemiah	Micah	Micah	Micah
1 Chronicles	Nahum	Nahum	Nahum
2 Chronicles	Habakkuk	Habakkuk	Habakkuk
	Zephaniah	Zephaniah	Zephaniah
	Haggai	Haggai	Haggai
	Zechariah	Zechariah	Zechariah
	Nehemiah	Nehemiah	Nehemiah
	Malachi	Malachi	Malachi

Chapter 8 – Where did out Bible come from?
I say Deuterocanonical, your say Apocrypha?

The books which were recognized as Scripture in the Greek Orthodox Church and those recognized in the Roman Catholic Church do not correspond exactly to the list of books commonly called "Apocrypha" by Protestants. The Protestant Apocrypha includes all of the books normally included in manuscripts of the Latin Vulgate. But three of these (1 and 2 Esdras and the Prayer of Manasseh) were omitted from the list published by the Council of Trent when it fixed the Roman Catholic canon. (Apparently these omissions were unintentional. The "Decree Concerning the Canonical Scriptures" specified that the books were to be recognized "as they are contained in the old Latin Vulgate.") The Eastern Orthodox churches (including the Greek, the Russian, the Ukrainian, the Bulgarian, the Serbian, the Armenian, and others) do not recognize 2 Esdras because it was not in the Septuagint, and they recognize some books which were present in many manuscripts of the Septuagint but not in the Vulgate (Psalm 151, 3 and 4 Maccabees).

Greek Orthodox Canon	**Protestant Apocrypha**	**Catholic Deuterocanonical**
1 Esdras	1 Esdras	
	2 Esdras	
Tobit	Tobit	Tobit
Judith	Judith	Judith
Additions to Esther	Additions to Esther	Additions to Esther
Wisdom of Solomon	Wisdom of Solomon	Wisdom of Solomon
Ecclesiasticus	Ecclesiasticus	Ecclesiasticus
Baruch	Baruch	Baruch
Epistle of Jeremiah	Epistle of Jeremiah	Epistle of Jeremiah
Song of the Three Children	Song of the Three Children	Song of the Three Children
Story of Susanna	Story of Susanna	Story of Susanna
Bel and the Dragon	Bel and the Dragon	Bel and the Dragon
Prayer of Manasseh	Prayer of Manasseh	
1 Maccabees	1 Maccabees	1 Maccabees
2 Maccabees	2 Maccabees	2 Maccabees
3 Maccabees		
4 Maccabees		
Psalm 151		

Chapter 8 – Where did our Bible come from?

The New Testament has no problems?

So you might ask – is the New Testament is different from the Hebrew Bible in that there is no argument or issues with the books included there? No – same kind of issues exist with the New Testament.

OK – so what does this all mean? Most people are looking for a 'perfect' Bible so they can follow its instructions, but if you have been reading this book so far you will realize that very few people really accept the writings in scriptures as they are now anyway – a more 'perfect' bible will really make no difference, because no matter how perfect the book may be, the reader is flawed, opinionated and unwilling to accept what the scriptures say. Isn't that right?

The BIG question is – if the Bible is not **completely and utterly** 'scientifically accurate' (from every perspective) then what is its purpose? We believe the scriptures are inspired by God and inerrant, but how does this add up when we can see that there are many minor details that are not lining up?

Finally – a real question.

First, the Bible is inerrant in matters of Faith and Morals, not historically. If there are problems with the sequence of events, that is not an issue for the Bible.

Secondly, at the time of Christ, there was no defined list of all sacred books – there were many that were well known to be 'Holy Books' and the Scriptures were primarily the Torah alone. The Jews, however, venerated many books that we pay no attention to at all now. If the followers of Christ were *supposed to* latch onto a set of Scriptures and use those for individual direction, don't you think SOMEONE would have said that in the New Testament? Christ would have said 'Follow everything in the Torah, except Leviticus, and observe all the writings of Isaiah.' But He said nothing like that.

The full Hebrew Canon was probably not finalized at the time of Christ, and would not be finalized until much later (possibly as late as c.800 AD). The New Testament was not started until (possibly) several years after the Ascension of Christ - why did it take so long for the New Testament to be written and finally accepted? Why didn't Jesus write the whole thing himself? Better still, why is it that God Himself did not simply write a perfect book himself for us to use as a basis for our faith? Christ could have distributed complete versions of the King James Bible in Greek if that was what He wanted to do. He did not.

Chapter 8 – Where did our Bible come from?

Muslims believe that Mohammed was given a perfect set of instructions from Allah and that is what they use. They believe that the Arabic version of the Koran is literally written word for word by Allah himself through an angel - Archangel Gabriel. The Mormons believe that the Angel Moroni delivered the Book of Mormon to Joseph Smith who then translated it perfectly into English. Why did the God of Abraham 'fail' to do the same for us? If we were to use a book as a basis for Christ's Church, would that document be present at the beginning? Clearly, the Scriptures were intended to give us direction and inspiration, but not personally written by God. We know that "All Scripture is inspired by God" as Paul says – not actually written by Him. It is by the Scriptures that we come to learn about God.

Back to Scriptures!

Personally, I am a big fan of the Scriptures, and they are invaluable to better understand God – but do not confuse them as an authority for running a Church! You and I are not authorized to rush out and establish a church - Christ set up ONE structure to deliver the Truth to you – the same one used in the early Church. Establishing a new church for yourself based **on you** and **what you think** is the ultimate rejection of the message of Christ, who wanted His flock to be together, and to listen to His voice. Were you crucified for the redemption of the world? I do not think so, so then why do you feel empowered to establish your own church?

Who established the Church you attend (if you attend one)? Was it set up by Jesus Himself, or some 'reformer' who decided that Jesus really did not know what He was doing?

After 1,500 years, some people decided that Jesus really was not competent to establish a Church that would withstand the passage of time, so they set about to 'fix' it. Apparently they thought that the Church could not withstand the Gates of Hell[124]. The reformers dedicated themselves (and the lives of their followers) to fixing the mistake that Jesus left for us.

Did they fix it? Perhaps that is a matter of opinion, but it seems that splitting Christ's Church into 36,000+ quarreling factions hardly seems an improvement. Fighting over personal interpretations of scripture was not something anyone should approve of.

---

[124] Mt 16:18 - And I say also to you that you are Peter, and on this rock I will build my church; and **the gates of hell shall not prevail against it.**

Chapter 8 – Where did our Bible come from?

The Church leaders – The apostles plus Paul – taught the Truth themselves, and rejected false teachings[125]. They did not hand out Bibles and say 'Here – read this and figure it for yourselves.' How could they? The scriptures were not available to hand out copies, and most people could not read anyway. The New Testament was not written yet, and truly it was not needed, as the actual people who followed Christ were there to show people the way. Why did Christians not use a Bible as their source of Authority?

- There were no Bibles for another 300+ years.
- Most people could not read anyway.
- The Apostles were called to action, not writing (Mt 28:19, etc.)
- Primarily because the teaching authority of Christ's Church came from its leaders, as inspired by Christ Himself (Lk 10:16).

Here is the secret, something that should be obvious to everyone – Christ/God did not write a book for instruction because He knew (as you should know) that mankind will warp any book to mean what *they want it to mean*. Written words are powerless to control how people understand them. Jesus knew this – that is why He established His Church on the *hearts of men*, as predicted in the Hebrew Scriptures[126], and specifically He gave control of the whole Church to a group of good men. Please read the chapter on the Church for more detail.

Certainly, the early Church leaders referred to the Hebrew Bible (Old Testament) often as supporting scriptures, but the new faith was a living faith, written on the hearts of the Apostles, and they were charged with guiding the faithful, and correcting the errant. Today, most Christians accept Scripture as inerrant in teaching faith and morals, but subject to interpretation of tradition.[127] On inerrancy Vatican II made an important qualification as stated here: *"The Books of Scripture must be acknowledged as teaching firmly, faithfully, and without error that truth which God wanted put into the sacred writings for the sake of our salvation."*

So now you are saying "Great, well I feel also empowered to interpret scriptures, and so why should I not go out and teach what I

---

[125] 2 Thessalonians 2 :15 " Hold fast to the traditions you received from us "

[126] Jer 31:33 – "I will put my law within them and write it on their hearts and minds"

[127] The simple majority of Christians are catholic, and accept the teachings of the Vatican II resolutions

Chapter 8 – Where did our Bible come from?

believe Jesus tells me in my heart?" Lots of reasons – lets quote the original Church leader:

> *"But false prophets also arose among the people, just as **there will also be false teachers among you, who will secretly introduce destructive heresies**, even denying the Master who bought them, bringing swift destruction upon themselves. And many will follow their sensuality, and because of them the way of the truth will be maligned; and **in their greed they will exploit you with false words**; their judgment from long ago is not idle, and their destruction is not asleep."*[128]

What does all of this mean?

Given that <u>only the Church</u> is empowered to interpret Scripture, according to Peter, and that no matter how smart you or I may be (I think I am very clever indeed☺), there is no reason to believe we are smarter and wiser than all of the dedicated theologians for the past 2,000 years. We should dedicate ourselves to learning from those who are knowledgeable, and not trying to reinvent the wheel. I can tell you from experience that just learning what others know about Scriptures is enough to keep anyone occupied from one lifetime, and the endless wisdom of the Church will satisfy anyone's curiosity.

But you do have to work at it – wisdom is not delivered to you without a lot of work.

The Bible is not a stand-alone book – the Church that Christ established is here to help you understand the message of Jesus.

---

[128] 2 Pet 2:1-3

Chapter 9 – The Eucharist

John 6:25-70 is a section of the New Testament that has led to outrageous flights of fancy since the 16th Century. Today many Christians seem to have forgotten how to read, and make crazy assumptions rather than accept a plain statement. So how can someone offer His body and blood to everyone? More to the point, why would He?

In Short:

The basis for the Eucharist began in Genesis. When Abraham met with Melchizedek, the venerable Priest of God offered a sacrifice of Bread and Wine. This was where the children of Israel continued an older tradition – Moses instituted the Bread of the Presence, which was constantly offered in the Temple – a weekly offering of Bread and Wine, prepared by the Priests. The Passover meal also emphasized Bread and Wine, culminating in the new Covenant which is 'in the blood' offered at the Eucharistic celebration. This was no leap of invention, but a solid continuation of the Tradition of the Jews, but now taking on a new role for Christians. It becomes the 'Body and Blood' of Christ, just as He said.

Long Version:

The Bread of Life

Do you know why the early Church was persecuted by the Jews and Romans? The Jews persecuted Christians because they were angered by Jesus of Nazareth in many ways – his unorthodox teachings and ultimately because he claimed to be 'The Son of Man' – a term used for the Messiah.

Why did the Romans care one way or the other? For the first century they did not. Then the People of the Way (the name of early Christians) or the Followers of Christus (as Josephus refers to them) fell into disrepute for breaking one of the few laws the Romans had regulating religion.

Romans regulated a lot of things, but they typically stayed out of matters of religion. They tolerated almost anything, and in the time of Claudius, there was reputed to be a statue dedicated to 'Christus' in the Pantheon, a place which recognized all the gods of Rome. There was no restriction on burial practices, except that no one could be buried in a Roman city – there were places outside the walls where a burial could

Chapter 9 – The Eucharist

take place, but only cremation was allowed in the City itself – this was strictly for health reasons, not theological.

As far as Religious practices for the living, almost anything was tolerated within the temples and during funerals. One thing was expressly forbidden however – cannibalism. It was in this area that the followers of Christus were to become persecuted. It became generally known that all followers of Christus shared and ate the body or their Savior on a regular basis. When asked, the Christian would admit that this was true – they did indeed eat His body and drink His blood. As a result of this, the Christians had to retreat to the Catacombs, where they could celebrate their Eucharistic Celebrations uninterrupted (under Roman law). An explanation of the Roman understanding of Christianity is explored in the Octavius [129]. In this writing the author explains the Roman understanding of the 'Christian Perversions' by describing the incorporation of a human child into the preparation of the bread used in their secret ceremonies.

What do you think of that? It was *all just a misunderstanding*? No, the Early Church was 100% confident that the Eucharistic Celebration truly transformed the bread and wine into the Body and Blood of their savior – a position still held today officially by most Christians worldwide. No Children were involved, but the misunderstanding is easy enough to understand – the transformation of the bread into the literal flesh and blood of *anyone* was hard to comprehend. The commitment of the Early Church cannot be overstated. The early Martyrs were mostly executed for refusing to deny the true presence in the Eucharist. To this day, people are still dying to protect that most precious sacrament.

OK – so where in the Bible does it say that? Read John 6.

"Then Jesus declared, "*I am the bread of life. Whoever comes to me will never go hungry, and whoever believes in me will never be thirsty. But as I told you, you have seen me and still you do not believe. All those the Father gives me will come to me, and whoever comes to me I will never drive away. For I have come down from heaven not to do my will but to do the will of him who sent me. And this is the will of him who sent me that I shall lose none of all those he has given me, but raise them up at the last day. For my Father's will is that everyone who looks to the Son and believes on him shall have eternal life, and I will raise them up at the last day.*"

---

[129] The Octavius, A Christian Debate by Minucius Felix, A.D. 130–200

Chapter 9 – The Eucharist

At this the Jews there began to grumble about him because he said, **"I am the bread that came down from heaven."** They said, "Is this not Jesus, the son of Joseph, whose father and mother we know? How can he now say, 'I came down from heaven'?"

"Stop grumbling among yourselves," Jesus answered. "No one can come to me unless the Father who sent me draws them, and I will raise them up at the last day. It is written in the Prophets: 'They will all be taught by God.' Everyone who has heard the Father and learned from him comes to me. No one has seen the Father except the one who is from God; only he has seen the Father. Very truly I tell you, the one who believes has eternal life. **I am the bread of life.** Your ancestors ate the manna in the wilderness, yet they died. But **here is the bread** that comes down from heaven, which anyone may eat and not die. **I am the living bread** that came down from heaven. Whoever **eats this bread** will live forever. **This bread is my flesh**, which I will give for the life of the world."

Then the Jews began to argue sharply among themselves, "**How can this man give us his flesh to eat?**"

Jesus said to them, "Very truly I tell you, unless you **eat the flesh of the Son of Man and drink his blood**, you have no life in you. Whoever **eats my flesh and drinks my blood** has eternal life, and I will raise them up at the last day. **For my flesh is real food and my blood is real drink**. Whoever **eats my flesh and drinks my blood** remains in me, and I in them. Just as the living Father sent me and I live because of the Father, so the one who **feeds on me** will live because of me. **This is the bread** that came down from heaven. Your ancestors ate manna and died, but whoever **feeds on this bread** will live forever." He said this while teaching in the synagogue in Capernaum.

On hearing it, many of his disciples said, "This is a hard teaching. Who can accept it?"

Aware that his disciples were grumbling about this, Jesus said to them, "Does this offend you? Then what if you see the Son of Man ascend to where he was before! The Spirit gives life; the flesh counts for nothing. The words I have spoken to you—they are full of the Spirit and life. Yet there are some of you who do not believe." For Jesus had known from the beginning which of them did not believe and who would betray him. He went on to say, "This is why I told you that no one can come to me unless the Father has enabled them."

From this time many of his disciples turned back and no longer followed him.

"You do not want to leave too, do you?" Jesus asked the Twelve.

Chapter 9 – The Eucharist

Simon Peter answered him, "Lord, to whom we shall go? You have the words of eternal life. We have come to believe and to know that you are the Holy One of God."

The term for Flesh above (in Greek) is the word Sarx, which literally means 'Corpse'. The translators into Greek understood this to mean that it was necessary to eat the Corpse of the Messiah. The Early Church believed this literally, and the celebration of the Last Supper was a careful reenactment of the creation of the Body and Blood of the Christ so that the faithful could eat and drink as specified by the savior himself.

Many denominations quibble over this passage – odd that people committed to literal belief in scripture deny clear speech as quoted above. "It is a metaphor – all Jesus wants us to do is believe in Him". Really?

This section of John is immediately after the great miracle of the Loaves and Fishes. The symbol of a fish is forever associated with Christianity because of the miracle of the loaves and fishes THAT THESE PEOPLE HAD JUST WITNESSED. This was not, as some would infer, a simple trick to get people to share their food, but a true miracle which astounded the crowd – these people witnessed the multiplication of the loaves and fishes – they did not hear a rumor and possibly misunderstood – they were there. They were clearly able to accept Jesus was important and a miracle maker greater than any since Moses, and they were asking Him what to believe in. If it was simply that they had to believe in Jesus personally, that would be no problem at all. They did REALLY believe in Him and accepted His authority.

Yet after Jesus made his declaration that they HAD to eat his body they left him in droves. Almost all of his followers left Him at that point, except the 12 apostles. The Jews believed in, but did not understand, that they had to eat the Body and Blood to be righteous and to attain salvation through the New Covenant. The details of this process would be explained at the last supper.

"This is My Blood of the covenant, which is poured out for many" **(Mk 14:23-25, Mt 26:27-28, Lk 22:19-20)** was the phrase used by Christ at the last supper – He gave those present a cup of His Blood (His words, not mine) and had them drink is BECAUSE this was the blood of the new covenant. Those who drank participated in this new covenant – those who did not eat and drink did not.

Have you consumed the Body and Blood of Christ? If you have, then you are a part of the new covenant with Him. If not (you ate and drank something 'symbolizing' the body and blood) then you are not a part of His covenant. Why? BECAUSE THE COVENANT IS IN HIS

Chapter 9 – The Eucharist

BLOOD! He says so in the Gospels of Matthew, Mark and Luke – if you want to live, you have to eat His body and drink His blood. *His words –* not mine. You should listen to what Jesus said.

So many times I hear the counter arguments:
- How can He give us His Body to eat?
- Why would He do that?
- Are you saying Christians have to be Cannibals?
- Eating His body is against all laws – is He going to disregard the Law?

First of all, we have to choose not to be like the Jews in **Jn 6:52** who grumble and fail to believe Him, or are you like Peter in **Jn 6:68**? By the way, did you notice that Jn 6:66 reads: "*As a result of this many of His disciples withdrew and did not walk with Him anymore.*" How about that? The infamous verse 666 in John relates to the disciples leaving Jesus because he challenged them to believe in His message – to Eat His Body and Drink His Blood. Do you want to agree with those who left Him in **Jn 6:66** or with those who trusted Him?

Where did the Eucharist come from?

As we have discussed before, God has and has always had a plan. Jesus did not wake up one day and decide that he wanted to use Bread to convert into His body – this was deeply rooted, all the way back, in sacred tradition.

Genesis

Adam and Eve were believed to have practiced sacrifices, although this is not explicitly mentioned in the account in Genesis, the Talmudic writers believed this is where the practice began. In Genesis 3:21, the gift of animal skins from God was believed to be the result of the first sacrifice, and was to set the pattern for animal sacrifices to follow. By the time of Noah, the practice was established, as Noah offered a sacrifice when he arrived on dry land after the flood, and he was commanded to being along animals for that purpose (Genesis 8:20-22). Noah's righteous son, Shem (Gen. 5:32) was the progenitor of Abraham (1 Chronicles 1:24-27.) and the father of the Semitic people (meaning 'from Shem'). He was the Patriarch that followed Noah, and was therefore the High Priest of their faith. In Hebrew Tradition, Shem inherited the High Priestly garments from Noah, who had been given the original garments from Adam, and was then trained in the traditions of

Chapter 9 – The Eucharist

the pre-flood faith. It was assumed that he held the keys to priesthood and was the great high priest of his day when he stood next to Abraham. His blessing showed that the patriarchs passed on the priesthood to him.

Abraham and Shem were related – their family tree is as follows: Noah fathered Shem, who fathered Arpachshad, who fathered Kenan, who fathered Shelah, who fathered Eber, who fathered Peleg, who fathered Rehu, who fathered Serug, who fathered Nahor, who fathered Terah who was the father of Abraham. So Abraham was the 11th generation from Noah.

In Chazalic literature—specifically Targum Jonathan, Targum Yerushalmi, and the Babylonian Talmud— the name of Melchizedek (מלכי־צדק) is another title for Shem, the son of Noah. The name Melchizedek means "King of Righteousness" (Heb. 7:1-2). He was known as the great high priest (Alma 13:14), priest of the most high God (Gen. 14:18) ordained as priest after the order of the 'Son of God' (Heb 7:3). He is also known as Abram/ Abraham's ecclesiastical leader (Gen. 14:19) (Gen. 14:20) (Heb. 7:4) and the King of Salem (Gen. 14:18.) It is Melchizedek that introduces the first use of Bread and Wine as the preferred 'pure' sacrifice for the God of Abraham in Genesis 14:18-20:

"And Melchizedek king of Salem brought out bread and wine; and he was priest of God the Most High. And he blessed him, and said: 'Blessed be Abram of God Most High, Maker of heaven and earth; and blessed be God the Most High, who has delivered your enemies into your hands.' And he gave him a tenth of all."

This offering of the Bread and Wine would remain, but rarely mentioned until the Exodus. When the Children of Israel were wandering in the wastes they were fed by the Bread from heaven – which they clearly associated with the bread from Melchizedek. Some of this bread from heaven was put into a jar and placed in the Ark of the Covenant (Heb 4:9) and the sacrifice of Melchizedek was perpetuated in the Tent/Temple with the Bread of the Presence (Exodus 25:30 and 39:36) as stated below:

*"The ark of the testimony and its poles and the mercy seat; the table, all its utensils, and the **bread of the Presence**; the pure gold lampstand, with its arrangement of lamps and all its utensils, and the oil for the light."*

The use of this bread and wine sacrifice was codified in Lev 24:5 where the 'Bread of the Presence of God' or 'Bread of the Face of God' would always be present in the Temple.

In Mt 12:4, Jesus explains how His disciples were allowed to work on the Sabbath, as they were just following the rules set aside for the Priests, who had to prepare the Bread of the Presence every Sabbath as

Chapter 9 – The Eucharist

part of their duties. He explained that the Bread of the Presence was allowed for priests alone to eat, but King David and his men were allowed to eat it. According to Leviticus, only Levite Priests (that is, men from the tribe of Levi) were allowed to eat this special bread. This made King David and his men (by inference) Priests of a different kind in Psalm 110 and Heb 7:17. This also meant that Jesus (from the tribe of Judah, just like David) and his men (also not Levites) were also priests along the same lines.

The golden altar of the Bread of the Presence was in the outer room of the tabernacle where the Ark of the Covenant was kept in Solomon's temple, and it was in Herod's Temple also, even though the Ark of the Covenant was no longer in that Temple. The Table of the Bread of the presence, with the wine libation associated with it, was in this chamber with the Lamp Stand called the Menorah and Altar of Incense. See an image showing the three major items below:

On the left we have the Menorah, in the center is the Altar of Incense and on the right is the Table of the Bread of the Presence. Behind the curtain was the Ark of the Covenant, although this was missing in the Second Temple period.

From the Levitical texts, there were 5 kinds of offerings – the Burnt Offering (Lev 1, 6:8-13, 8:18-21 and 16:24), the Grain Offering (Lev 2, 6:14-23), the Peace offering (Lev 3, 7:11-34), the Sin offering (Lev 4, 5:1-13, 6:24-30 and 8:14-17) and finally the Trespass Offering (Leviticus 5:14-19, 6:1-7 and 7:1-6).

The Grain Offering was an offering of Grain, fine flour, olive oil, incense, baked bread (cakes or wafers), salt; no yeast or honey; accompanied burnt offering and peace offering (along with drink offering) which was typically wine. The primary purpose of this offering was a voluntary act of worship; the recognition of God's goodness and provisions as a devotion to God.

Chapter 9 – The Eucharist

The Feast of Unleavened Bread was also established to begin the night after the Passover and celebrates Israel being delivered from bondage in Egypt. Lev. 23:6. A morning and evening sacrifice was offered. Only unleavened bread is eaten and meat of the sacrifices. Exodus 12:19 states the seriousness of the commandment from God.

"Seven days shall there be no leaven found in your houses: for whosoever eats that which is leavened, even that soul shall be cut off from the congregation of Israel, whether he is a stranger, or born in the land."

Leaven is symbolic of sin and the Passover was a memorial to God's delivering them from slavery in Egypt, but also a time of repentance and the putting away of sin. Galatians 5:9 says, *"A little leaven leavens the whole lump."* Leaven when placed in a lump of flour with begin to grow and spread until it permeates the whole lump. The picture is that of one diligently searching for and getting rid of sin even the smallest sin in one's life. Even as a little leaven (sin) will spoils the whole of the lump, therefore any and all sin is to be confessed and put out of one's life.

Paul explains that in the Eucharistic Celebration the Christian is to examine (1 Cor. 11:28) and to judge (1 Cor. 11:31) himself in regard to having un-confessed or remaining sin in his life.

The regular daily sacrifice was offered after the special offering. The 1st and 7th day like a Sabbath everyone rested with the exception of those preparing the food. That was a reference to Sundays being special.

On the 2nd day, a barley sheaf of the new harvest was symbolically offered to the Lord, by waving it before the Lord (not burned). Those attending may offer a burnt offering of not less than sixteen grains of corn, a festive offering of not less than 32 grains, and a peace or joy offering (Deut. 27:7) determined by the giver (Deut. 16:16-17).

In Corinthians Paul referred to the Passover and Unleavened Bread:

"Purge out therefore the old leaven, that you may be a new lump, as you are unleavened. For even Christ our Passover is sacrificed for us: Therefore let us keep the feast, not with old leaven, neither with the leaven of malice and wickedness; but with the unleavened bread of sincerity and truth.[130]"

---

[130] 1 Corinthians 5:7-8

Chapter 9 – The Eucharist

What does all of this mean?

The tradition of the Unleavened Bread probably reaches all the way back to the earliest days, when it was offered to show our love of God, and His love for us. Now only a very few Churches offer or are able to offer the 'Bread of Life' in the Eucharist. Many denominations will tell you that they have communion services just like the Catholics and Orthodox Churches, but they are also quick to correct you if you ask if their crouton and grape juice is literally the 'Body and Blood' of Christ, as mentioned in the Eucharistic blessing. The Jews rejected the teaching of the Eucharist in Jn 6:66 – be sure that you accept it.

'Food' for thought.

Chapter 10 – There is something about Mary…?

For some reason, many denominations have a personal vendetta against Mary, the mother of Jesus. Not sure why, but let's look into why the early Church had a special place in their hearts for this highly favored lady. Remember – she was Jesus' real mother, and no matter how you may have been taught, being rude to the Savior's mom is not going to win you any points with the Judge.

In Short:
The subject of Mary, the mother of Jesus, has been a strange one for many people. Many people these days pretty much ignore her role in the life of Christ, but historically she has been considered a vital figure in Christianity. Her role as the Virgin in prophecy from Isaiah is vital in establishing Jesus as Messiah, and her suitability for that role shows something special. Archangel Gabriel refers to her as 'Full of Grace' – a term not used anywhere else in the Bible (except for Jesus Himself), and he used it as a title, which confused Mary. The brother of Jesus, James the Just, wrote a pre-gospel[131] about his stepmother, Mary, where he explains that she was a sworn Virgin, and remained so her whole life. Why then do we have so much consternation about her in the modern churches?

Long Version:
Since the beginning, the Christian Church has considered it a matter of fact that Mary, the mother of Jesus, was a sworn life-long virgin, to fulfill the Prophecy of Isaiah *"Therefore the Lord himself will give you a sign: The virgin will conceive and give birth to a son, and will call him Immanuel."*[132] It is interesting to note that the verse from Isaiah in Hebrew uses the word "הָעַלְמָה" or "hā·'al·māh" (Strong 5959), which actually means a "young woman" in Hebrew. This may be the source of confusion, as the Virgin aspect of this word is not solely implied by it. In fact, the word has nothing to do with virginity – it is only by inference we would assume that a young girl is a virgin. That is, if we rely on the MT version of the text. The early Church used the Greek version of

---

[131] This is the Protoevangelium of James
[132] Isaiah 7:14, Mt 1:23

Chapter 10 – There is something about Mary…?

scripture, as the MT version would not be available for at least 600 years!

So where did the Virgin quote from Matthew come from if not from the Hebrew Scriptures? The fact is that it came from the Septuagint! The word used in the Septuagint is "σημεῖον" (parthanos) which means a **sworn virgin**, not just a young girl. Many religions of the time, including Judaism, had virgins who were dedicated to the service of their gods. The Vestal virgins (at the temple of Vesta) were famous throughout the Roman Empire for their virginity and service to their god. In Judaism, the entire sect of the Essenes were practicing celibacy, and for centuries they 'procreated' only through adoption For this reason, the writers and readers of the New Testament would be familiar with the word used in this passage, and the idea of a Virgin sworn to the service of a god. It is only very recently that people reject the idea.

The Septuagint was the preferred scripture of the Christians and the Jews in the Diaspora in general, as anyone could read the Greek version, while a substantial amount of study was necessary to understand the Hebrew (see my section on Ivrit in Chapter 8). The Septuagint is now known to be a much older translation than the Modern Hebrew Scriptures, and therefore authoritative over those more modern Hebrew Scriptures (the Septuagint was translated around 300 BC while the Hebrew Scriptures we use today are from about 800 AD – 1,100 years more recent versions!).

What other evidence exists about the Virginity of Mary? Let's consider the annunciation (Luke chapter 1 – in Lk 1:27) where she is described as a 'Virgin' betrothed to Joseph. The Greek word here is "παρθένον" or 'Parthanos' – a chaste person. When the Angel announces that this Virgin will have a child, she is confused. Let's read that section again:

*Luke 1:29 Mary was greatly troubled at his words and wondered what kind of greeting this might be. 30But the angel said to her, "Do not be afraid, Mary; you have found favor with God. 31**You will conceive** and give birth to a son, and you are to call him Jesus. 32He will be great and will be called the Son of the Most High. The Lord God will give him the throne of his father David, 33and he will reign over Jacob's descendants forever; his kingdom will never end."*

*34**"How will this be,"** Mary asked the angel, **"since I am a virgin?"** (parthanos)*

*35The angel answered, "The Holy Spirit **will come** on you, and the power of the Most High will overshadow you. **So the holy one to be born will be called the Son of God.**"*

Chapter 10 – There is something about Mary...?

OK – so there are 3 major points here in the text:
1. The Angel announces that Mary WILL become pregnant and have a son. NOT that she IS pregnant – will become.
2. Mary does not understand how this can happen, as she is a sworn Virgin. She is not stupid – women do know how children are conceived, and Mary is engaged to be married. The logical assumption would be that her first son would be the child that is foretold here. This is the same sort of event as the Angels promising Abraham a son, Sampson's mother being promised a son, any many more children born by natural means. In each case, the event would be impossible due to the mother's age – but not in this case. Mary is at an ideal age to have children, yet somehow she cannot understand how it can happen. She must have sworn to be, and remain always, a virgin.
3. The Angel explains how a Virgin, who has every intention to remain a Virgin, can become pregnant and why. Gabriel says that the Holy Spirit will overshadow her, and that is because this is a fulfillment of Prophecy ("So the holy one to be born will be called the Son of God" as the prophecy detailed.) This would not be a violation of Mary's oath of virginity. Joseph may have trouble with it, though, and he does.

For some reason, this idea of Mary being a sworn Virgin really annoys people today. Why else would Mary be confused about becoming a mother? Most women would be happy – not only to become pregnant with a Son, but with the Messiah! Most people would be happy about this announcement – why would she be confused unless she was a sworn Virgin, and turning up pregnant would present obvious problems.

Was Mary Pregnant at the Annunciation?
The common objection to this argument is "She was confused because she had *not yet* been with a man". This argument has two problems:
1. The Angel is saying that Mary WILL become pregnant – **not** that she is now pregnant.
2. Mary's question is often translated as "I know not a man?" What does that mean? It **does not mean** "I do not yet know a man" – it is much more general. She does not know a man (in a Biblical sense). Therefore she is a sworn Virgin.

Other objections would relate to a virgin as defined as a girl that has *not yet* had relations, but this is temporary. A married girl would

Chapter 10 – There is something about Mary…?

normally expect to stop being a virgin pretty soon. There are two problems with this idea:
1. If she planned to stop being a virgin, why would she be surprised that she would have a son?
2. Why would a prophecy (as in Isaiah) specify something that almost EVERY JEWISH FEMALE was qualified for? Why even bring up the prophecy if we are saying a young girl/virgin would have a son. Almost all sons were born to young girls.

What is the big deal there?

As a parallel with Abraham, whose wife Sarah could not have children due to advanced age, Mary could not have children due to her vow of chastity. Remember, God works the miraculous in events of great importance so that people know that something important is going on. Mary could not have children for a reason – that is, she swore not to.

The Birds and the Bees in the first century

Modern people have some assumptions that the people in the first century did not have. One of these is that children are half from their mother, and half from their father. The Jews believed that children came from their father only.

Think about it – when a woman can have children, we call her 'fertile' – like a field. She can sustain life in her womb. In fact, this is not really an adequate description – she has to have an egg in the right place, and it has to be able to (once fertilized) implant in the lining of the womb. A mother is not merely a place for children to grow!

How about for men? Men are said to have 'seed' – again, seeds are planted in fertile ground to grow plants. They do not match with anything else to become a plant – they just grow. The assumption for the early Jews was that the father alone had children *through* his wife or wives. That is why there was no concept of half-brothers or half-sisters – if they shared the same father, then from a Jewish frame of mind, they *were literally brothers and sisters* regardless of who the mother was.

Knowing this is important to understanding many stories in the Bible. When Sarah decides to provide her maid (Hagar) as a means for Abraham to have a child (through Hagar) she does go on the basis that the child born would be Abraham's son, through the maid servant who is owned by Sarah. Even though the child would be from another woman, Sarah owned the other woman and the child would be a child of Abraham, not a child of Abraham and Hagar. In this case, it did not work out well for poor Ishmael.

Chapter 10 – There is something about Mary…?

Brothers and Sisters of Christ

The existence of 'Brothers and Sisters' of Christ presents a problem for some. There are two traditional explanations for these 'Brethren' of Christ – they are cousins, or they are children of Joseph. St. Jerome believed that the 'brothers' of Christ are just cousins, who were close Jesus in age, so they were showing up for that reason, and as Jews really called every person of the same family group who lived together "Brothers" or "Sisters": Jerome is saying that this is just all a big misunderstanding. Jerome espoused this opinion because he believed that Jesus came from a 'Perfect' family where Joseph and Mary were both celibate.

The second traditional understanding is that these 'brothers and sisters' were in fact children of Joseph. The other children of Joseph were in fact brothers and sisters of Jesus because of the fact that Mary was Joseph's wife, regardless of the fact that the children were not hers but those of Joseph from an earlier marriage.

In this text I mention both theories – the Protoevangelium and the theory proposed by Jerome, but I do have to say that Jerome's theory seems somewhat less supportable than James'. Either is considered valid by the Magisterium, so either is acceptable for us. I recommend being aware of both, and understanding the two positions, so that you can make up your own mind on the subject.

In order to understand the concept of 'brother' in Jewish society, we have to look in Hebrew to see if there is a term for 'half-brother'. A quick word search will show that there is no reference in the Bible to half siblings – no half-brothers or half-sisters. That means that there were none? Hardly – there are many half-brothers in scripture. Many of the Children of Israel were half-brothers. Joseph, for example, was a true brother to Benjamin, but only a half-brother to the rest. Why then were these half or step brothers just called 'brothers'?

In Jewish terms, all children of a father are brothers and sisters by definition. There was no official differentiation, but clearly in the case of Joseph, son of Israel, there was a lot of sibling rivalry between children of various wives. How does this bear on Jesus and His brothers?

All the children of Joseph, either from Mary or a previous wife, would be brothers and sisters in Hebrew society. The biggest separations occur (importantly for us) with who takes care of whose mother. Women with no children have to look after themselves upon the death of their husband. Traditionally, the eldest son inherits a 'double portion' of the inheritance, but there is nothing for the wives. Women with children could rely on their children to look after them, and they did – that was required by the 10 commandments and the Law. If a man had multiple

Chapter 10 – There is something about Mary...?

wives, each wife would have her children to look after her after his demise. The family often did not have to look after anyone else.

Look at the situation in scripture relating to Jesus and Mary. When Jesus died, His mother would, traditionally, be looked after by her other children. In Mary's case, Jesus had to ask John (not a relative) to look after Mary. Why? Where were her 'other children'?

There were no other children

That is why Jesus did what He did. So what did Jesus' family really look like? How can we find out? Consider the Protoevangelium of James, the brother of Jesus.

The 'Protoevangelium' or the 'Gospel of James' is pretty cool – and quite intertwined with the Gospels. The Early Church Fathers refer to it, so it had some recognition in the early Church, and probably accounts for the explanations that have traditionally been used to explain questions about Mary. It is referred to in early writings, and the Letter of James was included, but not this other writing of James the Just. Several Church Fathers wrote on this subject (Ignatius, Polycarp, Irenaeus, Justin Martyr, Ebion, Theodotus of Byzantium, and Valentinus) – all support James' explanation for the 'Brothers' of Jesus.

Neither the Gospel accounts nor the early Christians had the idea that Mary bore other children besides Jesus. The faithful knew, through the witness of Scripture and Tradition, that Jesus was Mary's **only** child and that she remained a lifelong virgin.

The Protoevangelium of James was written by the Brother of Jesus (James the Just, Bishop of Jerusalem) when memories of her life were still vivid in the minds of many. As a brother of Jesus and son of Joseph, James is ideally suited to give details on Mary's life as a witness like no other.

According to the world-renowned patristics scholar, Johannes Quasten: "The principal aim of the whole writing [*Protoevangelium of James*] is to prove the perpetual and inviolate virginity of Mary before, in, and after the birth of Christ" (*Patrology*, 1:120–1)[133].

To begin with, the *Protoevangelium* records that when Mary's birth was prophesied, her mother, St. Anne, vowed that she would devote the child to the service of the Lord, as Samuel had been by his mother (1 Sam. 1:11). Mary would thus serve the Lord at the Temple, as women had for centuries (1 Sam. 2:22), and as Anna the prophetess did at the

---

[133] Much of this section is from information supplied on the Catholic Answers website, an excellent resource for answers to difficult questions.

Chapter 10 – There is something about Mary...?

time of Jesus' birth (Luke 2:36–37). A life of continual, devoted service to the Lord at the Temple meant that Mary would not be able to live the ordinary life of a child-rearing mother. Rather, she was vowed to a life of perpetual virginity.

However, due to considerations of ceremonial cleanliness, it was eventually necessary for Mary, a consecrated "virgin of the Lord," to have a guardian or protector who would respect her vow of virginity. During the years that she was menstruating, she was ritually unclean and therefore not allowed in the Temple. Once she reached menopause, she could return, as Anna had. Thus, according to the *Protoevangelium*, Joseph, an elderly widower who already had children, was chosen to be her spouse. (This would also explain why Joseph was apparently dead by the time of Jesus' adult ministry, since he does not appear during it in the gospels, and since Mary is entrusted to John, rather than to her husband at the crucifixion).

According to the *Protoevangelium*, Joseph was required to regard Mary's vow of virginity with the utmost respect. The gravity of his responsibility as the guardian of a virgin was indicated by the fact that, when she was discovered to be with child, he had to answer to the Temple authorities, who thought him guilty of defiling a 'virgin of the Lord'. Mary was also accused of having forsaken the Lord by breaking her vow. Keeping this in mind, it is an incredible insult to the Blessed Virgin to say that she broke her vow by bearing children other than her Lord and God, who was conceived through the power of the Holy Spirit.

Thus the perpetual virginity of Mary has always been reconciled with the biblical references to Christ's brethren through a proper understanding of the meaning of the term "brethren." The understanding that the brethren of the Lord were Jesus' stepbrothers (children of Joseph) rather than half-brothers (children of Mary) was the most common one until the time of Jerome (fourth century).

Again, it was Jerome who introduced the possibility that Christ's brethren were actually his cousins, since in Jewish idiom cousins were also referred to as "brethren." The Catholic Church allows the faithful to hold either view, since both are compatible with the reality of Mary's perpetual virginity.

Today most Protestants are unaware of these early beliefs regarding Mary's virginity and the proper interpretation of "the brethren of the Lord." And yet, the Protestant Reformers themselves—Martin Luther, John Calvin, and Ulrich Zwingli—honored the perpetual virginity of Mary and recognized it as the teaching of the Bible, as have other, more modern Protestants.

Chapter 10 – There is something about Mary...?

The Protoevangelium of James

"And behold, an angel of the Lord stood by [St. Anne], saying, 'Anne! Anne! The Lord has heard your prayer, and you shall conceive and shall bring forth, and your seed shall be spoken of in all the world.' And Anne said, 'As the Lord my God lives, if I beget either male or female, I will bring it as a gift to the Lord my God, and it shall minister to him in the holy things all the days of its life.' . . . And [from the time she was three] Mary was in the temple of the Lord as if she were a dove that dwelt there" [134].

"And when she was twelve years old there was held a council of priests, saying, 'Behold, Mary has reached the age of twelve years in the temple of the Lord. What then shall we do with her, lest perchance she defile the sanctuary of the Lord?' And they said to the high priest, 'You stand by the altar of the Lord; go in and pray concerning her, and whatever the Lord shall manifest to you, that also will we do.' . . . [A]nd he prayed concerning her, and behold, an angel of the Lord stood by him saying, 'Zechariah! Zechariah! Go out and assemble the widowers of the people and let them bring each his rod, and to whomsoever the Lord shall show a sign, his wife shall she be. . . . And Joseph [was chosen]. . . . And the priest said to Joseph, 'You have been chosen by lot to take into your keeping the Virgin of the Lord.' But Joseph refused, saying, 'I have children, and I am an old man, and she is a young girl'" [135].

"And Annas the scribe came to him [Joseph] . . . and saw that Mary was with child. And he ran away to the priest and said to him, 'Joseph, whom you did vouch for, has committed a grievous crime.' And the priest said, 'How so?' And he said, 'He has defiled the virgin whom he received out of the temple of the Lord and has married her by stealth'" [136].

"And the priest said, 'Mary, why have you done this? And why have you brought your soul low and forgotten the Lord your God?' . . . And she wept bitterly saying, 'As the Lord my God lives, I am pure before him, and know not man.'"

Was the Protoevangelium Authentic?

The Protoevangelium was considered authentic by the early church fathers (I include some of their opinions on it on the following pages). Certainly, it is always a good idea to question sources of all kinds – 'Is it

---

[134] *Protoevangelium of James* 4, 7 [A.D. 120]
[135] *Protoevangelium of James* 8-9
[136] *Protoevangelium of James* 15

Chapter 10 – There is something about Mary...?

a valid source' is always something to be considered when dealing with a text that is not is the Bible itself. I do not recommend that the text of Protoevangelium be considered scriptural, but as with any historical document (and this certainly was known and considered authoritative before the year 248) it can be considered a witness to the events recorded in it, but not scriptural. There are many similar documents from this period that, while important witnesses to the events of the period, these cannot be considered scripture, because there may be some things left out or unconsidered in the writings themselves. Even with the best intentions, all authors have biases and limitations which are bound to impact their writings. That does not mean they are inaccurate or invalid.

Regardless of possible inconsistencies with our faith, we should also remember that any document of this age, when it was written, was considered accurate by those around it at that time. Clearly no one thought it to be fraudulent.

When Origen wrote about the Protoevangelium in 248 AD he considered it accurate, and to do so, as a Church Father and Bishop, he had to have good reason. He was much closer to the events and traditions at that time, and so I do consider the Protoevangelium to be useful on his witness alone! In addition, the events presented in the Protoevangelium mesh perfectly with the Gospels, and support the early traditions about Mary, so I believe it is appropriate to consider the Protoevangelium as a reference text.

Origen

"The Book [the Protoevangelium] of James [records] that the brethren of Jesus were sons of Joseph by a former wife, whom he married before Mary. Now those who say so wish to preserve the honor of Mary in virginity to the end, so that body of hers which was appointed to minister to the Word . . . might not know intercourse with a man after the Holy Spirit came into her and the power from on high overshadowed her. And I think it in harmony with reason that Jesus was the firstfruit among men of the purity which consists in [perpetual] chastity, and Mary was among women. For it were not pious to ascribe to any other than to her the firstfruit of virginity" (Commentary on Matthew 2:17 [A.D. 248]).

Hilary of Poitiers

"If they [the brethren of the Lord] had been Mary's sons and not those taken from Joseph's former marriage, she would never have been given over in the moment of the passion [crucifixion] to the apostle John as his mother, the Lord saying to each, 'Woman, behold your son,' and

to John, *'Behold your mother'* [John 19:26–27), as he bequeathed filial love to a disciple as a consolation to the one desolate" (*Commentary on Matthew* 1:4 [A.D. 354]).

Athanasius

"Let those, therefore, who deny that the Son is by nature from the Father and proper to his essence deny also that he took true human flesh from the ever-virgin Mary" (*Discourses Against the Arians* 2:70 [A.D. 360]).

Epiphanius of Salamis

"We believe in one God, the Father almighty, maker of all things, both visible and invisible; and in one Lord Jesus Christ, the Son of God... who for us men and for our salvation came down and took flesh, that is, was born perfectly of the holy ever-virgin Mary by the Holy Spirit" (*The Man Well-Anchored* 120 [A.D. 374]).

"And to holy Mary, [the title] 'Virgin' is invariably added, for that holy woman remains undefiled" (*Medicine Chest Against All Heresies* 78:6 [A.D. 375]).

Jerome

"[Helvidius] produces Tertullian as a witness [to his view] and quotes Victorinus, bishop of Petavium. Of Tertullian, I say no more than that he did not belong to the Church. But as regards Victorinus, I assert what has already been proven from the gospel—that he [Victorinus] spoke of the brethren of the Lord not as being sons of Mary but brethren in the sense I have explained, that is to say, brethren in point of kinship, not by nature. [By discussing such things we] are... following the tiny streams of opinion. Might I not array against you the whole series of ancient writers? Ignatius, Polycarp, Irenaeus, Justin Martyr, and many other apostolic and eloquent men, who against [the heretics] Ebion, Theodotus of Byzantium, and Valentinus, held these same views and wrote volumes replete with wisdom. If you had ever read what they wrote, you would be a wiser man" (*Against Helvidius: The Perpetual Virginity of Mary* 19 [A.D. 383]).

"We believe that God was born of a virgin, because we read it. We do not believe that Mary was married after she brought forth her Son, because we do not read it.... You [Helvidius] say that Mary did not remain a virgin. As for myself, I claim that Joseph himself was a virgin, through Mary, so that a virgin Son might be born of a virginal wedlock" (ibid., 21).

Chapter 10 – There is something about Mary...?

Didymus the Blind

"It helps us to understand the terms 'first-born' and 'only-begotten' when the Evangelist tells that Mary remained a virgin 'until she brought forth her first-born son' [Matt. 1:25]; for neither did Mary, who is to be honored and praised above all others, marry anyone else, nor did she ever become the Mother of anyone else, but even after childbirth she remained always and forever an immaculate virgin" (*The Trinity* 3:4 [A.D. 386]).

Ambrose of Milan

"Imitate her [Mary], holy mothers, who in her only dearly beloved Son set forth so great an example of material virtue; for neither have you sweeter children [than Jesus], nor did the Virgin seek the consolation of being able to bear another son" (*Letters* 63:111 [A.D. 388]).

Pope Siricius I

"You had good reason to be horrified at the thought that another birth might issue from the same virginal womb from which Christ was born according to the flesh. For the Lord Jesus would never have chosen to be born of a virgin if he had ever judged that she would be so incontinent as to contaminate with the seed of human intercourse the birthplace of the Lord's body, that court of the eternal king" (*Letter to Bishop Anysius* [A.D. 392]).

Augustine

"In being born of a Virgin who chose to remain a Virgin even before she knew who was to be born of her, Christ wanted to approve virginity rather than to impose it. And he wanted virginity to be of free choice even in that woman in whom he took upon himself the form of a slave" (*Holy Virginity* 4:4 [A.D. 401]).

"It was not the visible sun, but its invisible Creator who consecrated this day for us, when the Virgin Mother, fertile of womb and integral in her virginity, brought him forth, made visible for us, by whom, when he was invisible, she too was created. A Virgin conceiving, a Virgin bearing, a Virgin pregnant, a Virgin bringing forth, a Virgin perpetual. Why do you wonder at this, O man?" (*Sermons* 186:1 [A.D. 411]).

"Heretics called Antidicomarites are those who contradict the perpetual virginity of Mary and affirm that after Christ was born she was joined as one with her husband" (*Heresies* 56 [A.D. 428]).

Chapter 10 – There is something about Mary...?

Leporius

"We confess, therefore, that our Lord and God, Jesus Christ, the only Son of God, born of the Father before the ages, and in times most recent, made man of the Holy Spirit and the ever-virgin Mary" (*Document of Amendment* 3 [A.D. 426]).

Cyril of Alexandria

"[T]he Word himself, coming into the Blessed Virgin herself, assumed for himself his own temple from the substance of the Virgin and came forth from her a man in all that could be externally discerned, while interiorly he was true God. Therefore he kept his Mother a virgin even after her childbearing" (*Against Those Who Do Not Wish to Confess That the Holy Virgin is the Mother of God* 4 [A.D. 430]).

Praying to the Saints and Mary to help us?

One of the biggest differences between the old religions (Catholic/Orthodoxy) and the new ones (less than 500 years old) is the focus on a Kingdom of God – not just Jesus. This concept is largely discarded or avoided in the Protestant reformation, and progressively attacked by more radical fundamentalists, gradually change the faith into a minimalist religion where the very basic elements are all that remain of a rich tapestry that existed in the first 1,500 years of the Church. The concept of 'The Church' as a complete community of believers is essential to the Christian understanding of heaven, and why so many people today have no trouble understanding hell, with its punishments, while they fail to grasp the opposite idea that Heaven is a huge community of love and worship of the Triune God, where individuals all come together to form the vine and branches of the mystical body of Christ, as described in the NT. When you strip away the Kingdom of God, you are left with you and Jesus. The Saints, Angels, Apostles, Kings of Heaven, Choirs of Angelic beings and community of Saints are clearly explained in the Scriptures, and all are in place in Heaven, giving us a much better understanding of that place that a 'Cloudy place with me and Jesus where I experience complete Joy all the time'. Reading the Heavenly scenes in Rev 20-22 shows how all of the Saints come together in the end to form the People of God, who with the Angels worship at the Altar of God and live together in a joyful communion. What are they doing? Offering intercessions to God – for whom? For us.

In Revelation 5:8, where John depicts the saints in heaven offering our prayers to God under the form of "golden bowls full of incense, which are the prayers of the saints." But if the saints in heaven are offering our prayers to God, then they must be aware of our prayers.

Chapter 10 – There is something about Mary…?

They are aware of our petitions and present them to God by interceding for us.

The intercession of fellow Christians—which is what the saints in heaven are—also clearly does not interfere with Christ's unique role as mediator because in the four verses immediately before 1 Timothy 2:5, Paul *says* that Christians should intercede:

"First of all, then, I urge that supplications, prayers, intercessions, and thanksgivings be made for all men, for kings and all who are in high positions, that we may lead a quiet and peaceable life, godly and respectful in every way. This is good and pleasing to God our Savior, who desires all men to be saved and to come to the knowledge of the truth" (1 Tim. 2:1–4).

Clearly, then, intercessory prayers offered by Christians on behalf of others is something "good and pleasing to God," not something infringing on Christ's role as mediator.

God has forbidden contact with the dead for the purpose of foretelling the future – this does not apply to requesting prayers from the dead. What God has forbidden is the necromantic practice of conjuring up spirits. *"There shall not be found among you any one who burns his son or his daughter as an offering, anyone who practices divination, a soothsayer, or an augur, or a sorcerer, or a charmer, or a medium, or a wizard, or a necromancer. . . . For these nations, which you are about to dispossess, give heed to soothsayers and to diviners; but as for you, the Lord your God has not allowed you so to do. The Lord your God will raise up for you a prophet like me from among you, from your brethren—him you shall heed"* (Deut. 18:10–15)

The question of saints in heaven responding to petitions no doubt comes from anti-Catholic Loraine Boettner:

"How, then, can a human being such as Mary hear the prayers of millions of Roman Catholics, in many different countries, praying in many different languages, all at the same time? Let any priest or layman try to converse with only three people at the same time and see how impossible that is for a human being. . . . The objections against prayers to Mary apply equally against prayers to the saints. For they too are only creatures, infinitely less than God, able to be at only one place at a time and to do only one thing at a time. How, then, can they listen to and answer thousands upon thousands of petitions made simultaneously in many different lands and in many different languages? Many such petitions are expressed, not orally, but only mentally, silently. How can Mary and the saints, without being like God, be present everywhere and know the secrets of all hearts?" (Roman Catholicism, 142-143).

Chapter 10 – There is something about Mary...?

If you believe that the people in Heaven are limited in the same way that we are (in the body here on earth) then this is a legitimate argument – however, the 'Glorified Body' of the resurrection appears to be unlimited in ways that we are limited – similar to Angelic bodies in some ways. Prayers to Angels and from Angels is well documented in the OT and NT:

Psalms 103, we pray, *"Bless the Lord, O you his angels, you mighty ones who do his word, hearkening to the voice of his word! Bless the Lord, all his hosts, his ministers that do his will!"* (Ps. 103:20-21). And in Psalms 148 we pray, *"Praise the Lord! Praise the Lord from the heavens, praise him in the heights! Praise him, all his angels; praise him, all his host!"* (Ps. 148:1-2).

Not only do those in heaven pray with us, they also pray for us. In the book of Revelation, we read: *"[An] angel came and stood at the altar [in heaven] with a golden censer; and he was given much incense to mingle with the prayers of all the saints upon the golden altar before the throne; and the smoke of the incense rose with the prayers of the saints from the hand of the angel before God"* (Rev. 8:3-4).

Those in heaven who offer to God our prayers aren't just angels, but humans as well. John sees that *"the twenty-four elders [the leaders of the people of God in heaven] fell down before the Lamb, each holding a harp, and with golden bowls full of incense, which are the prayers of the saints"* (Rev. 5:8). The simple fact is that the saints in heaven offer to God the prayers of the saints on earth.

Why ask a Saint in Heaven to pray for you in addition to someone on earth? One such benefit is that the faith and devotion of the saints can support our own weaknesses and supply what is lacking in our own faith and devotion. Jesus regularly helped one person based on another person's faith (e.g., Matt. 8:13, 15:28, 17:15–18, Mark 9:17–29, Luke 8:49–55). Clearly someone in Heaven has proved that he or she is able to be a good advocate as preferred by the Lord. God answers in particular the prayers of the righteous.

James declares: *"The prayer of a righteous man has great power in its effects. Elijah was a man of like nature as us and he prayed fervently that it might not rain, and for three years and six months it did not rain on the earth. Then he prayed again and the heaven gave rain, and the earth brought forth its fruit"* (Jas. 5:16–18). Yet those Christians in heaven are more righteous, since they have been made perfect to stand in God's presence (Heb. 12:22-23), than anyone on earth.

Chapter 10 – There is something about Mary...?

So what does all of this mean?

Mary was a lifelong virgin, as was Jesus and many other saints throughout history who emulate Christ. If you prefer Jerome's explanation to that of James the Just is not as important as recognizing the perpetual virginity of Mary and Jesus.

Regarding praying to Mary and the Saints - do we need to pray to the dead people – saints or not – for intercession? No one prays to *dead* saints, because those in heaven are more alive than we are. The Lord is God of the living, not of the dead. The fervent prayer of a righteous man is very powerful (Jas 5:16). Those in heaven are surely righteous, since nothing unclean can enter heaven (Rev 21:27). Those in heaven are part of the Mystical Body of Christ and have not been separated from us by death, but surround us as a great cloud of witnesses (Heb 12:1). They stand before the throne of God and offer our prayers to him (Rev 5:8) and cheer us on as we run the good race. Intercession among members of the body of Christ is pleasing to God (1 Tim 2:1-4) and even commanded by him (Jn 15:17). Those in heaven have a perfected love, so how could they *not* intercede for us? Christ is the vine, and we are the branches; if we are connected to him, we are inseparably bound together as well. Can the eye say to the hand, *"I need you not"*? Neither are we to say that we don't need the prayers of our brothers and sisters (alive here with us, or in heaven), because salvation is a family affair.

Do not be quick to dismiss Mary and the Saints – we are all parts of the Body of Christ, and there is much to learn from fellow pilgrims while we travel to Heaven.

The Cheat Sheet and how to use it
So, with all you could be asked about – how do you remain ready to answer at a moment's notice? Do you need to memorize everything?

In Short:
Time is of the essence in maintaining a conversation with someone who has memorized their attack points. No matter how knowledgeable a person may seem, they do not understand the teachings of Christ unless they are Catholic. Not to say all Catholics get it either, but non-Catholics are missing something. Exactly *what* is the problem – it could be anything from a long list of errors. That is why you need a familiar cheat sheet – it gives you the right Bible verse to defuse their argument, and nudge them in the right direction. Read this sheet – line by line, and read the associated Bible verse. Know it, and you will begin to know your faith.

Long Version:
This collection of Bible and other quotes is a quick list – there are MANY more than this, but before we get into the specific material, let's be sure we understand why we quote scriptures to others, and where we get our direction from.

First of all, for Catholics, the Magisterium of the Church is the final say in matters of Faith and Morals. The Bible is important to us, but is NOT the final say in anything. Why?

Because Jesus established the Magisterium of His Church, not the Bible. The bible was collated by the Church's Bishops and councils, not the other way around. The Church made the Bible, not vice versa. It is important to remember that we (all of us, not just Catholics) only have a Bible because the Church decided that it was important to have a collection of sacred books that could reliably be read in Church to educate the People.

So when someone 'Only accepts the Bible' you might point out to them that the Bible was determined by councils of Catholic Bishops, and the only reason it was published or made important was because the Church decided that it should be so.

As many have said in the past – "They like our cookbook, but hate our cooking." The Bible is certainly a Catholic creation, and it was never intended to contain all of the instructions necessary for Christians. The Magisterium was intended and directed by

The Cheat Sheet and how to use it

Christ himself to tell the People of God how to live and what to do. When Peter got the keys to the Kingdom of God, he was instructed to be a caretaker of that kingdom *"I will give you the keys of the kingdom of heaven; and whatever you bind on earth shall have been bound in heaven, and whatever you loose on earth shall have been loosed in heaven."*[137]

So the Church under Peter, and those who follow who maintain his office, have authority to teach and affirm the message of Christ – no one else. No book is qualified to lead a Church, no matter what the Fundamentalists believe. There is no valid basis for this sort of behavior – the Bible is a collection of books, selected by Catholics, to help the Magisterium to stay true to the Gospel.

The Scriptures, however, as the sole leg the Fundamentalists have to stand on, can be used to explain to them (from 'their' own book) how off-base they really are. Therefore, we have a cheat sheet.

I just mention all of this in case you become confused while reading or hearing scriptures – the Church is the final authority, not Scriptures. A proper understanding of the Scriptures will always be in line with the teachings of the Church. If you are in doubt, research it in the Catechism or the publications of the Magisterium.

What do we do with this Cheat Sheet?

Let's start this off by reviewing what you should be doing anyway – Praying, reflecting, and reading the catechism and Scriptures. Every day you should do this for at least an hour, and use the cheat sheet to polish your understanding. I use mine as a piece of note paper and a reminder of what to read.

The Bible is not a series of one liners – the text is intended to be read in context, and in the light of the entire collection. The elements may seem confused or uncertain, but that is just because you do not fully understand – not one word is out of place. The references are astonishingly deep, once you understand it in context. Many people fail to understand the Scriptures because they take it as a series of one line statements – it is not. Every day, I see new depth myself (after 30 years of study). So when something comes up that sounds bad ("Call no man your

---

[137] MT 16:19

The Cheat Sheet and how to use it

father"[138], for example) – read it and understand. Jesus is not saying that the term "Father" is somehow improper, but He is saying that your ultimate Father is God Himself, as in the Lord's Prayer ("Our Father,") What do you call the guy who raised you along with your mother? Don't the commandments remain in force – Honor your Father and Mother? Of course you do – the emphasis is placed by Christ to show just how much of a true Father God is, and therefore He acts as a true Father does. With understanding, the entire Bible makes sense in a Catholic context.

So read each quote, in context, and understand what it means, and why it supports the category it is in. For example – you may be mystified why Gen 1:2 is included to support the Holy Spirit. You may have to read it word for work until you realize – "Hey – the *"Spirit of God was over the Waters"* means that God created the world through Water and the Holy Spirit – ok – that is just like Baptism. Wow!"

If in doubt – ask someone at the Parish or go to Catholic Answers. Apologetics is a team sport! Do not stop until you understand what is going on – for your own peace of mind. Understanding and removing doubt helps you to be a better Christian. Do not be upset if something you have always believed is not quite correct – we are all learning here. No one knows everything – most of us are lucky to know something. Anything at all.

* This symbol means that this quote is an apparent contradiction, but is in fact not. Some people will quote these references to try to prove an incorrect idea, so you should know these and why they do not disprove anything.

The Cheat Sheet is in Appendix 1.

---

[138] Mt 23:9

Appendix 1: The Cheat Sheet:

Sola scriptura (Scripture Alone)
Jn 21:25 ... Not everything is in the Bible.
2 Thess 2:15; 2 Tim 2:2; 1 Cor 11:2; 1 Thess 2:13 ... Oral tradition.
2 Tim 3:15-16 "All Scripture is ... profitable for teaching, for reproof, for correction, for training in righteousness." Not Sola Scriptura.
Acts 2:42 ... Early Christians followed apostolic tradition.
2 Pet 3:16 ... Bible hard to understand, get distorted.
2 Jn 1:12; 3 Jn 1:13-14 ... More oral tradition.
2 Pet 1:20-21 ... No personal interpretation.
Acts 8:31; Heb 5:12 ... Guidance needed to interpret scriptures.
Lk 3:2, Lk 5:1, Acts 4:31, 6:2, 6:7, 8:14, 11:1, 12:24 ...Word of God more than just what is written in Scripture.

Sola fide (Faith Alone)
James 2:14-26 ... What good is faith w/o works?
Heb 10:26 ... Must avoid sin.
James 5:20 ... "Earning" forgiveness.
Lk 6:46; Mt 7:21; Mt 19:16-21; Jn 5:29 ... Must do will of God.
1 Cor 9:27 ... "Buffet my body ..."
Phil 2:12; 2 Cor 5:10; Rom 2:6-10, 13, 3:31; Mt 25:32-46; Gal 6:6-10; Rev 20:12 ... Works have merit.
Mt 25:31-46 – People are judged on works, not faith
1 Jn 2:3-4; 1 Jn 3:24; 1 Jn 5:3 ... Keep commandments.

Catholic Bible (73) not Protestant Bible (66)
First Bible Canon Developed up to AD 397 at the third Council of Carthage. Protestant Bible invented starting around the 17th Century or the 1646 Westminster Confession, 1249 yrs. later! The Protestant Bible had 66 books, while the Catholic has the original 73 books. Deuterocanonical books were used in NT: 2 Mach 6:18-7:42 ... Heb 11:35; Wisdom 3:5-6, 1 Pet 1:6-7, Wisdom 13:1-9, Rom 1:18-32, Septuagint version of OT quoted in NT, noticeably different from Hebrew version: Is 7:14 ... Mt 1:23; Is 40:3 ... Mt 3:3; Joel 2:30-31 ... Acts 2:19-29; Ps 95:7-9 ... Heb 3:7-9 etc.

Salvation (once and for all?)
1 Cor 9:27 ... After preaching ... I myself disqualified.
1 Cor 10:12 ... Paul thinks that he stands ... lest he fall.
Phil 2:12 ... Work out salvation with fear and trembling.
Heb 4:1 ... Fear of failing to reach salvation.
1 Jn 5:16, 17 ... Some sins are mortal, some not.
Rom 11:21, 22 ... Spare branches, continue or be cut off.

Appendix 1 - Apologetics Cheat Sheet

Purgatory
Mt 5:48 - Be perfect as your heavenly Father is perfect
Heb 12:14 - Strive for that holiness without which cannot see God
James 3:2 - We all fall short in many respects
Rev 21:27 - Nothing unclean shall enter heaven
James 1:14-15 - When sin reaches maturity gives birth to death
2Sam 12:13-14 - David, though forgiven, still punished for his sin
Mt 5:26 - You will not be released until paid last penny
Mt 12:32 - Sin against Holy Spirit unforgiving in this age or next
Mt 12:36 - Account for every idle word on judgment day
2Macc 12:44-46 - Atoned for dead to free them from sin
1Cor 3:15 - Suffer loss, but saved as through fire
1Pet 3:18-20; 4:6 - Jesus preached to spirits in prison
2Tim 1:16-18 - Paul prays for dead friend Onesiphorus
1Cor 15:29-30 - Paul mentions people baptizing for the dead

Hell
Is 33:11, 14 - Who of us can live with the everlasting flames?
Mt 25:41 - Depart, you accursed, into the eternal fire
Mt 25:46 - These will go off to eternal punishment
Lk 3:16-17 - The chaff will burn in unquenchable fire
2Thess 1:6-9 - These will pay the penalty of eternal ruin
Lk 12:59; 1 Cor 3:15; 1 Pet 1:7; Mt 5:25-26 ... Temporary agony.
Heb 12:6-11 ... God's painful discipline.
Mt 12:32 ... No forgiveness ... nor in the age to come.
1 Pet 3:19 ... Purgatory (limbo?).
Rev 21:27 ... Nothing unclean shall enter heaven.
Heb 12:23 ... Souls in heaven are perfect.
Col 1:24; 2 Sam 12:14 ... "Extra" suffering.
2 Mac 12:43-46 ... Sacrifice for the dead.
2 Tim 1:15-18 ... Prayer for Onesiphorus for "that Day."
1 Jn 5:14-17 ... Mortal/venial sins

Eucharist
Mt 26:26-27; Mk 14:22, 24; Lk 22:19-20; 1 Cor 10:24-25 ... This is my body ... this is my blood.
1 Cor 11:26-30 ... Sinning against the body and blood.
Jn 6:32-58 ... Long discourse on Eucharist.
Gen 14:18; Ps 110:4; Heb 7:1-17 ... Melchizedek.
Acts 2:42 ... Breaking of bread.
Ps 27:1-2; Is 9:18-20; Is 49:26; Micah 3:3; Rev 17:6, 16 ... Symbolic interpretation of Jn 6 inappropriate.
Rev 6:9, 8:3-5, 9:13, 11:1, 14:18, 16:7...Altar in heaven

Appendix 1 - Apologetics Cheat Sheet

Baptism
Gen 1:2 – Holy Spirit participating in New Creation with Water
Acts 2:38 – Repent and be baptized for the forgiveness of sins
Heb 6:1-3 – Baptism is one of 6 basic Christian necessities
Acts 22:16 - "Get up, be baptized and wash your sins away"
Acts 19:2-3 – "What Baptism did you receive?" Methodology matters!
Romans 6:3-4 – Baptism can "Set free from sin"
Colossians 2:11-12 – Baptism allows us to participate in the death and resurrection of Christ. No Baptism, no salvation!

Baptism of infants
Acts 2:38-39; Acts 16:15, 16:33, 18:8; 1 Cor 1:16 ... Suggests baptism of all, incl. children.
Jn 3:5; Rom 6:4 ... Necessity of baptism.
Col 2:11-12 ... Circumcision (normally performed on infants c.f. Gen 17:12) replaced by baptism.

Forgiveness of sins
Jn 20:22-23 ... "If you forgive ... they are forgiven."
Mt 18:18 ... Binding on earth and heaven.
2 Cor 5:18 ... Ministry of reconciliation.
Jas 5:14-16 ... Forgiveness of sins, anointing of the sick, confession.
Gn 2:16-17 - The day you eat of that tree, you shall die
Gn 3:11-19 - God's punishment for eating of the tree
Rom 5:12-19 - Many became sinners through one man's sin
1Cor 15:21-23 - By a man came death; in Adam all die
Eph 2:1-3 - We all once lived in the passions of our flesh

Church/Papacy
Mt 10:1-4; Mk 3:16-19; Lk 6:14-16; Acts 1:13; Lk 9:32 ... Peter always mentioned first, as foremost apostle.
Mt 18:21; Mk 8:29; Lk 12:41; Jn 6:69 ... Peter speaks for group.
Acts 2:14-40 ... Pentecost: Peter who first preached.
Acts 3:6-7 ... Peter worked first healing.
Acts 10:46-48 ... Gentiles to be baptized revealed to Peter.
Jn 1:42 ... Simon is renamed Peter. This is very rare.
Mt 16:18-19 ... "On this Rock ... keys ... bind ... loose"
Is 22:22; Rev 1:18 ... Keys as symbol of authority.
Jn 21:17 ... "Feed my sheep"
Lk 22:31-32 ... "Simon ... strengthen your brethren".
Lk 10:1-2, 16; Jn 13:20; 2 Cor 5:20; Gal 4:14; Acts 5:1-5 ... "Vicars" (substitutes) of Christ.
Mk 6:20; Lk 1:70, 2:23; Rom 12:1; Act 3:21, 1 Cor 7:14; Eph 3:5; Col 1:22 ... Humans can be holy ("call no one holy").

Appendix 1 - Apologetics Cheat Sheet

Church and authority
Acts 2:42 ... Doctrine, community, sacred rite (bread).
Eph 5:25-26 ... Christ loved the Church.
1 Tim 3:15 ... Church is pillar/foundation of truth.
Mt 16:18; 20:20 ... Christ protects Church.
Heb 13:17 ... Obey the Church.
Mt 18:17-18 ... Church as final authority.
Mt 23:2 ... Pharisees succeeded Moses (seat of Moses).
1 Cor 5:5; 1 Tim 1:20 ... Excommunication.

Priesthood and worship
*1Tim 4:1-3 - Forbidding marriage is a doctrine of demons
*1Tim 3:2 - Bishop must be married only once
Eph 5:21-33 - Marriage is good: holy symbol of Christ & church
Mt 19:12; 1 Cor 7:32, 33 - Celibacy praised by Jesus, who was chaste
Jer 16:1-4 - Jeremiah told not to take wife & have children
1Cor 7:8 - St. Paul was celibate
1Cor 7:32-35 - Celibacy recommended for full-time ministers
2Tim 2:3-4 - No soldier gets entangled in civilian pursuits
1Tim 5:9-12 - Pledge of celibacy taken by older widows
Acts 1:15-26; 2 Tim 2:2; Tit 1:5 ...Unbroken succession.
Acts 15:6, 23; 1 Tim 4:14, 5:22; 1 Tim 5:17; Jas 5:13-15 ...
Presbyters/elders (priests) were ordained, preached and taught the flock, administered sacraments.
Lk 16:24; Rom 4; 1 Cor 4:14-15; Acts 7:2; 1 Thess 2:11; 1 Jn 2:13-14 ...
"Call no one father"?
1 Cor 7:7-9 ... Paul unmarried.
Gen 14:18; Ps 110:4; Heb 7:1-17 ... Melchizedek.
Rev 4:8 ... "Vain repetition"?
1 Kg 8:54; 2 Chr 6:13; Ezra 9:5; Mt 17:14; Lk 5:8 ... Kneeling.
Rev 8:3-4 ... Incense.
1 Cor 12 ... Different roles of members of body.

Mary - Perpetual Virginity
Lk 1:34 - How can this be, since I do not know man
Lk 2:41-51 - Age 12, Jesus evidently only son of Mary
Mk 6:3 - "The son of Mary" not "a son of Mary"
*Mt 13:55-56 - Brothers James, Joseph, Simon & Jude
Mt 27:56 - Mary the mother of James & Joseph also
Jn 19:25 - Mary the wife of Clopas
Jn 19:26 - Entrusted Mary to John, not a younger sibling
Jn 7:3-4 - Brothers advise like elders: "go to Judea, manifest self" unthinkable for younger siblings (see next verse)
Mk 3:21 - Set out to seize him, "he is out of his mind"
Mt 28:20 - I am with you always, until the end of the age
1Tim 4:13 - Until I arrive, attend to reading, teaching...

Appendix 1 - Apologetics Cheat Sheet

1Cor 15:25 - He must reign until has enemies underfoot
Lk 1:80 - John in desert until day of his manifestation
Ex 13:2; Nb 3:12 - Consecrate first -born that opens womb
Ex 34:20 - First-born among your sons you shall redeem
Gen 5:24; Heb 11:5; 2 Kings 2:1-13 ... Enoch and Elijah taken to heaven.
Lk 1:28 ... Annunciation – she is a Virgin, does not understand how she can have children EVER.
Lk 1:42-48 ... Blessed are you among women.
2 Tim 4:8, Jas 1:12, 1 Pet 5:4, Rev 2:10 ... Coronation awaits saints.
Jn 2:1-5 ... Mary's intercession.

Saints
Mk 12:26-27 ... "Not God of the dead, but of the living."
Jn 15:1-8 ... Vine and its branches.
1 Cor 12:25-27; Rom 12:4-5 ... Body of Christ.
Eph 6:18; Rom 15:30; Col 4:3; 1 Thess 1:11 ... Intercessory prayer.
Jos 5:14; Dan 8:17; Tob 12:16 ... Veneration of angels united with God (Mt 18:10).
1 Cor 13:12; 1 John 3:2 ... Saints also united with God.
Lk 20-34-38 ... Those who died are like angels.
2 Mac 15:11-16 ... Deceased Onias and Jeremiah interceded for Jews.
Rev 8:3-4; Jer 15:1 ... Saints' intercession.

Statues, images and relics
Ex 25:18-22, 26:1, 31; Num 21:8-9 God commands images made.
1 Kings 6:23-29, 35, 7:29 ... Solomon's temple: statues & images.
Acts 19:11, 12 ... Paul's handkerchiefs and aprons.
2 Kg 13:20-21 ... Elisha's bones.
Acts 5:15-16 ... Peter's shadow.
Mt 9:20-22 ... Jesus' Tallit (Prayer Shawl) cures woman.

Justification
1 Jn 1:7, 2 Pet 1:9 ... Purified from sins.
Jn 1:29, Heb 9:26-28 ... Takes away sin.
Ps 50:3, Ps 102:12, Is 43:25 ... Blot out, clear away sin.
Rom 2:13, Rom 3:20 ... Future justification.
Heb 11:8...Gen 12:1-4; Rom 4:2-3...Gen 15:6; Jas 2:21-23...Gen 22:1-18 ... Justifications of Abraham.
2 Pet 1:4 ... Become partakers of the divine nature.
Eph 2:10 – We are created in Christ for Good Works
Gal 2:20 – Christ lives through us, and our works are His

Appendix 1 - Apologetics Cheat Sheet

Contraception
Gn 38:9-10 God killed Onan for spilling seed [see next]
Dt 25:5-10 - Penalty for defying Levitical law: not death
Gn 1:27-28 (Gn 9:1, 35:11) - Be fruitful and multiply
Ps 127:3-5 - Children gift from God, blessed is a full quiver
1Chr 25:5 - God gave 14 sons & 3 daughters to exalt him
1Chr 26:4-5 - God indeed blessed Obededom with 8 sons
Hos 9:10-17 - Israel is punished with childlessness
Ex 23:25-26 - Blessings promised: no miscarrying, barrenness
Lv 21:17-20 - Crushed testicles is called a defect & blemish
Dt 23:1 - No one castrated shall enter the assembly
Dt 25:11-12 - Punishment for potential damage to genitals
Rom 1:25-27 - Natural function of women = childbearing
1Tim 2:11-15 - Women saved through the bearing of children
Acts 5:1-11 - Ananias/Saphira slain - withholding part of gift
Gal 6:7 - God is not mocked-accepting pleasure, denying fruit
Mt 21:19, Mk 11:14 - Jesus cursed fruitless fig tree
Gal 5:20, Rv 9:21, 21:8 - Greek pharmakeia = causes abortions
1Cor 6:19-20 - Body temple of the Holy Spirit, glorify God with body

Homosexuality
Gn 1:27 - Complementarity of sexes reflects God's inner unity
Gn 2:21-24 - Transmission of life through total self-donation - one flesh
Gn 19 - Original sin deteriorates to Sodom's sin, destroyed
Lv 18:22 - Called abomination, cut off from people (v.29)
Lv 20:13 - Both shall be put to death for abominable deed
Rom 1:27 - Called unnatural, shameful, and a perversity
1Cor 6:9 - Active homosexuals won't inherit kingdom of God
1Tim 1:9-10 - Those who engage in such acts called sinners

Drinking Wine
Gn 27:25 - Isaac brought Jacob wine, and he drank
* Dt 14:23-26 - Spend money on sheep, wine, & strong drink
* Prov 20:1 - Wine is a mocker, unwise to be led astray by it
Eccl 9:7 - Drink your wine with merry heart - God approves
Is 25:6 - God will provide feast of rich foods & choice wines
Is 5:11 - Woe to those who rise early & run after strong drink
Is 5:22 - Woe to those who are heroes at drinking wine
* Luke 7:33-34 - Son of man eats & drinks: behold glutton & drunk
Jn 2:2-10 - Miracle at Cana: water turned into good wine
* Eph 5:18 - Do not get drunk with wine, that is debauchery
1Tim 5:23 - Drink a little wine for the sake of your stomach

Appendix 1 - Apologetics Cheat Sheet

Communion of Saints
Eph 1:22-23 - He is head of the Church, which is His body
Eph 5:21-32 - Christ is the head of the Church, Savior of the body
Col 1:18, 24 - He is head of the body, the Church
1Cor 12:12-27 - If I suffer, all suffer; if I am honored, all rejoice
Rom 12:5 - We are one body in Christ, individual parts of one another
Eph 4:4 - One body, one Spirit, called to one hope
Col 3:15 - You were called in one body
Rom 8:35-39 - Death cannot separate us from Christ
Rom 12:10 - Love one another with mutual affection
1Thess 5:11 - Encourage, build up one another
Gal 6:2 - Bear one another's burdens
Gal 6:10 - Let us do good to all, especially those in family of faith

Intercessory Prayer of Saints
Rom 15:30 - Join me by your prayers to God on my behalf
Col 4:3, 1Thess 5:25 - Pray for us
2Thess 1:11 - We always pray for you
2Thess 3:1 - Finally, brothers, pray for us
Eph 6:18-19 - Making supplication for all the saints & for me
Tob 12:12 - Angel presents Tobit & Sarah's prayer to God
Ps 148 - David calls upon angels
Zech 1:12 - Angel intercedes for Jerusalem
Mk 12:25, Mt 22:30 - Men in heaven are as the angels
Rev 5:8 - Those in heaven offer prayers of the holy ones to God
*Saints dead, prayer is necromancy (Dt 18:10-11)
Mk 12:26-27 - He is God of the living, not of the dead
Mk 9:4 - Jesus seen conversing with Elijah & Moses
Lk 9:31 - Elijah & Moses aware of earthly events
Rev 6:9-11 - Martyrs under altar want earthly vindication
Heb 12:1 - We are surrounded by a cloud of witnesses
Lk 16:19-30 - Departed rich man intercedes for brothers
Rev 20:4 - Saw the souls of those who had been beheaded
Wis 3:1-6 - The souls of the just are in the hand of God
2Macc 15:7-16 - Dead Onias & Jeremiah pray for the Jews
Jas 5:16 Prayers of righteous man
1 Cor. 13:12 - I shall understand fully
1 John 4: 20-21 - Whoever loves God must love his brother
1 Cor 12:21 - Parts of Christ's Body cannot say to other parts, "I do not need you".
*1Tim 2:5 - "One mediator between God and man"
1Tim 2:1-7 - Offer prayers, petitions for all men
1Pet 2:5 - Be a holy priesthood to offer sacrifices through Christ
Mk 10:18 - Only God is good
Mt 25:23 - Well done my good and faithful servant
Jn 10:11-16 - I am good shepherd; one flock I shepherd

Appendix 1 - Apologetics Cheat Sheet

Jn 21:15-16 - Feed my lambs, tend my sheep
Eph 4:11 - He gave some as apostles...others as pastors
Heb 3:1, 7:24, 9:12-13 - Jesus eternal high priest; one sacrifice
Rev 1:6, 5:10 - He made us a kingdom of priests for God

Veneration of Saints
Jos 5:14 - Joshua fell prostrate in worship before angel
Dan 8:17 - Daniel fell prostrate in terror before Gabriel
Tob 12:16 - Tobiah & Tobit fall to ground before Raphael
Mt 18:10 - Angels in heaven always behold face of God (we venerate angels because of their great dignity, which comes from their union with God. Saints also are united with God)
1Jn 3:2 - We shall be like him, we shall see him as he is
1Thess 1:5-8 - You become an example to all the believers
Heb 13:7 - Remember leaders, consider/imitate their faith & life

Relics
2 Kgs 13:20-21 - Contact with Elisha's bones restored life
Acts 5:15-116 - Cures performed through Peter's shadow
Acts 19:11-12 - Cures through face cloths that touched Paul

Statues
*Ex 20:4-5 - Do not make and worship any graven images
Ex 25:18-19 - Make two cherubim of beaten gold
Num 21:8-9 - Moses made bronze serpent & put on pole
1Kgs 6:23-29 - Temple had engraved cherubim, trees, flowers
1Kgs 7:25-45 - Temple had bronze oxen, lions, pomegranates

Scandals in the Church
Jer 32:32-35 - OT leaders & priests offered child sacrifices
2Kgs 23:7 - OT cult prostitutes in the temple of the Lord
Jn 4:22 - In spite of their infidelity, salvation is from Jews
Mk 14:43-46 - Judas betrayed Jesus
Mk 14:66-72 Peter denied him
Jn 20:24-25 Thomas refused to believe his resurrection
Mk 14:50 - They all left him and fled in garden of Gethsemane
Rom 3:3-4 - Will their infidelity nullify fidelity of God? No!
2Tim 2:13 - If we are unfaithful, God remains faithful
Mt 13:24-30 - Parable of the weeds among the wheat
Mt 13:47-48 - Parable of net that collects good and bad

Appendix 1 - Apologetics Cheat Sheet

Fasting
*1Tim 4:3 - Condemns anti-flesh heretics
* Mk 7:19 - Christ declared all food clean
* 1Tim 4:4-5 - Everything created by God is good
Dan 10:3 - Daniel refused to eat choice foods for 3 weeks
Mt 9:15 - Christ's followers will fast once he is gone
Mt 6:16-18 - Jesus gave regulations concerning how to fast

Divinity of Jesus
Jn 1:1 - The Word was God
Jn 1:14-15 - Glory of Father's only Son, full of grace and truth
Jn 8:19 - If you knew me, you would know my Father
Jn 8:58-59 - I assure you, before Abraham was, I AM
Jn 10:30-33 - The Father and I are one (see Ex 3:14, 20:7; Lev 19:12, 24:14-16)
Jn 10:38 - The Father is in me and I am in the Father
Jn 12:45 - Whosoever sees me sees the one who sent me
Jn 14:8-12 - Whoever had seen has seen the Father
Jn 20:28 - Jesus accepts Thomas's "my Lord and my God"
Col 2:9 - In him dwells whole fullness of deity bodily
Acts 20:28 - Church of God he acquired with his blood
Eph 1:7 - In him we have redemption by his blood
1Jn 1:7 - Blood of his Son Jesus cleanses from all sin
Tit 2:13 - Glory of our great God and Savior, Jesus Christ

Time of Second Coming Unknown
Mt 24:44 - Be prepared, Jesus coming at unexpected hour
Mt 25:13 - Stay awake, you know neither the day nor hour
Mk 13:35-37 - Watch, unknown when lord of house coming
Lk 12:46 - Master will come like a thief in night
1Thess 5:2-3 - Day of Lord will come like a thief in night
2Pet 3:9-10 - Day of lord will come like a thief
Rev 3:3 - If not watchful, will come like a thief
Mt 24:36 - No one but Father alone knows day and hour

Repetitious Prayer
*Mt 6:7 - Do not babble like pagans with their many words
*1Kgs 18:25-29 - Example of vain repetition: call Baal for hours
Mt 26:44 - Jesus prayed a third time, saying the same thing again
Lk 18:13 - Collector kept beating breast & praying: be merciful
Rev 4:8 - Repeat day & night, "Holy, holy, holy is the Lord"
1Thess 5:17 - Pray without ceasing
Ps 136 (26X 'His steadfast love endures forever')
Mt 6:9-13 Our Father

Appendix 1 - Apologetics Cheat Sheet

Holy Spirit a Person, Not a Force
Jn 14:26 - "He will teach you all things"
Acts 8:29 - "And the Spirit said to Philip, 'Go up...''
Acts 13:2 - "Holy Spirit said, 'Set apart for me...'"
Rom 8:27 - "Spirit intercedes for the saints..."
1Cor 2:11 - No one understands the thoughts of God, but Spirit
1Cor 12:11 - Spirit apportions to each as he wills
Eph 4:30 - "Do not grieve the Holy Spirit of God"
Gen 1:2 – Holy Spirit participating in Creation with Water

Judgment
Mt 5:22 – Even calling another a Fool will be enough for Hell..
Mt 10:15 – Rejecting Apostles will bring destruction like Sodom
Mt 12:36-42 – You must account for every careless word
Mt 25:31 – Judgment Description in Gospels – judged by Deeds
Lk 10:14 – Rejecting the message of Christ leads to destruction
Jn 3:19 – Jesus not brought to judge the world, but those who love the light and does good will be acceptable to God.
Jn 5:22-30 – The Son has authority to Judge.
Jn 7:24 - Do not judge by appearance
Jn 8:16 – If I do Judge, My judgment is true b/c God is with Me
Jn 9:39 – For Judgment I came into this world
Jn 12:31 – Now judgment is on this world
Jn 16:8-11 – Holy Spirit will come and convict the world
Rom 2:1-5 – Do not Judge – God alone Judges
1 Cor 4:5, Rom 14:3-13 – Do not judge others
1 Cor 5:3 – Paul renders judgment
1 Cor 11:29 – Taking the Eucharist unworthily brings Judgment
2 Cor 5:10 – All Christians must appear before the Judgment seat
1 Tim 5:24 – Sins of men bring Judgment
Heb 6:2 – Judgment one of 6 basic Christian beliefs
Heb 9:27 – All men die once then judgment
Heb 10:27 – If you continue to sin after baptism, you are lost
Jam 2:13 – Judgment merciless to those who show no mercy
1 Pet 4:17 – Obey the Gospel or fear judgment
2 Pet 2:4-11 – God cast Angels, ancient world, Sodom, etc. into Hell, unrighteous will be condemned
2 Pet 3:7 – Ungodly men destroyed at judgment
1 Jn 4:17 – Perfect love provides confidence for judgment
Jude 1:5-15 – Judgment of the unfaithful will be terrible
Rev 14:7, Rev 15:4, Rev 16:7, Rev 17:1, Rev 18:10, Rev 18:20, Rev 19:2, Rev 20:4-15, Rev 21:8, Rev 22:1 – The Judgment process in Revelation.

Appendix 2: The list of the Popes

1. St. Peter (32-67)
2. St. Linus (67-76)
3. St. Anacletus (Cletus) (76-88)
4. St. Clement I (88-97)
5. St. Evaristus (97-105)
6. St. Alexander I (105-115)
7. St. Sixtus I (115-125)
8. St. Telesphorus (125-136)
9. St. Hyginus (136-140)
10. St. Pius I (140-155)
11. St. Anicetus (155-166)
12. St. Soter (166-175)
13. St. Eleutherius (175-189)
14. St. Victor I (189-199)
15. St. Zephyrinus (199-217)
16. St. Callistus I (217-22
17. St. Urban I (222-30)
18. St. Pontain (230-35)
19. St. Anterus (235-36)
20. St. Fabian (236-50)
21. St. Cornelius (251-53)
22. St. Lucius I (253-54)
23. St. Stephen I (254-257)
24. St. Sixtus II (257-258)
25. St. Dionysius (260-268)
26. St. Felix I (269-274)
27. St. Eutychian (275-283)
28. St. Caius (283-296)
29. St. Marcellinus (296-304)
30. St. Marcellus I (308-309)
31. St. Eusebius (309 or 310)
32. St. Miltiades (311-14)
33. St. Sylvester I (314-35)
34. St. Marcus (336)
35. St. Julius I (337-52)
36. Liberius (352-66)
37. St. Damasus I (366-83)
38. St. Siricius (384-99)
39. St. Anastasius I (399-401)
40. St. Innocent I (401-17)
41. St. Zosimus (417-18)
42. St. Boniface I (418-22)
43. St. Celestine I (422-32)
44. St. Sixtus III (432-40)
45. St. Leo I (the Great) (440-61)
46. St. Hilarius (461-68)
47. St. Simplicius (468-83)
48. St. Felix III (II) (483-92)
49. St. Gelasius I (492-96)
50. Anastasius II (496-98)
51. St. Symmachus (498-514)
52. St. Hormisdas (514-23)
53. St. John I (523-26)
54. St. Felix IV (III) (526-30)
55. Boniface II (530-32)
56. John II (533-35)
57. St. Agapetus I (535-36)
58. St. Silverius (536-37)
59. Vigilius (537-55)
60. Pelagius I (556-61)
61. John III (561-74)
62. Benedict I (575-79)
63. Pelagius II (579-90)
64. St. Gregory I (the Great) (590-604)
65. Sabinian (604-606)
66. Boniface III (607)
67. St. Boniface IV (608-15)
68. St. Adeodatus I (615-18)
69. Boniface V (619-25)
70. Honorius I (625-38)
71. Severinus (640)
72. John IV (640-42)
73. Theodore I (642-49)
74. St. Martin I (649-55)
75. St. Eugene I (655-57)
76. St. Vitalian (657-72)
77. Adeodatus (II) (672-76)
78. Donus (676-78)
79. St. Agatho (678-81)
80. St. Leo II (682-83)
81. St. Benedict II (684-85)
82. John V (685-86)
83. Conon (686-87)
84. St. Sergius I (687-701)
85. John VI (701-05)
86. John VII (705-07)
87. Sisinnius (708)
88. Constantine (708-15)
89. St. Gregory II (715-31)
90. St. Gregory III (731-41)
91. St. Zachary (741-52)
92. Stephen III (752-57)
93. St. Paul I (757-67)
94. Stephen IV (767-72)

Appendix 2: The List of Popes

95. Adrian I (772-95)
96. St. Leo III (795-816)
97. Stephen V (816-17)
98. St. Paschal I (817-24)
99. Eugene II (824-27)
100. Valentine (827)
101. Gregory IV (827-44)
102. Sergius II (844-47)
103. St. Leo IV (847-55)
104. Benedict III (855-58
105. St. Nicholas I (858-67)
106. Adrian II (867-72)
107. John VIII (872-82)
108. Marinus I (882-84)
109. St. Adrian III (884-85)
110. Stephen VI (885-91)
111. Formosus (891-96)
112. Boniface VI (896)
113. Stephen VII (896-97)
114. Romanus (897)
115. Theodore II (897)
116. John IX (898-900)
117. Benedict IV (900-03)
118. Leo V (903)
119. Sergius III (904-11)
120. Anastasius III (911-13)
121. Lando (913-14)
122. John X (914-28)
123. Leo VI (928)
124. Stephen VIII (929-31)
125. John XI (931-35)
126. Leo VII (936-39)
127. Stephen IX (939-42)
128. Marinus II (942-46)
129. Agapetus II (946-55)
130. John XII (955-63)
131. Leo VIII (963-64)
132. Benedict V (964)
133. John XIII (965-72)
134. Benedict VI (973-74)
135. Benedict VII (974-83
136. John XIV (983-84)
137. John XV (985-96)
138. Gregory V (996-99)
139. Sylvester II (999-1003)
140. John XVII (1003)
141. John XVIII (1003-09)
142. Sergius IV (1009-12)
143. Benedict VIII (1012-24)
144. John XIX (1024-32)
145. Benedict IX (1032-45)
146. Sylvester III (1045)
147. Benedict IX (1045)
148. Gregory VI (1045-46)
149. Clement II (1046-47)
150. Benedict IX (1047-48)
151. Damasus II (1048)
152. St. Leo IX (1049-54)
153. Victor II (1055-57)
154. Stephen X (1057-58)
155. Nicholas II (1058-61)
156. Alexander II (1061-73)
157. St. Gregory VII (1073-85)
158. Blessed Victor III (1086-87)
159. Blessed Urban II (1088-99)
160. Paschal II (1099-1118)
161. Gelasius II (1118-19)
162. Callistus II (1119-24)
163. Honorius II (1124-30)
164. Innocent II (1130-43
165. Celestine II (1143-44)
166. Lucius II (1144-45)
167. Blessed Eugene III (1145-53)
168. Anastasius IV (1153-54)
169. Adrian IV (1154-59)
170. Alexander III (1159-81)
171. Lucius III (1181-85)
172. Urban III (1185-87)
173. Gregory VIII (1187)
174. Clement III (1187-91)
175. Celestine III (1191-98)
176. Innocent III (1198-1216)
177. Honorius III (1216-27)
178. Gregory IX (1227-41)
179. Celestine IV (1241)
180. Innocent IV (1243-54)
181. Alexander IV (1254-61)
182. Urban IV (1261-64)
183. Clement IV (1265-68)
184. Blessed Gregory X (1271-76)
185. Blessed Innocent V (1276)
186. Adrian V (1276)
187. John XXI (1276-77)
188. Nicholas III (1277-80)
189. Martin IV (1281-85)
190. Honorius IV (1285-87)
191. Nicholas IV (1288-92)
192. St. Celestine V (1294)
193. Boniface VIII (1294-1303)
194. Blessed Benedict XI (1303-04)

Appendix 2: The List of Popes

195. Clement V (1305-14)
196. John XXII (1316-34)
197. Benedict XII (1334-42)
198. Clement VI (1342-52)
199. Innocent VI (1352-62)
200. Blessed Urban V (1362-70)
201. Gregory XI (1370-78)
202. Urban VI (1378-89)
203. Boniface IX (1389-1404)
204. Innocent VII (1404-06)
205. Gregory XII (1406-15)
206. Martin V (1417-31)
207. Eugene IV (1431-47)
208. Nicholas V (1447-55)
209. Callistus III (1455-58)
210. Pius II (1458-64)
211. Paul II (1464-71)
212. Sixtus IV (1471-84)
213. Innocent VIII (1484-92)
214. Alexander VI (1492-1503)
215. Pius III (1503)
216. Julius II (1503-13)
217. Leo X (1513-21)
218. Adrian VI (1522-23)
219. Clement VII (1523-34)
220. Paul III (1534-49)
221. Julius III (1550-55)
222. Marcellus II (1555)
223. Paul IV (1555-59)
224. Pius IV (1559-65)
225. St. Pius V (1566-72)
226. Gregory XIII (1572-85)
227. Sixtus V (1585-90)
228. Urban VII (1590)
229. Gregory XIV (1590-91)
230. Innocent IX (1591)
231. Clement VIII (1592-1605)
232. Leo XI (1605)
233. Paul V (1605-21)
234. Gregory XV (1621-23)
235. Urban VIII (1623-44)
236. Innocent X (1644-55)
237. Alexander VII (1655-67)
238. Clement IX (1667-69)
239. Clement X (1670-76)
240. Blessed Innocent XI (1676-89)
241. Alexander VIII (1689-91)
242. Innocent XII (1691-1700)
243. Clement XI (1700-21)
244. Innocent XIII (1721-24)
245. Benedict XIII (1724-30)
246. Clement XII (1730-40)
247. Benedict XIV (1740-58)
248. Clement XIII (1758-69)
249. Clement XIV (1769-74)
250. Pius VI (1775-99)
251. Pius VII (1800-23)
252. Leo XII (1823-29)
253. Pius VIII (1829-30)
254. Gregory XVI (1831-46)
255. Blessed Pius IX (1846-78)
256. Leo XIII (1878-1903)
257. St. Pius X (1903-14)
258. Benedict XV (1914-22)
259. Pius XI (1922-39)
260. Pius XII (1939-58)
261. Blessed John XXIII (1958-63)
262. Paul VI (1963-78)
263. John Paul I (1978)
264. Blessed John Paul II (1978-2005)
265. Benedict XVI (2005-2013)
266. Francis (2013—)

Appendix 3: A Chronology of Early Church Writings

Old Testament		New Testament	
Job--	Unknown	James--	A.D. 44-49
Genesis--	1445-1405 B.C.	Galatians--	A.D. 49-50
Exodus--	1445-1405 B.C.	Matthew--	A.D. 33-60
Leviticus--	1445-1405 B.C.	Mark--	A.D. 33-60
Numbers--	1445-1405 B.C.	1 Thessalonians--	A.D. 51
Deuteronomy--	1445-1405 B.C.	2 Thessalonians--	A.D. 51-52
Psalms--	1410-450 B.C.	1 Corinthians--	A.D. 55
Joshua--	1405-1385 B.C.	2 Corinthians--	A.D. 55-56
Judges--	c. 1043 B.C.	Romans--	A.D. 56
Ruth--	c. 1030-1010 B.C.	Luke--	A.D. 60-61
Song of Solomon--	971-965 B.C.	Ephesians--	A.D. 60-62
Proverbs--	c. 971-686 B.C.	Philippians--	A.D. 60-62
Ecclesiastes--	940-931 B.C.	Philemon--	A.D. 60-62
1 Samuel--	931-722 B.C.	Colossians--	A.D. 60-62
2 Samuel--	931-722 B.C.	Acts--	A.D. 62
Obadiah--	850-840 B.C.	1 Timothy--	A.D. 62-64
Joel--	835-796 B.C.	Titus--	A.D. 62-64
Jonah--	c. 775 B.C.	1 Peter--	A.D. 64-65
Amos--	c. 750 B.C.	2 Timothy--	A.D. 66-67
Hosea--	750-710 B.C.	2 Peter--	A.D. 67-68
Micah--	735-710 B.C.	Hebrews--	A.D. 67-69
Isaiah--	700-681 B.C.	Jude--	A.D. 68-70
Nahum--	c. 650 B.C.	John--	A.D. 80-90
Zephaniah--	635-625 B.C.	1 John--	A.D. 90-95
Habakkuk--	615-605 B.C.	2 John--	A.D. 90-95
Ezekiel--	590-570 B.C.	3 John--	A.D. 90-95
Lamentations--	586 B.C.	Revelation--	A.D. 50-70
Jeremiah--	586-570 B.C.		
1 Kings--	561-538 B.C.		
2 Kings--	561-538 B.C.		
Daniel	536-530 B.C.		
Haggai--	c. 520 B.C.		
Zechariah--	480-470 B.C.		
Ezra--	457-444 B.C.		
1 Chronicles--	450-430 B.C		
2 Chronicles--	450-430 B.C.		
Esther--	450-331 B.C.		
Malachi--	433-424 B.C.		
Nehemiah--	424-400 B.C..		

Appendix 3: A Chronology of Early Church Writings

Other Early Church Writings

30-60 Passion Narrative
40-80 Lost Sayings Gospel Q
50-60 **1 Thessalonians**
50-60 **Philippians**
50-60 **Galatians**
50-60 **1 Corinthians**
50-60 **2 Corinthians**
50-60 **Romans**
50-60 **Philemon**
50-80 **Colossians**
50-90 Signs Gospel
50-95 **Book of Hebrews**
50-120 Didache
50-140 Gospel of Thomas
50-140 Oxyrhynchus 1224 Gospel
50-200 Sophia of Jesus Christ
65-80 **Gospel of Mark**
70-100 **Epistle of James**
70-120 Egerton Gospel
70-160 Gospel of Peter
70-160 Secret Mark
70-200 Fayyum Fragment
70-200 Testaments of the Twelve Patriarchs
73-200 Mara Bar Serapion
80-100 **2 Thessalonians**
80-100 **Ephesians**
80-100 **Gospel of Matthew**
80-110 **1 Peter**
80-120 Epistle of Barnabas
80-130 **Gospel of Luke**
80-130 **Acts of the Apostles**
80-140 1 Clement
80-150 Gospel of the Egyptians
80-150 Gospel of the Hebrews
80-250 Christian Sibyllines
90-95 **Apocalypse of John**
90-120 **Gospel of John**
90-120 **1 John**
90-120 **2 John**
90-120 **3 John**
90-120 **Epistle of Jude**
93 Flavius Josephus
100-150 **1 Timothy**
100-150 **2 Timothy**
100-150 **Titus**
100-150 Apocalypse of Peter
100-150 Secret Book of James
100-150 Preaching of Peter
100-160 Gospel of the Ebionites
100-160 Gospel of the Nazoreans
100-160 Shepherd of Hermas
100-160 **2 Peter**
100-200 Odes of Solomon
101-220 Book of Elchasai
105-115 Ignatius of Antioch
110-140 Polycarp to the Philippians
110-140 Papias
110-160 Oxyrhynchus 840 Gospel
110-160 Traditions of Matthias
111-112 Pliny the Younger
115 Suetonius
115 Tacitus
120-130 Quadratus of Athens
120-130 Apology of Aristides
120-140 Basilides
120-140 Naassene Fragment
120-160 Valentinus
120-180 Apocryphon of John
120-180 Gospel of Mary
120-180 Dialogue of the Savior
120-180 Gospel of the Savior
120-180 2nd Apocalypse of James
120-180 Trimorphic Protennoia
130-140 Marcion
130-150 Aristo of Pella
130-160 Epiphanes On Righteousness
130-160 Ophite Diagrams
130-160 2 Clement
130-170 Gospel of Judas
130-200 Epistle of Mathetes to Diognetus
140-150 Epistula Apostolorum
140-160 Ptolemy
140-160 Isidore
140-170 Fronto
140-170 Infancy Gospel of James
140-170 Infancy Gospel of Thomas
140-180 Gospel of Truth
150-160 Martyrdom of Polycarp
150-160 Justin Martyr
150-180 Excerpts of Theodotus
150-180 Heracleon
150-200 Ascension of Isaiah
150-200 Acts of Peter
150-200 Acts of John
150-200 Acts of Paul
150-200 Acts of Andrew
150-225 Acts of Peter and the Twelve
150-225 Book of Thomas the Contender
150-250 Fifth and Sixth Books of Esra
150-300 Authoritative Teaching
150-300 Coptic Apocalypse of Paul
150-300 Discourse on the Eighth and Ninth
150-300 Melchizedek
150-400 Acts of Pilate
150-400 Anti-Marcionite Prologues

Appendix 3: A Chronology of Early Church Writings

160-170 Tatian's Address to the Greeks
160-180 Claudius Apollinaris
160-180 Apelles
160-180 Julius Cassianus
160-250 Octavius of Minucius Felix
161-180 Acts of Carpus
165-175 Melito of Sardis
165-175 Hegesippus
165-175 Dionysius of Corinth
165-175 Lucian of Samosata
167 Marcus Aurelius
170-175 Diatessaron
170-200 Dura-Europos Gospel Harmony
170-200 Muratorian Canon
170-200 Treatise on the Resurrection
170-220 Letter of Peter to Philip
175-180 Athenagoras of Athens
175-185 Irenaeus of Lyons
175-185 Rhodon
175-185 Theophilus of Caesarea
175-190 Galen
178 Celsus
178 Letter from Vienna and Lyons
180 Passion of the Scillitan Martyrs
180-185 Theophilus of Antioch
180-185 Acts of Apollonius
180-220 Bardesanes
180-220 Kerygmata Petrou
180-230 Hippolytus of Rome
180-250 1st Apocalypse of James
180-250 Gospel of Philip
182-202 Clement of Alexandria
185-195 Maximus of Jerusalem
185-195 Polycrates of Ephesus
188-217 Talmud
189-199 Victor I
190-210 Pantaenus
193 Anonymous Anti-Montanist
193-216 Inscription of Abercius
197-220 Tertullian
200-210 Serapion of Antioch
200-210 Apollonius
200-220 Caius
200-220 Philostratus
200-225 Acts of Thomas
200-250 Didascalia
200-250 Books of Jeu
200-300 Pistis Sophia
200-300 Coptic Apocalypse of Peter
203 Acts of Perpetua and Felicitas
203-250 Origen

Appendix 4: A table of the Early Church Canons

Some of the early known canons are:

- The Muratorian Fragment (c. 170 AD)
- Melito (c. 170 AD)
- Origen (c. 240 AD)
- Eusebius of Caesarea (c. 324 AD)
- Cyril of Jerusalem (c. 350 AD)
- Hilary of Poitiers (c. 360 AD)
- The Cheltenham List (c. 360 AD)
- Council of Laodiocia (c. 363 AD)
- Letter of Ananasius (367 AD)
- Gregory of Nazianzus (c. 380 AD)
- Amphilochius of Iconium (c. 380 AD)
- Apostolic Canons (c. 380 AD)
- Epiphanius of Salamis (c. 385 AD)
- St. Jerome (c. 390 AD)
- St. Augustine (c. 397 AD)
- **Third Council of Carthage (c. 397 AD)**
- Codex Claromontanus (c. 400 AD)
- Rufinus of Aquileia (c. 400 AD)
- Innocent I (c. 405 AD)
- Decree of Gelasius (c. 550 AD)
- Sixty Canonical Books (c. 7th Cent. AD)
- Stichometery of Nicephorus (810 AD)

A table of some of the canons are shown on the following pages – the explanation of the symbols used in these tables is shown below:

Explanation on the Symbols:

Allowable	A
Deuterocanonical	D
Rejected	R
Questioned	Q
Included in Canon	●
Not Mentioned	-

Appendix 4: Some of the Early Church Canons

A table of some of the Canons are shown below –
The Old Testament:

Book	Date Written	170 AD - Muratorian Fragment	170 AD - Melito	240 AD - Origen from Eusebius	324 AD - Eusebius	350 AD - Cyril of Jerusalem	360 AD - Hilary of Poitiers	360 AD - The Cheltenham List	363 AD - Council of Laodicea	367 AD - Athanasius of Alexandria	380 AD - Gregory of Nazianzus	380 AD - Amphilochius of Iconium	380 AD - Apostolic Canons	385 AD - Epiphanius of Salamis	390 AD - St. Jerome	397 AD - St. Augustine	397 AD - Third Council of Carthage	400 AD - Codex Claromontanus	400 AD - Rufinus of Aquileia	405 AD - Innocent I	550 AD - Decree of Gelasius	7th Cent. AD - Cat. o/t Sixty Canonical Books	810 AD - Stichometery of Nicephorus
Genesis	1445-1405 B.C.	-	●	●	-	●	●	●	●	●	●	●	●	●	●	●	●	●	●	●	●	●	●
Exodus	1445-1405 B.C.	-	●	●	-	●	●	●	●	●	●	●	●	●	●	●	●	●	●	●	●	●	●
Leviticus	1445-1405 B.C.	-	●	●	-	●	●	●	●	●	●	●	●	●	●	●	●	●	●	●	●	●	●
Deuteronomy	1445-1405 B.C.	-	●	●	-	●	●	●	●	●	●	●	●	●	●	●	●	●	●	●	●	●	●
Numbers	1445-1405 B.C.	-	●	●	-	●	●	●	●	●	●	●	●	●	●	●	●	●	●	●	●	●	●
Joshua	1405-1385 B.C.	-	●	●	-	●	●	●	●	●	●	●	●	●	●	●	●	●	●	●	●	●	●
Judges	c. 1043 B.C.	-	●	●	-	●	●	●	●	●	●	●	●	●	●	●	●	●	●	●	●	●	●
Ruth	c. 1030-1010 B.C.	-	●	●	-	●	●	●	●	●	●	●	●	●	●	●	●	●	●	●	●	●	●
1 Kings	561-538 B.C.	-	●	●	-	●	●	●	●	●	●	●	●	●	●	●	●	●	●	●	●	●	●
2 Kings	561-538 B.C.	-	●	●	-	●	●	●	●	●	●	●	●	●	●	●	●	●	●	●	●	●	●
3 Kings/1 Samuel	931-722 B.C.	-	●	●	-	●	●	●	●	●	●	●	●	●	●	●	●	●	●	●	●	●	●
4 Kings/2 Samuel	931-722 B.C.	-	●	●	-	●	●	●	●	●	●	●	●	●	●	●	●	●	●	●	●	●	●
1 Chronicles/Book of Days	450-430 B.C.	-	●	●	-	●	●	●	●	●	●	●	●	●	●	●	●	-	●	●	●	●	●
2 Chronicles/Book of Days	450-430 B.C.	-	●	●	-	●	●	●	●	●	●	●	●	●	●	●	●	-	●	●	●	●	●
1 Ezra	457-444 B.C.	-	●	●	-	●	●	●	-	●	●	●	●	●	●	●	●	●	●	●	●	●	●
2 Ezra/Nehemiah	424-400 B.C.	-	●	●	-	●	●	●	-	●	●	●	●	●	?	●	●	●	●	●	●	●	●
Psalms	1410-450 B.C.	-	●	●	-	●	●	●	●	●	●	●	●	●	●	●	●	●	●	●	●	●	●
Proverbs	c. 971-686 B.C.	-	●	●	-	●	●	●	-	●	●	●	-	●	●	●	●	●	●	●	●	A	●
Ecclesiastes	940-931 B.C.	-	●	●	-	●	●	●	-	●	●	●	-	●	●	●	●	●	●	●	●	-	●
Song of Solomon	971-965 B.C.	-	●	●	-	●	●	●	-	●	●	●	-	●	●	●	●	●	●	●	●	A	R
Sirach		-	-	-	-	-	-	-	A	-	●	Q	A	●	●	●	●	-	●	●	-	A	R
Wisdom of Sirach		-	-	-	-	-	-	-	-	-	-	-	-	-	-	-	●	-	D	-	-	-	R
Wisdom of Solomon		●	-	-	-	-	-	-	A	-	-	Q	A	●	●	●	●	D	●	●	●	A	R
Isaiah	700-681 B.C.	-	●	●	-	●	●	●	●	●	●	●	●	●	●	●	●	●	●	●	●	●	●
Jeremiah	586-570 B.C.	-	●	●	-	●	●	●	●	●	●	●	●	●	●	●	●	●	●	●	●	●	●
Baruch		-	?	●	-	●	?	●	●	?	?	●	?	?	?	●	?	?	-	?	●	●	
Lamentations	586 B.C.	-	?	●	-	●	?	●	●	?	?	●	?	?	?	●	?	?	-	?	●	●	
Daniel	536-530 B.C.	-	●	●	-	●	●	●	●	●	●	●	●	●	●	●	●	●	●	●	●	●	●
Ezekiel	590-570 B.C.	-	●	●	-	●	●	●	●	●	●	●	●	●	●	●	●	●	●	●	●	●	●
Job	Unknown	-	●	●	-	●	●	●	●	●	●	●	●	●	●	●	●	●	●	●	●	●	●
Esther	450-331 B.C.	-	-	●	-	●	●	●	●	A	-	A	A	●	●	●	●	●	●	●	●	A	R
Tobit		-	-	-	-	-	-	●	-	A	-	-	-	-	A	●	●	●	D	●	●	A	R
Judith		-	-	-	-	-	-	●	-	A	-	-	-	●	A	●	●	●	D	●	●	A	R
1 Maccabees		-	-	●	-	-	-	●	-	-	-	-	-	-	A	●	●	●	D	●	●	A	R
2 Maccabees		-	-	●	-	-	-	●	-	-	-	-	●	-	A	●	●	●	D	●	●	A	R
3 Maccabees		-	-	●	-	-	-	-	-	-	-	-	●	-	-	-	-	-	D	-	-	A	R
4 Maccabees		-	-	-	-	-	-	-	-	-	-	-	-	-	-	-	-	-	D	-	-	A	-
Hosea	750-710 B.C.	-	●	-	-	●	●	●	●	●	●	●	●	●	●	●	●	●	●	●	●	●	●
Amos	c. 750 B.C.	-	●	-	-	●	●	●	●	●	●	●	●	●	●	●	●	●	●	●	●	●	●
Micah	735-710 B.C.	-	●	-	-	●	●	●	●	●	●	●	●	●	●	●	●	●	●	●	●	●	●
Joel	835-796 B.C.	-	●	-	-	●	●	●	●	●	●	●	●	●	●	●	●	●	●	●	●	●	●
Obadiah	850-840 B.C.	-	●	-	-	●	●	●	●	●	●	●	●	●	●	●	●	●	●	●	●	●	●
Jonah	c. 775 B.C.	-	●	-	-	●	●	●	●	●	●	●	●	●	●	●	●	●	●	●	●	●	●
Nahum	c. 650 B.C.	-	●	-	-	●	●	●	●	●	●	●	●	●	●	●	●	●	●	●	●	●	●
Habakkuk	615-605 B.C.	-	●	-	-	●	●	●	●	●	●	●	●	●	●	●	●	●	●	●	●	●	●
Zephaniah	635-625 B.C.	-	●	-	-	●	●	●	●	●	●	●	●	●	●	●	●	●	●	●	●	●	●
Haggai	c. 520 B.C.	-	●	-	-	●	●	●	●	●	●	●	●	●	●	●	●	●	●	●	●	●	●
Zechariah	480-470 B.C.	-	●	-	-	●	●	●	●	●	●	●	●	●	●	●	●	●	●	●	●	●	●
Malachi	433-424 B.C.	-	●	-	-	●	●	●	●	●	●	●	●	●	●	●	●	●	●	●	●	D	
Life of Adam and Eve		-	-	-	-	-	-	-	-	-	-	-	-	-	-	-	-	-	-	-	-	●	D
Book of Enoch		-	-	-	-	-	-	-	-	-	-	-	-	-	-	-	-	-	-	-	-	D	D
Lamech		-	-	-	-	-	-	-	-	-	-	-	-	-	-	-	-	-	-	-	-	D	-
The Patriarchs		-	-	-	-	-	-	-	-	-	-	-	-	-	-	-	-	-	-	-	-	D	D
The Prayer of Joseph		-	-	-	-	-	-	-	-	-	-	-	-	-	-	-	-	-	-	-	-	D	D
Eldad and Modad		-	-	-	-	-	-	-	-	-	-	-	-	-	-	-	-	-	-	-	-	D	D
The Testament of Moses		-	-	-	-	-	-	-	-	-	-	-	-	-	-	-	-	-	-	-	-	D	D
Assumption of Moses		-	-	-	-	-	-	-	-	-	-	-	-	-	-	-	-	-	-	-	-	D	D
The Revelation of Elias		-	-	-	-	-	-	-	-	-	-	-	-	-	-	-	-	-	-	-	-	D	D
The Vision of Isaiah		-	-	-	-	-	-	-	-	-	-	-	-	-	-	-	-	-	-	-	-	D	-
The Revelation of Zephaniah		-	-	-	-	-	-	-	-	-	-	-	-	-	-	-	-	-	-	-	-	-	D
The Revelation of Zechariah		-	-	-	-	-	-	-	-	-	-	-	-	-	-	-	-	-	-	-	-	-	-
The Revelation of Ezra		-	-	-	-	-	-	-	-	-	-	-	-	-	-	-	-	-	-	-	-	-	-
Book of Abraham		-	-	-	-	-	-	-	-	-	-	-	-	-	-	-	-	-	-	-	-	-	D
Book of Zacharias		-	-	-	-	-	-	-	-	-	-	-	-	-	-	-	-	-	-	-	-	-	D
Pseudepigraphica of Baruch, Habakkuk, Ezekiel, and Daniel		-	-	-	-	-	-	-	-	-	-	-	-	-	-	-	-	-	-	-	-	-	D

Appendix 4: Some of the Early Church Canons

A table of some of the Canons are shown below – The New Testament:

Book	Date Written	170 AD - Muratorian Fragment	170 AD - Melito	240 AD - Origen from Eusebius	324 AD - Eusebius	350 AD - Cyril of Jerusalem	360 AD - Hilary of Poitiers	360 AD - The Cheltenham List	363 AD - Council of Laodicea	367 AD - Athanasius of Alexandria	380 AD - Gregory of Nazianzus	380 AD - Amphilochius of Iconium	380 AD - Apostolic Canons	385 AD - Epiphanius of Salamis	390 AD - St. Jerome	397 AD - St. Augustine	397 AD - Third Council of Carthage	400 AD - Codex Claromontanus	400 AD - Rufinus of Aquileia	405 AD - Innocent I	550 AD - Decree of Gelasius	7th Cent. AD - Cat. o/t Sixty Canonical Books	810 AD - Stichometry of Nicephorus
Gospel of Matthew	A.D. 50-60	●	-	●	●	●	-	●	●	●	●	●	●	●	●	●	●	●	●	●	●	●	●
Gospel of Mark	A.D. 50-60	●	-	●	●	●	-	●	●	●	●	●	●	●	●	●	●	●	●	●	●	●	●
Gospel of Luke	A.D. 60-61	●	-	●	●	●	-	●	●	●	●	●	●	●	●	●	●	●	●	●	●	●	●
Gospel of John	A.D. 80-90	●	-	●	●	●	-	●	●	●	●	●	●	●	●	●	●	●	●	●	●	●	●
Acts	A.D. 62	●	-	●	●	●	-	●	●	●	●	●	●	●	●	●	●	●	●	●	●	●	●
Romans	A.D. 56	●	-	A	●	●	-	●	●	●	●	●	●	●	●	●	●	●	●	●	●	●	●
1 Corinthians	A.D. 55	●	-	A	●	●	-	●	●	●	●	●	●	●	●	●	●	●	●	●	●	●	●
2 Corinthians	A.D. 55-56	●	-	A	●	●	-	●	●	●	●	●	●	●	●	●	●	●	●	●	●	●	●
Galatians	A.D. 50-60	●	-	A	●	●	-	●	●	●	●	●	●	●	●	●	●	●	●	●	●	●	●
Ephesians	A.D. 60-62	●	-	A	●	●	-	●	●	●	●	●	●	●	●	●	●	●	●	●	●	●	●
Philippians	A.D. 60-62	●	-	A	●	●	-	●	●	●	●	●	●	●	●	●	●	●	●	●	●	●	●
Colossians	A.D. 60-62	●	-	A	●	●	-	●	●	●	●	●	●	●	●	●	●	●	●	●	●	●	●
1 Thessalonians	A.D. 51	●	-	A	●	●	-	●	●	●	●	●	●	●	●	●	●	●	●	●	●	●	●
2 Thessalonians	A.D. 51-52	●	-	A	●	●	-	●	●	●	●	●	●	●	●	●	●	●	●	●	●	●	●
Philemon	A.D. 60-62	●	-	A	●	●	-	●	●	●	●	●	●	●	●	●	●	●	●	●	●	●	●
Titus	A.D. 62-64	●	-	A	●	●	-	●	●	●	●	●	●	●	●	●	●	●	●	●	●	●	●
1 Timothy	A.D. 62-64	●	-	-	●	●	-	●	●	●	●	●	●	●	●	●	●	●	●	●	●	●	●
2 Timothy	A.D. 66-67	●	-	-	●	●	-	●	●	●	●	●	●	●	●	●	●	●	●	●	●	●	●
Hebrews	A.D. 50-95	-	-	Q	Q	●	-	-	●	●	●	A	●	●	●	●	●	-	●	●	●	●	●
James	A.D. 44-49	-	-	-	Q	●	-	-	●	●	●	●	●	●	●	●	●	-	●	●	●	●	●
1 Peter	A.D. 64-65	-	-	●	●	●	-	●	●	●	●	●	●	●	●	●	●	●	●	●	●	●	
2 Peter	A.D. 67-68	-	-	Q	Q	-	-	●	●	●	●	A	●	●	●	●	●	●	●	●	●	●	●
1 John	A.D. 90-95	●	-	●	●	●	-	●	●	●	●	●	●	●	●	●	●	●	●	●	●	●	●
2 John	A.D. 90-95	●	-	●	Q	-	-	●	●	●	●	A	●	●	●	●	●	●	●	●	●	●	●
3 John	A.D. 90-95	-	-	-	Q	-	-	●	●	●	●	A	●	●	●	●	●	●	●	●	●	●	●
Jude	A.D. 68-70	●	-	A	Q	●	-	-	●	●	●	A	●	●	●	●	●	●	●	●	●	●	-
Revelation/Apocalypse of John	A.D. 94-96	●	-	●	R	-	-	●	-	●	-	A	-	●	●	●	●	●	●	●	●	●	R
1 Clement	A.D. 80-140	-	-	-	-	-	-	-	-	-	-	-	●	-	-	-	-	-	-	-	-	D	D
2 Clement	A.D. 130-160	-	-	-	-	-	-	-	-	-	-	-	●	-	-	-	-	-	-	-	-	D	D
Revelation/Apocalypse of Peter	A.D. 100-150	●	-	-	R	-	-	-	-	-	-	-	-	-	-	Q	-	-	●	-	R	D	R
Acts of Peter	A.D. 150-200	-	-	-	Q	-	-	-	-	-	-	-	-	-	-	Q	-	-	-	-	R	-	-
Acts of Paul	A.D. 150-200	-	-	-	R	-	-	-	-	-	-	-	-	-	-	-	-	-	●	-	-	D	-
Circuit of John		-	-	-	-	-	-	-	-	-	-	-	-	-	-	-	-	-	-	-	-	-	D
Circuit of Paul		-	-	-	-	-	-	-	-	-	-	-	-	-	-	-	-	-	-	-	-	-	A
Circuit of Peter		-	-	-	-	-	-	-	-	-	-	-	-	-	-	-	-	-	-	-	-	-	D
Circuit of Thomas		-	-	-	-	-	-	-	-	-	-	-	-	-	-	-	-	-	-	-	-	-	D
Didache	A.D. 50-120	-	-	-	-	-	-	-	-	-	-	-	-	-	-	-	-	-	-	-	-	-	A
Gospel of Barnabas	A.D. 80-120	-	-	-	-	-	-	-	-	-	-	-	-	-	-	-	-	-	-	-	-	D	-
Gospel of Matthias		-	-	-	-	-	-	-	-	-	-	-	-	-	-	-	-	-	-	-	-	D	-
Gospel of Peter	A.D. 70-160	-	-	-	R	-	-	-	-	-	-	-	-	-	-	Q	-	-	-	-	-	-	-
Gospel of the Hebrews	A.D. 80-150	-	-	-	-	-	-	-	-	-	-	-	-	-	-	-	-	-	-	-	-	-	R
Gospel of Thomas	A.D. 50-140	-	-	-	R	R	-	-	-	-	-	-	-	-	-	-	-	-	-	-	R	-	D
Judas the Zealot		-	-	-	-	-	-	-	-	-	-	-	-	-	-	-	-	-	-	-	●	●	-
Preaching of Peter		-	-	-	Q	-	-	-	-	-	-	-	-	-	Q	-	-	-	-	-	R	-	-
Shepherd of Hermas	A.D. 80-100	A	-	-	R	-	-	-	-	A	-	-	-	-	A	-	-	●	R	-	-	-	D
Teaching of Ignatius	A.D. 105-115	-	-	-	-	-	-	-	-	-	-	-	-	-	-	-	-	-	-	-	-	D	D
Teaching of Polycarp	A.D. 110-140	-	-	-	-	-	-	-	-	-	-	-	-	-	-	-	-	-	-	-	-	D	D
Teachings of the Apostles		-	-	-	R	-	-	-	-	A	-	-	-	-	-	-	-	-	-	-	-	-	-
The Circuits and Teachings of the Apostles		-	-	-	-	-	-	-	-	-	-	-	-	-	-	-	-	-	-	-	-	-	-
The Epistle of Barnabas	A.D. 80-120	-	-	-	R	-	-	-	-	-	-	-	-	-	-	-	-	-	-	-	-	-	R
The History of James		-	-	-	-	-	-	-	-	-	-	-	-	-	-	-	-	-	-	-	-	D	-
The Judgement of Peter		-	-	-	-	-	-	-	-	-	-	-	-	-	-	-	-	-	-	-	R	-	-
The Revelation of Paul		-	-	-	-	-	-	-	-	-	-	-	-	-	-	-	-	-	-	-	-	D	-
The Two Ways		-	-	-	-	-	-	-	-	-	-	-	-	-	-	-	R	-	-	-	-	-	-

Appendix 5: Approved Eucharistic Miracles

- Siena, Italy -- August 17, 1730
- Amsterdam, Holland 1345
- Blanot, France -- March 31, 1331
- Bolsena-Orvieta, Italy
- Betania, Venezuela on December 8th, 1991
- Fiecht, 1310
- Seefeld, 1384
- Weiten-Raxendorf, 1411
- Bois-Seigneur-Isaac, 1405
- Bruges, 1203
- Brussels, 1370
- Herentals, 1412
- Herkenrode-Hasselt, 1317
- Liège (Corpus Christi), 1374
- Middleburg-Lovanio, 1374
- Eucharistic Miracle of the Caribbean Island of Martinique
- Morne-Rouge, 1902
- Tumaco, 1906
- Ludbreg, 1411
- Jordan / Arabian Desert - St. Mary of Egypt, 6th Century
- Scete, 3rd – 5th Century
- Avignon, 1433
- Blanot, 1331
- Bordeaux, 1822
- Dijon, 1430
- Douai, 1254
- Faverney, 1608
- La Rochelle, 1461
  Neuvy Saint Sépulcre, 1257
- Les Ulmes, 1668
- Marseille-En-Beauvais, 1533
- Paris, 1290
- Pressac, 1643
- Augsburg, 1194
- Benningen, 1216
- Bettbrunn, 1125
- Erding, 1417
- Kranenburg, District of Kleve, 1280
- Regensburg, 1255
- Walldürn, 1330
- Weingarten

Appendix 5: Approved Eucharistic Miracles

- Wilsnack, 1383
- Chirattakonam, 2001
- Saint-André de la Réunion, 1902
- Alatri, 1228
- Assisi (Saint Clare), 1240
- Asti, 1535
- Asti, 1718
- Bagno Di Romagna, 1412
- Bolsena, 1264
- Canosio, 1630
- Cascia, 1330
- Cava Dei Tirreni, 1656
- Dronero, 1631
  San Mauro La Bruca, 1969
- Ferrara, 1171
- Florence, 1230-1595
- Gruaro (Valvasone), 1294
- Lanciano, 700 A.D.
- Macerata, 1356
- Mogoro, 1604
- Morrovalle, 1560
- Offida, 1273-1280
- Patierno (Naples), 1772
- Rimini, 1227
- Rome, 6th – 7th Centuries
- Rome, 1610
- Rosano, 1948
- Saint Peter Damian, 11th Century
- Scala, 1732
- Siena, 1730
- Trani, 11th Century
- Turin, 1453
- Turin, 1640
- Veroli, 1570
- Volterra, 1472
- Alkmaar, 1429
- Amsterdam, 1345
- Bergen, 1421
- Boxmeer, 1400
- Boxtel-Hoogstraten, 1380
- Breda-Niervaart, 1300
- Meerssen, 1222-1465
- Stiphout, 1342

Appendix 5: Approved Eucharistic Miracles

- Eten, 1649
- Glotowo, 1290
- Krakow, 1345
- Poznan, 1399
- Santarém, 1247
- Alboraya-Almácera, 1348
- Alcalá, 1597
- Alcoy, 1568
- Caravaca de la Cruz, 1231
- Cimballa, 1370
- Daroca, 1239
- Gerona, 1297
- Gorkum-El Escorial, 1572
- Guadalupe, 1420
- Ivorra, 1010
- Moncada, 1392
- Montserrat, 1657
- O'Cebreiro, 1300
- Onil, 1824
- Ponferrada, 1533
- Saint John of the Abbesses, 1251
- Silla, 1907
- Valencia
- Zaragoza, 1427
- Ettiswil, 1447

Appendix 6: Approved Incorruptibles

Saint Agatha
Saint Agnes of Montepulciano
Blessed Andrew Franchi
Blessed Angela of Foligno
Saint Angela Merici
Blessed Angelo of Acri
Blessed Angelo of Chiavasso
Blessed Anthony Bonfadini
Blessed Anthony of Stroncone
Blessed Antonia of Florence
Saint Benedict the Moor
Saint Bernadette Soubirous
Saint Bernardine of Siena
Saint Catherine of Bologna
Saint Catherine of Genoa
Saint Cecilia
Saint Charles Borromeo
Saint Charles of Sezze
Saint Clare of Assisi
Saint Clare of Montefalco
Saint Crispin of Viterbo
Saint Didacus of Alcala
Saint Eustochium
Saint Fernando III
Saint Frances of Rome
Saint Francis de Sales
Blessed Francis of Fabriano
Venerable Francis Gonzaga
Blessed Gabriel Ferretti
Blessed Gandolph of Binasco
Blessed Helen Enselmini
Saint Ignatius of Laconi
Saint Ignatius of Santhia
Blessed Imelda Lambertini
Blessed James of Bitecto
Saint James of the March
Blessed James Oldo
Blessed James of Pieve
Blessed James of Strepar
Saint Jean-Marie-Baptiste Vianney
Blessed Jane Mary of Maille
Blessed Jane of Signa
Saint Jane of Valois
Saint John Bosco
Saint Joseph of Cupertino
Saint Louis Bertrand
Blessed Lucy of Narni
Blessed Margaret of Castello
Saint Margaret of Cortona
Blessed Margaret of Lorraine
Blessed Mark Marconi
Venerable Mary of Agreda
Blessed Mary Assunta Pollotta
Saint Mary Joseph Rossello
Blessed Mary Magdalene Martinengo
Blessed Matthia Nazzarei
Blessed Nicholas Factor
Saint Pacifico of San Severino
Saint Paschal Baylon
Blessed Philippa Mareri
Saint Pope Pius X
Saint Rose of Viterbo
Blessed Sebastian of Aparicio
Saint Seraphin of Montegranaro
Blessed Salome of Cracow
Saint Sperandia
Saint Veronica Giuliani
Saint Vincent Pallotti
Saint Zita
Saint Albert the Great
Saint Alphege of Canterbury
Blessed Alphonsus of Orozco
Saint Andrew Bobola
Blessed Angelo of Borgo San Sepolcro
Blessed Anna Maria Taigi
Saint Anthony Maria Zaccaria
Saint Antoninus
Blessed Arcangela Girlani
Saint Benezet
Blessed Bernard Scammacca
Blessed Bertrand of Garrigua
Saint Camillus de Lellis
Venerable Catalina de Cristo
Saint Catherine Labouré
Blessed Charbel Makhlouf
Saint Catherine dei Ricci
Saint Catherine of Siena
Saint Coloman
Saint Cuthbert
Saint Dominic Savio
Saint Edmund Rich of Canterbury
Saint Edward the Confessor
Saint Etheldreda
Blessed Eustochia Calafato

Appendix 6: Approved Incorruptibles

Saint Ezequiel Moreno y Diaz
Saint Francis of Paola
Saint Francis Xavier
Saint George Preca
Saint Germaine Cousin
Saint Guthlac
Annibale Maria di Francia
Saint Herculanus of Piegaro
Saint Hugh of Lincoln
Saint Idesbald
Saint Isidore the Farmer
Blessed James of Blanconibus
Venerable John of Jesus Mary
Saint Jane Frances de Chantal
Saint Jeanne de Lestonnac
Blessed John of Chiaramonte
Saint John of God
Saint John of the Cross
Saint John Southworth
Saint Josaphat
Saint Julie Billiart
Blessed Karl of Austria
Saint Louise de Marillac
Saint Luigi Orione
Saint Lucy Filippini
Saint Madeleine Sophie Barat
Blessed Mafalda of Portugal
Blessed Margaret of Savoy
Saint Maria Goretti
Venerable Maria Vela
Saint Martin de Porres
Blessed Mary Bagnesi
Saint Mary Magdalen de' Pazzi
Blessed Mary of the Divine Heart
Mother Mariana de Jesus Torres
Venerable Mother Maria of Jesus
Saint Nicholas of Tolentino
Blessed Osanna of Mantua
Saint Padre Pio of Pietrelcina
Blessed Paula Frassinetti
Saint Peregrine Laziosi
Blessed Peter Ghigenzi
Saint Philip Neri
Saint Pierre Julien Eymard
Saint Rita of Cascia
Saint Romuald
Saint Rose of Lima
Saint Rose Philippine Duchesne
Blessed Sibyllina Biscossi
Saint Silvan
Saint Stanislaus Kostka
Saint Teresa of Avila
Saint Teresa Margaret of Sacred Heart
Saint Ubald of Gubbio
Saint Vincent de Paul
Saint Waltheof
Saint Werburgh
Saint Withburga
Saint Wunibald

Bibliography/Recommended Reading

- Accetta, August D., Kenneth Lyons, and John Jackson. *"Nuclear Medicine and Its Relevance to the Shroud of Turin."* Paper presented at the Ovieto Worldwide Conference "Sindone 2000," August 27–29, 2000, Ovieto, Italy
- *A History of Christian Thought*, Paul Tillich, Touchstone Books, 1972. ISBN 0-671-21426-8Anonymous. *"Chronology of Byzantine Empire (330–1455 A.D*
- Akin, Jimmy (2010), "*The Fathers Know Best: Your Essential Guide to the Teachings of the Early Church*", (Catholic Answers, San Diego)
- *The Anathemas Against Origen*, by the Fifth Ecumenical Council (Schaff, Philip, "The Seven Ecumenical Councils", *Nicene and Post-Nicene Fathers*, Series 2, Vol. 14. Edinburgh: T&T Clark)
- *The Anathematisms of the Emperor Justinian Against Origen* (Schaff, *op. cit.*)
- Antonacci, Mark. *The Resurrection of the Shroud.* New York: M. Evans, 2000.
- Pope Benedict XVI," *Church Fathers from Clement of Rome to Augustine*", (Libreria Editrice Vaticana, Vatican City2008)
- Bennett, Janice. *Sacred Blood, Sacred Image: The Sudarium of Oviedo: New Evidence for the Authenticity of the Shroud of Turin.* San Francisco: Ignatius Press, 2001.
- Bettenson, Henry andMaunder, Chris. "Documents of the Christian Church." Oxford University Press, 1999
- Beveridge, Henry. trans. *Calvin's Tracts* (Calvin Translation Society, Edinburgh. 1849)
- "Blood on the Shroud of Turin." Applied Optics, 19/16 (1980), pp. 2742–2744.
- Bollone, B., M. C. Jurio, and M. Massaro. *"Identification of the Group of the Traces of Human Blood on the Shroud."* Shroud Spectrum International, 2 (1983), pp. 2–6.
- Brauer, Jerald. "*The Westminster Dictionary of Church History*", ed. (Philadelphia:Westminster, 1971)
- Britannica Online Encyclopedia. *Church Father (Christianity)* --
- Bruce, FF. *"The Canon of Scripture"*, Downers Grove, IL: InterVarsity Press, 1988. ISBN 0-8308-1258-X

- Bruce, FF. *"The Bible History Atlas"* Downers Grove, IL: InterVarsity Press, 1988. ISBN 0-8308-1258-X
- Bruce, FF. *"New Testament Documents: Are They Reliable?"* Downers Grove, IL: InterVarsity Press, 1981. (First published in 1943 as Are the New Testament Documents Reliable?) ISBN 0-8028-2219-3
- Burke, David G. *"Cross; Crucify."* In Geoffrey W. Bromiley, ed., International Standard Bible Encyclopedia, 1, pp. 825–830. Grand Rapids: Eerdmans, 1979.
- *Catechism of the Catholic Church – English translation* (U.S.A., 2nd edition) (English translation of the Catechism of the Catholic Church: Modifications from the Editio Typica, copyright 1997, United States Catholic Conference, Inc., Libreria Editrice Vaticana) (Glossary and Index Analyticus, copyright 2000, U.S. Catholic Conference, Inc.). ISBN 1-57455-110-8
- *Catholic Encyclopedia.* "Fathers of the Church". New York: Robert Appleton Company. 1913.
- *Compendium of the Catechism of the Catholic Church – English translation* (USCCB, 2006). ISBN 1-57455-720-3
- Cross, F. L., ed. *The Oxford Dictionary of the Christian Church.* New York: Oxford University Press. 2005, article *Platonism*
- Cross, Frank L., and Elizabeth A. Livingstone, eds. *Oxford Dictionary of the Christian Church.* Oxford: Oxford University Press, (1958) 1974.
- Damon, P. E., D. J. Donahue, B. H. Gore, A. L. Hatheway, A. J. T. Jull, T. W. Linick, P. J. Sercel, L. J. Toolin, C. R. Bronk, E. T. Hall, R. E. M. Hedges, R. Housley, I. A. Law, C. Perry, G. Bonani, S. Trumbore, W. Woelfli, J. C. Ambers, S. G. E. Bowman, M. N. Leese, and M. S. Tite. *"Radiocarbon Dating of the Shroud of Turin."* Nature, 337, February 16, 1989, pp. 611–618.
- Danin, Avinoam, Alan D. Whanger, Uri Baruch, and Mary Whanger. *Flora of the Shroud of Turin.* St. Louis: Missouri Botanical Garden Press, 1999.
- Durant, Will. *Caesar and Christ.* New York: Simon and Schuster. 1972
- Elliott, John. *1 Peter.* Doubleday, Toronto, 2000.
- Eusebius. *Ecclesiastical History (Historia ecclesiastica).* Greek with English translation by Kirsopp Lake. (Loeb

- Classical Library) Cambridge, MA and London: Harvard University Press. Vol. 1, 1926, reprinted 1998. Vol. 2, 1932, reprinted 2000.
- Evans, Craig A. "Crucifixion." In Katharine Doob Sakenfeld, ed., New Interpreter's Dictionary of the Bible, 1, pp. 806–807. Nashville: Abingdon, 2006.
- Fanti, Giulio, Barrie Schwortz, August Accetta, José A. Botella, Berns J. Buenaobra, Manuel Carreira, Frank Cheng, Fabio Crosilla, R. Dinegar, Helmut Felzmann, Bob Haroldsen, Piero Iacazio, Francesco Lattarulo, Giovanni Novelli, Joe Marino, Alessandro Malantrucco, Paul Maloney, Daniel Porter, Bruno Pozzetto, Ray Schneider, Niels Svensson, Traudl Wally, Alan D. Whanger, and Frederick Zugibe. *"Evidences for Testing Hypotheses about the Body Image Formation of the Turin Shroud."* Online, http://www.shroud.com/library.htm; scroll down to "Scientific Papers & Articles"
- Farmer, David Hugh "Ignatius of Antioch" in *The Oxford Dictionary of the Saints* (New York:Oxford University Press, 1987).
- France, R. T. (Robert). *The Gospel of Matthew.* (New International Commentary on the New Testament) Grand Rapids: William B. Eerdmans, 2007.
- Frei, Max. *"Nine Years of Palinological Studies on the Shroud."* Shroud Spectrum International, 1/3 (1982), pp. 3–7.
- Gasque, W. Ward & Ralph P. Martin (eds). *Apostolic History and the Gospel: Biblical and Historical Essays Presented to F. F. Bruce on his 60th Birthday.* Exeter: Paternoster; Grand Rapids, MI: William B. Eerdmans, 1970. ISBN 0-85364-098-X
- Hall, Christopher A. *"Reading Scripture with the Church Fathers"* (Aug 17, 1998) InterVarsity Press ISBN 0830815007
- Heller, John H. and Alan D. Adler. *"A Chemical Investigation of the Shroud."* Canadian Society of Forensic Science Journal, 14/3 (1981), pp. 81–103.
- Hoehner, Harold W. "Chronological Aspects of the Life of Christ", Zondervan Press, 1977. ISBN 0-310-26211-9
- Holmes, Michael W., (1992*), "The Apostolic Fathers"*, (Baker Academic, Grand Rapids MI)
- Iannone, John C. *"Floral Images and Pollen Grains on the Shroud of Turin: An Interview with Dr. Alan Whanger and Dr. Avinoam Danin,"* appeared online July, 1999.

- Jackson, John P. *"An Unconventional Hypothesis to Explain All Image Characteristics Found on the Shroud Image."* Paper presented at the Symposium on History, Science, Theology, and the Shroud, June 22–23, 1991, St. Louis, MO. Online, http://theshroudofturin.blogspot.com/2012/01/john-p-jackson-unconventional.html, accessed March 3, 2010.
- Jackson, John P., Eric J. Jumper, and D. Devan. *"Investigations of the Shroud of Turin by Computer Aided Analysis."* Paper presented at and published in the Proceedings of the 1977 United States Conference of Research on the Shroud of Turin, Colorado Springs, 1977, pp. 74–94.
- Jackson, John P., Eric J. Jumper, and William R. Ercoline. *"Correlation of Image Intensity on the Turin Shroud with the 3-D Structure of a Human Body Shape."* Applied Optics, 23/14 (1984), pp. 2244–2270.
- Josephus, Flavius, Whiston, William translator, "*The New Complete Works of Josephus*" (Kergel Publications, Grand Rapids MI(1999))
- Jumper, Eric J., Alan D. Adler, John P. Jackson, Sam F. Pellicori, John H. Heller, and J. R. Druzik. *"A Comprehensive Examination of the Various Stains and Images on the Shroud of Turin."* Archaeological Chemistry III, 205 (1984), pp. 447–476.
- Keating, Karl. *Catholicism and Fundamentalism: The Attack on "Romanism" by "Bible Christians"* (Ignatius Press, 1988)
- Keating, Karl. *What Catholics Really Believe* (Servant Publications, 1992)
- Keating, Karl. *Nothing but the Truth: Essays in Apologetics* (Catholic Answers, 2000)
- Keating, Karl. *The Usual Suspects: Answering Anti-Catholic Fundamentalists* (Ignatius Press, 2000)
- Keating, Karl. *Controversies: High-Level Catholic Apologetics* (Ignatius Press, 2001)
- Keating, Karl. *Holy War, Just War: Islam and Christendom at War* (Chronicles Press/The Rockford Institute 2007)
- Keener, Craig S. *The Gospel of John: A Commentary.* Peabody, MA: Hendrickson, 2 vols., 2003.
- Kugel, James L. *"The Bible as it was."* Harvard University Press, 1997 ISBN 0-674-06940-4

- Law, Timothy Michael. *"When God spoke Greek – the Septuagint and the making of the Christian Bible"*, Oxford University Press, 2013 ISBN 978-0-19-978172-0
- Langer, William L., comp. and ed. *An Encyclopedia of World History.* Boston: Houghton Mifflin, (1940, 1948, 1952) 1963.
- Laqueur, Walter. *The Changing Face of Antisemitism: From Ancient Times To The Present Day*, (Oxford University Press: 2006). ISBN 0-19-530429-2. 48
- Levada, Archbishop William J. (1994-02-07). "The New Catechism: An Overview". United States Conference of Catholic Bishops Office for the Catechism.
- Levi-Setti, Ricardo, G. Crow, and Y. L. Wang. *"Progress in High Resolution Scanning Ion Microscopy and Secondary Ion Mass Spectrometry Imaging Microanalysis."* Scanning Electron Microscopy 2 (1985), pp. 535–552.
- Lewy, Yohanan (Hans). "John Chrysostom" in *Encyclopaedia Judaica* (CD-ROM Edition Version 1.0), Ed. Cecil Roth (Keter Publishing House: 1997). ISBN 965-07-0665-8.
- Lombatti, Antonio, with Alan D. Whanger. *"Doubts concerning the Coins over the Eyes."* An email exchange which occurred following the appearance of Lombatti's article in the British Society for the Turin Shroud Newsletter 45, 1997, pp. 35–37. Online, http://www.shroud.com/library.htm; scroll down to "Scientific Papers & Articles" and click on author and title.
- MacDonald, Paul S. *"History of the Concept of Mind"* (Mar 2003) ISBN 0754613658
- Meacham, William. *"The Authentication of the Turin Shroud: An Issue in Archaeological Epistemology."* Current Anthropology 24/3 (1983), pp. 282–311. Online, http://www.shroud.com/library.htm; scroll down to "Scientific Papers & Articles" and click on author and title.
- Meyers, Eric M., James F. Strange, and Carol L. Meyers. *Excavations at Ancient Meiron, Upper Galilee, Israel, 1971–72, 1974–75, 1977.* Durham, NC: American Schools of Oriental Research and Duke University, 1981.
- Moreno, Guillermo Heras, José-Delfín Villalaín Bianco, and Jorge-Manuel Rodríquez Almenar. *"Comparative Study of the Sudarium of Oviedo and the Shroud of Turin."* Translated from Spanish by Mark Guscin. Paper presented at the Third

International Congress for the Study of the Shroud of Turin, June 5–7, 1998, Turin, Italy.
- Nicassio, Alexander. *"The Early Church Leaders, volume 1",* 2013 ISBN 9781490474861 736 pp
- Phillips, Thomas J. *"Shroud irradiated with neutrons?"* (Correspondence).   Nature, 337, February 1, 1989, p. 594.
- Pitre, Brant. *"Jesus and the Jewish roots of the Eucharist – unlocking the secrets of the Last Supper",* Doubleday 2011. ISBN 978-0-385-53184-9
- Pomazansky, Protopresbyter Michael (1973, in Russian), *Orthodox Dogmatic Theology,* Platina CA: Saint Herman of Alaska Brotherhood (published 1984. English trans.)
- Quigley, Christine.   *The Corpse: a History.*   Jefferson, NC: McFarland, 1996.
- *The Real Face of Jesus?* (DVD).   A&E Television Networks, 2008, 100 minutes.
- Rogers, Raymond N.   *"Comments on the Book The Resurrection of the Shroud by Mark Antonacci."*   Appeared online in 2001, http://www.shroud.com/library.htm; scroll down to "Scientific Papers & Articles" and click on author and title.
- Sarton, George. (1936). *"The Unity and Diversity of the Mediterranean World",* Osiris
- Scavone, Daniel C.   *"Book Review of The Turin Shroud: In Whose Image?* [by Lynn Picknett and Clive Prince, 1994]." Appeared online in 1996, http:/www.shroud.com/library.htm; scroll down to "Scientific Papers & Articles" and click on author and title.
- Secrets of the Dead: Shroud of Christ? (DVD).   PBS Home Video, 2004, 60 minutes.
- Shroud of Turin Education and Research Association (STERA), *"The Shroud of Turin Website."*   Barrie Schwartz, founder and executive director.   Online http://www.shroud.com
- Strong, James.   *The Strongest Strong's Exhaustive Concordance of the Bible.*   Revised and corrected John R. Kohlenberger III and James A. Swanson.   Grand Rapids: Zondervan, 2001.
- Tov, Emanuel. *The Text-Critical Use of the Septuagint in Biblical Research* (Jerusalem Biblical Studies 3; Jerusalem: Simor, 1981).

- Tov, Emanuel. Textual Criticism of the Hebrew Bible (2d rev. ed.; Minneapolis and Assen: Fortress Press/Royal Van Gorcum, 2001). ISBN 978-0-8006-3429-2
- Tov, Emanuel. *Hebrew Bible, Greek Bible, and Qumran—Collected Essays* (TSAJ 121; Tübingen: Mohr Siebeck, 2008).
- Tov, Emanuel. *"The Greek and Hebrew Bible—Collected Essays on the Septuagint"* (VTSup 72; Leiden/Boston/Cologne: E. J. Brill, 1999).
- *United States Catholic Catechism for Adults – English* "...resource for preparation of catechumens in the Rite of Christian Initiation of Adults and for ongoing catechesis of adults" (USCCB, 2006). ISBN 1-57455-450-6
- Pope Vigilius, *Constitution of Pope Vigilius*, 553
- Vignon, Paul. *The Shroud of Christ.* New York: E. P. Dutton, (translated from the French), 1902.
- Whanger, Alan, and Mary Whanger. *"Polarized Image Overlay Technique: A New Image Comparison Method and Its Applications."* Applied Optics, 24 (1985), pp. 766–772.
- Wilcox, Robert K. *The Truth about the Shroud of Turin: Solving the Mystery.* Washington: Regnery, 2010.
- Wilson, Ian. *The Blood and the Shroud: New Evidence that the World's Most Sacred Relic Is Real.* New York: Simon and Schuster, 1998.
- *The Shroud.* London, Toronto, Sydney: Bantam, 2010.
- *The Shroud of Turin: The Burial Cloth of Jesus Christ?* Garden City: Doubleday, 1978.
- Zugibe, Frederick T. *The Crucifixion of Jesus: A Forensic Inquiry.* New York: M. Evans, 2005.

Personal Notes: